Representing the Family

Representing the Family

Deborah Chambers

SAGE Publications
London • Thousand Oaks • New Delhi

First published 2001

Apart from any fair dealing for the purposes of research or
private study, or criticism or review, as permitted under the
Copyright, Designs and Patents Act, 1988, this publication
may be reproduced, stored or transmitted in any form, or by
any means, only with the prior permission in writing of the
publishers, or in the case of reprographic reproduction, in
accordance with the terms of licences issued by the Copyright
Licensing Agency. Inquiries concerning reproduction outside
those terms should be sent to the publishers.

SAGE Publications Ltd
6 Bonhill Street
London EC2A 4PU

SAGE Publications Inc
2455 Teller Road
Thousand Oaks, California 91320

SAGE Publications India Pvt Ltd
32, M-Block Market
Greater Kailash - I
New Delhi 110 048

British Library Cataloguing in Publication data

A catalogue record for this book is
available from the British Library

ISBN 0 7619 6472 X
ISBN 0 7619 6473 8 (pbk)

Library of Congress Control Number 2001131821

Typeset by SIVA Math Setters, Chennai, India
Printed and bound in Great Britain by Athenaeum Press,
Gateshead

CONTENTS

LIST OF ILLUSTRATIONS

ACKNOWLEDGEMENTS

The idea for this book emerged when, among my teaching commitments at Nottingham Trent University, I was asked to teach on undergraduate module called the 'Sociology of the Family', which made me realise that there was a need for a book on representations of the family. I thank the students who participated in the module for their stimulating class discussions. I am grateful to the Department of English and Media Studies at Nottingham Trent University for awarding me a sabbatical for a semester towards researching and writing this book, and to the Faculty of Humanities for providing a stimulating and friendly teaching and research culture.

I wish to thank John Tomlinson, Head of the Centre for Research in International Communication and Culture (CRICC), for his invaluable advice and support, and that of the Centre. I am grateful to the CRICC/Sage editorial board which was instrumental in the formulation of this book at an early stage of discussion with Sage. Tracey Skelton, John Tomlinson and Richard Johnson were managing editors of the board, and have been extremely helpful in their comments on my draft proposal. I would also like to express my gratitude to the following people for their advice and support, for intellectual inspiration, and for fruitful discussions: Roger Bromley, Rosalind Gill, Melanie Lenehan, Eleonore Koffman, Kathleen O'Mara, Liz Morrish, Parvati Raghuram, Chris Rojek, Estella Tincknell, Joost Van Loon. I also thank James Ryan and Joan Schwartz, who gave me advice while developing my ideas about family photograph albums for an essay in a book they are editing, *Picturing Place: Photography and the Geographical Imagination* (2001), and also the editors of the *European Journal of Cultural Studies*, Perti Alasuutari, Anne Gray and Joke Hermes, for publishing a paper on some of the subject matter of this book. Thanks go to Karen Wilkes for her library and archive help, which is warmly appreciated. I also wish to thank Terry McSwiney for her secretarial advice. I wish to convey kindest thanks to my friend and colleague Sandra Harris, Head of Department of English and Media Studies, for her encouragement and support throughout.

I gratefully acknowledge the funding support from the following institutions and funding bodies: the British Academy, for awarding me an overseas conference grant to present a paper on the subject of this book at the Social

Science History Society conference in the United States; the Department of English and Media Studies at Nottingham Trent University, for UK conference support; and the Australian Research Council, for a grant to conduct research, with Carol Liston and Chris Wieneke, on an oral history study of family photograph albums at the Women's Research Centre, University of Western Sydney, Nepean.

I thank Julia Hall, Senior Commissioning Editor at Sage, for her advice and encouragement; the anonymous readers; and the copyeditor at Sage for helpful comments on the proposal and draft manuscript. I wish to thank my friends, Lesley Musto and Adrian Musto, for enjoyable discussions about the subject matter of the book. And finally, thanks go to my family for their love and support.

Grateful acknowledgement is made for the following sources for permission to reproduce material in this book: Figures 1.1. and 4.4: by permission of PA Photo Agency; Figure 3.1: by permission of Thomas Rockwell and Curtis Publishing Company, Indiana, USA; Figure 4.1: by permission of The Reader's Digest Association Limited; Figures 4.2. and 4.3: by permission of MFI. Figure 5.1: by permission of Rex Features; and Figure 5.2: by permission of Camera Press.

CHAPTER 1

REPRESENTING 'THE FAMILY'

Deep anxieties about the family as a moral domain continue to be played out within the western anglophone media through the interconnection of official discourses and popular media representations of family values and public morality. During a time when these nations are engaged in struggles over local, national and international identities, the family continues to be fixed as a primary symbol of absolute values in some key contexts. Yet in other important contexts that fixity is being questioned and, seemingly, subverted and transcended. Increases in divorce, remarriage, post-divorce families, blended families, single parenthood, joint custody, abortion, cohabitation, two-career families, gay and lesbian partnerships and parenthood all contribute to a rising 'postmodern family' diversity that is undermining the orthodoxy of traditional family values. In this period of major shifts in the meanings, everyday practices and representations of 'family' we find that social and cultural theory, political debate and the news media claim 'the family' as a critical topic. It now occupies centre-stage.

Church leaders, the New Right and pro-family campaigners have interpreted empirical research on changes in the family as evidence of a 'decline in family values' within an ongoing discourse of 'family crisis'. It is somewhat misleading, however, to suggest that the traditional nuclear family is declining or no longer exists. On the one hand, it has only ever existed as a transitional phase of some people's lives. A variety of living arrangements are being experienced in western nations, including some complex multiple-occupancy households that have not, as yet, been given a satisfactory label. On the other hand, the modern nuclear family *does* exist and is flourishing as an ideal: as a symbol, discourse and powerful myth within the collective imagination. This cultural myth is a regulatory force that impacts on our lives at a very personal level. It structures emotions, modes of official knowledge, bodies, identities and definitions of public and private cultural space.

Within social theory, debates about the family have been hampered by a conceptual deficiency over the term 'family'. It is no longer possible to discuss the subject without framing the word in inverted commas, signifying the ambiguity surrounding it. As Smart and Neale (1999) point out, with few alternative conceptual frameworks to hand, it is difficult to unhinge this dominant narrative of 'family decline' in an effective way. In fact, the shortage of explicit definitions of the 'family' indicates a denial of the diversity of actual family forms. Recently, however, mainstream social theory has revisited the subject of the family by analysing the ways in which it is changing as a central element of the changing conditions of late modernity. Important in re-centring the family and intimate relationships in social and cultural theory has been the work of Giddens (1992), Beck (1992) and Beck and Beck-Gernsheim (1995). Approaching the family as an active site of transformation, they insist that it is not simply reacting to changes outside and beyond it but that it plays a fundamental part in contributing to the changes taking place in wider society.

By addressing a range of official, expert and popular media discourses of familialism, I explore some of the ways in which discourses and representations of white nuclear familialism, as an ideal and as a norm, are being both reproduced and challenged.[1] The underlying questions that have motivated this book are: who is representing the family in western anglophone nations, how is it being represented, and for what purposes? My intention, then, is to look at the family as an ideological construct in order to understand the ways in which *ideas* about it are represented through discourses, including those that influence and interact with ideas of 'family' as identity, kinship and location. I engage in a dialogue with recent debates about gender and sexuality, race and ethnicity within ideologies of the family in order to assess some of the principal ways in which a white nuclear version of familialism is being used, metaphorically, as a device and organising trope across popular culture, political rhetoric, official and 'expert' discourses to circumscribe social practices, frameworks of meaning and knowledge. Most problematically, mainstream approaches and perspectives within sociology and cultural studies often interrogate the relationship between factors of ethnic, gender and sexual identity, and family in ways that reflect and reinforce the idea of the nuclear family as *universal* in popular discourses of western anglophone societies.

Biological and medical codes of knowledge underpin the range of meanings and actions associated with belonging to a family, evoking ideas of 'family' as a natural phenomenon. Familialism is founded on the configuration of biological as well as racial difference. Investing in significations of the dominance of heterosexuality can only be legitimised by appeals to 'normal' and natural sexual behaviour. In fact, the search for biological explanations and solutions for social problems is so dominant that the 'biological' operates as a central device in mythologising the *naturalness* of the traditional nuclear family. Contemporary preoccupations evolve around the new biologism of genetic engineering, with its emphasis on biological blood ties as a defining criterion of 'familyness'. Its antecedents lie within eugenics and raced discourses of family, which I visit in Chapter 2. Overall, the book focuses on two key themes that have come to represent core arguments surrounding family values in western anglophone nations: namely the persistent privileging of white ethnicity and the regulation of heterosexuality and patriarchy through family values. These themes are examined by analysing the processes through which both whiteness and heterosexuality are naturalised and normalised by appropriating the nuclear family as a regulatory ideal that inferiorises and discredits alternative experiences, structures and meanings. The discussion works across certain binary oppositions centred on the categories of 'whiteness' and 'non-whiteness', 'heterosexuality' and 'homosexuality' as well as masculinity and femininity, and in so doing the book investigates the tensions posed by perceived dangers to 'the family' from within and beyond it.

Raising a number of themes and issues to be taken up in the book, this chapter begins by looking at ways in which the family is represented, and how family ideology is appropriated and circulated within the political rhetoric of western anglophone nations such as Britain and the United States. These issues are then examined in more depth within the chapters that follow. This chapter focuses on the political discourses of the British government and American politicians as an interesting contemporary example to draw out some of the main themes concerning the construction and circulation of ideas about the family. It then outlines some of the key problems surrounding academic discourses on the family, which have followed, remarkably closely, the same rhetoric as governments and reproduced similar biases in upholding a white, middle-class, aspirational, nuclear version of the family as a mythical norm. Debates in social theory about the postmodern family are introduced in this chapter to raise questions about the disjunction between the ideal and lived experiences of familism, which are then addressed in more depth in later chapters. In the following chapters I then look at the cultural methods used, together with historical and sociological sources and approaches, to study the way in which these ideological devices about family are deployed as discourses to privilege a particular version of morality and to structure raced, sexed, gendered, classed sets of identities in national contexts. The middle sections of the book are set up as two pairs of chapters around which key approaches are explored, that is, 'positive' followed by 'negative' representations in Chapters 3 and 4, and the 'modern family' followed by the 'hybrid family' in Chapters 5 and 6.

MORAL GODFATHERS AND POLITICAL RHETORIC ON FAMILY VALUES

At the centre of a storm of moral indignation over news media revelations of the pregnancy of two white 12-year-old girls, the British Prime Minister launched a 'new moral crusade' on family values in September 1999. The 'discovery' that Britain has the highest teenage pregnancies both in Europe and in western anglophone nations provided the context for Tony Blair's proposal for 'a partnership between government and the country to lay the foundations of that moral purpose'.[2] While they have been falling rapidly in continental western Europe, teenage pregnancies have neither risen nor fallen significantly in the UK in the last thirty years. Yet they have provided fuel for political rhetoric across this period. 'Problem families' are marked as the source of sexual anarchy against which the forces of good must be mobilised.[3] With a flourish of moral evangelism, Blair declared:

> The issue is how you could get to a situation where you have 12-year-old girls being made pregnant by 14-year-old fathers. We should be asking why.[4]

The 'we' being referred to is 'the nation'. The Prime Minister named his crusade the 'new national moral purpose' to promote a set of moral values about 'family life' and situate it within a discourse of nationhood.

On the other side of the Atlantic, five years earlier, US President Bill Clinton declared in an election season speech:

> That is a disaster. It is wrong. And someone has to say again, 'It is simply not right. You shouldn't have a baby before you're ready, and you shouldn't have a baby when you're not married.'[5]

Clinton's words echoed those of former vice-president, Dan Quayle, uttered in a speech made the previous day:

> The way a male becomes a man is by supporting his children.... What [the Democrats] cannot accept is that government proposals have failed. It is the family that can rebuild America.... The dissolution of the family, and in particular, the absence of fathers in the lives of millions of America's children is the single most critical threat [to our future].[6]

The carefully chosen words and phrases used in these political speeches evoke notions of family crisis and moral disintegration: 'disaster', 'dissolution of the family', 'absence of fathers', 'critical threat'. They work to create a deep sense of moral anxiety around the idea that the family is permanently under siege. The main emphasis is on the problem of the man's role in the family as father. Fatherhood is being singled out as the crucial part of the family under threat. Its absence delegitimises the family. Who, then, is the enemy? In order for the state to avoid being burdened by family welfare, the father must be reasserted as the 'head' of the family. He must not shirk his heavy responsibilities, so, as a reward, he is conferred a privileged status and identity within a system of patriarchy, not simply as a father, but as patriarch.

Family-values rhetoric is carefully reconstructed by each new generation of politicians in western anglophone nations in the steadfast belief that the discourse of family crisis will be a vote catcher. So definitions of family values get regularly acted out and contested on a very public stage. It also means that a distinctive, narrow version of the family unit is mythically evoked and performed through policy. Moreover, it ensures that debates about family values are firmly anchored in and invested with meanings about nation, nationhood, nationality and race. This pattern of struggle over family politics impacts on all of our lives through our personal and collective struggles to grapple with the gulf between representations, public policies and private lived experiences.

Nevertheless, it seems rather bizarre that two 12-year-old girls, the most vulnerable members of society, have come to be vilified as a profound threat to the moral fabric of the whole nation. Throughout the twentieth century and continuing into the twenty-first, women as potential and real mothers have constituted an ongoing threat to the nation at precisely the most vulnerable moment of their lives: as lone mothers, as working mothers and as unemployed mothers, as teenage mothers, and as pre-teenage mothers. It is equally bizarre that the government believes high teenage pregnancies can be reduced by introducing repressive curfews for children and adolescents. The link made between sex, family morality and the nation gives the government an excuse to restrict people's liberties in extraordinary ways.

Yet the Prime Minister's 'moral' crusade is not about morality at all. It does not open up debates about citizenship and respect for others. In fact, as I argue in Chapter 6 in relation to Section 28 of the British Local Government Act of 1988, it *forecloses* such debates. It is about the search for ways of reducing welfare provision to families in the wake of lone motherhood and rising post-divorce families by recovering a traditional version of fatherhood as patriarch, and reconstructing hegemonic masculinities, through forms of state regulation. The state is co-opting the idea of 'morality' as a strategy with which to recover and reassert the traditional family, and, in particular, fatherhood as a privileged status and essential ingredient in the making of the 'stable family'.[7] This theme is played out in contemporary mainstream films, and is the main topic of Chapter 4. It leads to serious dilemmas, not least of which is about the difficulties experienced by the education system in teaching sex education to children without offending traditional family values. These dilemmas are analysed in Chapter 6 in the context of the political arguments about Section 28 and the British Labour government's proposal, in 2000, to introduce classes in the value of marriage and parenthood training in the national curriculum of secondary schools as a central part of its plan to extend its political influence to the sphere of personal morality.

By naming his crusade 'the new national moral purpose', the British Prime Minister was able to link the powerful idea of familial morality with the 'national interest' and the moral health of the 'nation'. A key feature of Tony Blair's rule has been his move to take on the role of the nation's 'moral godfather', thus setting him apart from President Bill Clinton (beleaguered and tarnished during this same period by the international media exposure of his extra-marital activities). The British Labour government's plans culminated in a series of initiatives and announcements in 1999 to inculcate respect for stability in sexual relationships and a sense of responsibility in the bringing up of children. The government launched a £10 million drive to halve the number of schoolgirl pregnancies and to persuade those who *do* become mothers not to drop out of education. Predictably, a particular type of relationship and parenting is promoted: a heterosexual union within marriage, the traditional nuclear family, and also the desirability of conventional parenting.

Contemporary political leaders and other public actors use culturally available rhetorics about the family to account for their own practices and mobilise support for their actions (Morgan, 1999). They are marked by contradictions and highly emotive homilies that rely on scapegoating specific, vulnerable groups in society. After the General Election in 1997, the new Labour Prime Minister, Tony Blair, displayed his perfect nuclear family outside No. 10 Downing Street as a positive contrast to the 'sleaze' being replaced (see Figure 1.1). At first glance, the image seems to appeal to the genre of family photography as the front door of the family home, which is both home and office, operates as a powerful domestic symbol for framing the family members as a single unit in the same way as does the humble photograph from my own family's album in Chapter 3 (Figure 3.2). Yet this is unmistakably a photograph of a patriarch who has just achieved extraordinary power. This power is evoked by the triumphant look on the Prime Minister's face, by the raised hand hailing the press crowd, and also by the way the other hand is wrapped around his son's shoulder in a gesture of ownership: of his model family. When Tony Blair came into office there were also strong symbolic connections (reinforced by the press photographs and comments from the news media) between the images of his young family and the past images of the martyred US President Kennedy, who had been the first American President in a long while to enter office with a young family in 1960. The news media were fascinated by the idea of young children living and playing in the White House, and similarly in Downing Street.

The new Labour Prime Minister immediately exploited the theme of the family in his first major Conference speech, in which he said:

> We cannot say we want a strong and secure society when we ignore its very foundations: family life. This is not about preaching to individuals about their private lives. It is addressing a huge social problem. Attitudes have changed. The world has changed, but I am a modern man leading a modern country and this is a modern crisis. Nearly 100,000 teenage pregnancies every year; elderly parents with whom families cannot cope; children growing up without role models they can respect and learn from; more and deeper poverty; more crime; more truancy; more neglect of educational opportunities, and above all more

FIGURE 1.1   Britain's new Prime Minister, Tony Blair, with his family standing outside the door of No. 10 Downing Street, London, 1997. Pool photo by Sean Dempsey/PA. (By permission of PA Photo Agency.)

unhappiness. Every area of this government's policy will be scrutinised to see how it affects family life. Every policy examined, every initiative tested, every avenue explored to see how we strengthen our families.[8]

Within this text, the family is identified as both the *source* and the potential *saviour* of society's ills. In order for this to work, good families must be identified and separated from bad, 'dysfunctional' families. Otherwise, in an attempt to fudge the causes of familial breakdown, 'the family' could be interpreted as somehow threatened *by itself*: by its own shortcomings and inability to cope with change as a defunct institution. So Blair uses the device of identifying a category of 'bad families', and treats them as a threat to 'good families'. This is done by identifying the problem of teenage pregnancies, along with crime, truancy and educational opportunity neglect, as a menace to families and to 'modern' society. He makes claims for his status as a 'modern man', meaning an open-minded, sensitive, 'new man', leading a 'modern' developed country, projected in direct opposition to a conservative and old-fashioned man (as in his predecessor, John Major) who led an ex-imperial power. Blair's 'modernity' legitimises his claim for the mythical nuclear version of 'family' as the 'proper' and 'normal' version. By then declaring that all aspects of government policy will be scrutinised for their effects on family life so as to strengthen 'the family', it becomes clear that the nuclear ideal is the only version that the government is going to promote as genuinely familial, and that other identities, modes of parenting and living arrangements are to be discredited and pathologised in opposition to it. Thus, teenage pregnancies and 'bad families' constitute a crucial platform on which to stage a moral panic whenever the government wants to portray the idea of a crisis in 'family' values. The family is upheld as an ahistorical, fixed and timeless institution yet as also weak, vulnerable, under siege. All the changes going on around the family in a 'modern country' are leading to a modern crisis that the family itself must be protected from. In his desire to convey a crusade of national proportions, then, Blair declares that government policy will be the saviour of family life so that the 'good family' can gain the strength to save the nation – from bad families.

Significantly, when Tony Blair gave his public announcements about the Balkan war when Britain joined the United States in 1999 in the United Nations' bombing of Serbian military targets, he drew on the rhetoric of the family to show the nation that he 'cared' in a considered way about the human suffering caused by the war. Through carefully televised presentations Blair portrayed himself as calm and ordered, as the sensitive, caring yet powerful statesman, by referring to 'wives', 'sons', 'fellow human beings', 'families'. This public image of a measured, caring and sensitive national leader was dependent on familial rhetoric. It was sharply contrasted by Blair's references to the Yugoslav leader, Slobodan Milošević, at which point he switched to highly aggressive emotional terms of betrayal, barbarity, of a 'killing machine'.[9]

The media announcement in November 1999 of the impending arrival of the Blair baby, in May 2000, provided a further opportunity for the public celebration of images of the ideal nuclear family: 'Proof that if you vote Labour you too can be a middle-aged, regular guy who can have it all and more', as it was put in the *Mail on Sunday*.[10] Leo Blair came into the world as the First Baby in office for 150 years, at Downing Street. What was particularly ironic was the revelation that Cherie Blair's pregnancy was unplanned. Unplanned pregnancies are fine as long as you are not an adolescent, you are married, middle-class, a successful career wife of the Prime Minister and can afford to pay for private child care support to ensure minimum disruption to a busy lifestyle. A further irony, after the clever use of the family in the Prime Minister's visual declaration as a regular family man standing for wholesome family values, was the anger expressed by the Blair family when the press broke an agreement to respect the privacy of children and took photographs of the private christening of baby Leo Blair in July 2000. The tension between the call for family privacy and the call for media publicity raises significant questions about the way that the public world of the news media and political rhetoric mediate the stage management of family-values discourse. The Prime Minister's reaction was to cancel the ritual annual summer holiday news media photoshoot of the Blair family.

While teenage and pre-teenage motherhood is systematically demonised through political rhetoric as evidence of a breakdown in traditional, modern family values, an ongoing morality tale is being played out about the sexual perversions and exploits of white married men in high political office in the British and American news media – with the important exception of Britain's 'moral godfather', Tony Blair. This theme is analysed in further depth in Chapter 6. Interestingly, this news media condemnation contrasts sharply with current Hollywood films, in which a tale of responsible and caring middle-class fatherhood is being celebrated within a recovery of the figure of the 'new, caring, sensitive man', which is the focus of Chapter 4. Although the former discourse is 'factual' and the latter is 'fictional', both are engaged in an exploration and narrativisation of the parameters of 'good' and 'bad' family values. In the anglophone press, white married men are being publicly problematised through sexual scandals.

Following in the wake of the sexual indiscretions of British Members of Parliament, the American President, Bill Clinton, then disgraced his family through the international media exposure of his affair with Monica Lewinsky and a string of other women. In the same year, 1999, a prominent married British Tory politician, Michael Portillo, publicly admitted a homosexual past so as to 'clear the air' of public conjecture about his sexual history and make a bid for power in the British Conservative Party.[11] These recurrent revelations seem to indicate a crisis of hegemonic masculinity.[12] It is being evoked as a perverse masculine individualism that threatens the moral foundations of the ideal, nuclear version of familialism, and yet, at the same time, there is an ambivalent tolerance of this mode of masculinity being demonstrated by the news media.

Along with single mothers and problem families, white middle-class men and men in high office are being targeted as the cause of the crisis in family values and the rise of a particular perverse, 'dysfunctional' version of the family. Yet, significantly, this kind of scandalous reporting has not undermined the privileging of white fatherhood in the popular and news media. Individual men are vilified but the status of paternity is valorised. Bill Clinton has been forgiven by the nation, wives are shown standing by their unfaithful husbands, and men's sexual perversions somehow get bracketed off from 'the dysfunctional family'. At the height of Clinton's public shaming exposed by the press via the explosive Starr report, the British tabloid newspaper, the *Mirror* (12 September 1998) ran a double headline across its inside pages: 'I LOVE YOU DAD ... I'LL COPE. CHELSEA'S MESSAGE TO HER DISGRACED FATHER.'

SOCIOLOGICAL RESEARCH ON THE FAMILY AND CONSTRUCTIONS OF RACE

Academic research and debates in the social sciences in the United States and Britain continue to prioritise the nuclearised family form as an object of study (Van Every, 1999), and to take the Anglo-white nuclear family as the norm against which to measure 'other' family forms. Family sociology is deeply implicated, along with governments, in linking an attributed 'breakdown' of the family with a collapse of social cohesion. Remarkably, the institution of the white, English-speaking family has avoided being marked in terms of race and ethnicity within these debates. One of the unintended outcomes has been the privileging of a particular, narrow set of cultural relationships and dispositions as the norm, and the condemning and marginalising of other cultures and ways of living as somehow transitional. But, significantly, insufficient attention has been paid to the continuities, parallels and differences between representations of the family within political rhetoric, public policy, academic discourses and the popular media.

Sociological theories of the family typically invent 'the family' as a relatively bounded unit that exchanges with other equally relatively bounded units in society (Bernardes, 1997; Morgan, 1996). Many accounts of the family consist of checklists and categories of information collected to be tabulated and quantified for scientific analysis of 'the family' as an economic unit, residential household type, kinship network, and so on, and then presented as the manifestation of identified trends and generalities (Morgan, 1999: 14). An example of this is the methodological approach and summaries of the influential British government statistical journal *Social Trends*. While theoretical accounts are increasingly representing the family in terms of 'change', 'decline', or 'de-institucionalisation', it continues to be treated as a unit, as a coherent whole that somehow *ought to be* static and unchanging. Van Every (1999) points out that there is a serious and unhelpful slippage between family/household, couple/marriage and marriage/parenthood in sociological research on the family.

In the United States, the early 'classic' research of the 1950s and 1960s on American families approached non-Hispanic white families as the normative group by which to judge all American families, and the findings were often generalised to the whole of the American population (Roschelle, 1997). Much North American research on minority families has invested in the search for differences between black and 'standard white' *nuclear* families, between 'minorities' and Anglo-Americans. For example, extended households are said to be stronger among blacks than whites in USA. Lower incomes have been associated with a higher incidence of extended family structures, thereby evoking a natural interconnection between whiteness, nuclearity and middle classness. Comparison between Mexican American, black and Anglo families with male heads of household have reinforced rather than critically exposing patriarchal structures. The 'cultural approach' in American family sociology argues that African Americans and Chicanos attach no special importance to the nuclear family and give primary emphasis to the extended kinship network. But no social or historical explanation is offered to explain why one minority group might value extended families more than another. The unique socio-political histories, migration patterns and cultural norms of the ethnic groups that make up 'white', English-speaking people in western anglophone nations are ignored within such approaches (Roschelle, 1997). The tendency has been to look at those histories separately for an understanding of their separate ethnic and national identities. The impact on the meanings surrounding the family has been to reinforce the universality of the white, middle-class nuclear family.

In fact, the entire framework of the African American culture of poverty perspective within American family sociology is predicated on the assumption of a white, middle-class, normative model that is absent of strong extended kinship ties. This assumption inherently denies an African cultural heritage that characterises the black family. So black family traits, like extended kinship networks, are viewed as deviant and disorganised. The portrayal of black women as 'matriarchs' allows the dominant white group to blame African American women for the failure of black children to achieve, rather than to recognise racism as a socially detrimental force. By arguing that black poverty is passed on intergenerationally by a pathological value system, attention is diverted away from the political and economic inequality affecting black mothers and their children.

During the mid-1960s, American academics such as Moynihan (1965) blamed black occupational and economic inequality on family instability. The high number of female-headed households in urban areas, resulting from lack of well-paid permanent jobs for black men, was blamed on 'cultural pathology'. Being founded on a middle-class, white, normative model, the culture of poverty approach towards Latino families followed the same ethnocentric, racist biases as the studies of black families. Underlying this kind of approach is an assumption of the superiority of white middle-class culture and the devaluation of all other family forms (Staples and Mirande, 1980). But in contrast to studies of the black family, this approach focuses on male dominance and female passivity as the key explanation of Latino family 'disorganisation'. Chicano families are typically presented as radically different from the dominant (presumably egalitarian) Anglo-American family. The primary focus of this perspective is on the debilitating effects of machismo, that is, the spiritual, physical and sexual domination of men over women. In this way, the social and economic inequalities experienced by Chicanos are blamed solely on the patriarchal structure of the Chicano family (Mirande, 1985). Even though there is a large body of evidence from feminist research showing that the Anglo-white family is a mechanism for creating and maintaining women's oppression and is characterised by a strict division of power and gender roles, the 'culture of poverty' theorists characterise the Anglo family as a model of egalitarianism that the 'non-white' family should emulate.

Moreover, social scientists tend to lump all Latino groups together as if they share the same socio-historical experiences. Thus, the explanations for Chicano pathology are also applied to Puerto Rican families. Puerto Rican families are declared to be characterised by disorganisation, attributed to inherent flaws in their culture, including a strict differentiation of gender roles (Padilla, 1987). Puerto Rican men are presented as dictatorial and, like Chicano men, overtly concerned with their machismo. Puerto Rican women are depicted as self-sacrificing, chaste and dependent. Women are considered inferior to men and as having to defer to male authority. Low-income Puerto Ricans were said to be so completely obsessed with sex that it was seen to be the cause of most of the friction within the family (Lewis, 1966).

These research approaches emphasise negative social attributes that are held to be inherent qualities of ethnic minority families in the United States. A lack of deferred gratification among low-income minority families is seen as a sign of family disorganisation rather than a consequence of long-term economic and political deprivation. Significantly, proponents of the 'pathological approach' acknowledge the prevalence of extended kinship and social support networks, yet they judge them against the white, middle-class nuclear ideal, and therefore perceive extended families to be inherently pathological and end up focusing their analysis exclusively on marital disruption and female-headed households. Fierce arguments surrounding the 'culture of poverty' approach and the accusations of racism levelled against the infamous Moynihan (1965) report led to a reluctance by 'liberal' scholars to examine behaviour 'that might be construed as unflattering or stigmatising to racial minorities' (Roschelle, 1997: 6) for fear of being labelled racist. As a result, the growing problems of poverty concentration, joblessness and social dislocation in American inner-city ghettos were virtually ignored by social scientists for many years after the controversy had subsided (Wilson, 1991).

The 'strength resiliency' perspective that countered the 'culture of poverty' approach focuses on the positive aspects of black family life such as the strength of parent–child ties, informal social support networks, extended families and shared community responsibility for child care (Aschbrenner, 1978). The diversity of African American black families is now acknowledged (Billingsley, 1968, 1992; Nobles, 1974). But it depicts black women as dominating and castrating and ignores the effects of contemporary economic institutions on the development of family organisation. The 'adaptive' approach varies again by romanticising the black woman as strong and self-sufficient, and ultimately responsible for the survival of the black community (McCray, 1980). This tendency is evident in the feminist depiction of Aboriginal women in Australia. A celebration of the strong black mother represents an important attempt by black scholars to replace negative stereotypes with positive interpretations of black women, but it is still problematic. At the same time, it has been recognised by African American women that an Afro-centric, feminist analysis of motherhood is needed, one that debunks the image of both the matriarch and the super-strong black mother and presents a more realistic depiction of the dynamics of black motherhood (Collins, 1990).

Sociological perspectives on minority families in America have tended to collapse ethnic groupings into 'family types' that get either romanticised or condemned. In their various ways, the culture of poverty and cultural relativity approaches both privilege an Anglo-American familism by penalising or marking other ethnic groups for being extended rather than nuclear, for being over-reliant on relatives beyond the household, for being authoritarian families rather than conforming to the ideal of companionate marriages, for having too many children, for a lack of middle-class aspirations, for being poor. Most interpretations within these approaches either make unsubstantiated generalisations that fail to recognise the internal diversity of families or they exaggerate the differences as a way of pathologising them as inherently deviant and dysfunctional. The bitter debates on welfare reform that have flared across the United States in the last decade have centred on claims by politicians, academics and policy experts that if institutional forms of social support are withdrawn, impoverished families would still be able to survive because they rely on a wide network of extended family relatives. These political discourses about poor families and welfare reform exhibit increasingly racist undertones that are legitimised by reference to a white, middle-class nuclear ideal. Imposing of social policy that presumes some kind of family safety nets among non-white minority communities is likely to have deeply harmful effects on the lives of many people (Roschelle, 1997).

In Britain, studies of race and families have tended to focus on Caribbean and Asian families. Soon after their migration to post-war Britain, Caribbean families were labelled as deviant, prompting the quest for explanation, classification and derivation (Chamberlain, 1999: 129). Echoing aspects of North American social scientific approaches to non-white families in which white, middle-class nuclear families were treated as the norm, the main concern in Britain has been with conjugal and union status of couples and on the role of women in childrearing and family support. But sociological research has also focused on matrifocality and male marginality. Families in which women have power and take on the role of 'head of household' do not conform to the patriarchal structure represented as the norm in Anglo nuclear families, and so they constitute a threat to this perceived norm. When Britain's National Census revealed a higher proportion of single-mother-headed households among the British African-Caribbean community, it was discovered that it correlated with higher levels of 'welfare dependency' and social deviance within that community (for example, Dench, 1996). The dysfunctionality of non-white families arose out of government fears of the financial drain of non-nuclear families, with no male head of household, on the welfare system.

The implications for British Caribbean families of the colonial legacy of slavery, and of twentieth-century migration, are historical processes that have been persistently neglected within research. So have the damaging effects of institutional racism which are still being experienced in Britain today. It is only recently that research has begun to be conducted on the role of migration as a crucial dynamic in the culture of families, including the ways in which the extended family supported and enabled migration (Chamberlain 1995, 1997). As Chamberlain (1999: 129) states, 'Regarding migration and the family from the perspective of the Caribbean begins to shift the analytic framework away from what is perceived as "abnormality" to points of cultural survival and retention.'

Like the American research on minority families, current British research persists in the assumption of a two-parent norm that is not necessarily relevant to a West Indian context, where there are many half siblings and stepsiblings and membership of multiple- and trans-nuclear families. The underlying structures of racism that operate within academic and political discourses on the family are crucial aspects of the systematic privileging of the anglophone, white nuclear ideal. The white nuclear family cannot be elevated to the status of an ideal without inferiorising other cultures. The inferiorisation of non-white families operates both materially and at the level of representations through academic research that supports political rhetoric, welfare reform and family policy. This raises important questions about whiteness as a category that is naturalised by avoiding being marked as raced.

WHITE STUDIES

The global circulation of utopian images and meanings of white, western familialism in academic, popular media, political and policy representations and discourses raises questions about the implications of universalising a particular version of whiteness through familial signifiers. Whiteness may not be experienced or recognised as white consciousness in many regions but it is implicated in the 'othering' and subordination of other raced subjectivities. The historical, social and cultural construction of the white race is currently being addressed as a site of material and cultural privilege in the emerging area of white studies in the United States. The analysis of racial identity has been broadened by shifting attention beyond the African-American roots of mainstream white culture to its white colonial roots and contemporary identities. White studies is looking at the ways in which white identities were historically constructed and how 'whiteness' has been experienced through fluctuating processes of inclusion and exclusion (Giroux, 1997). Authors such as Roediger (1994) and Ignatiev (1995) emphasise the relational nature of identities and the arbitrary nature of white racial identity in its whole range of social contexts. A crucial issue is the identification of whiteness as an element of cultural identity that is *lived* and yet rarely recognised as a racial identity invested with power. Within cultural studies, whiteness has been identified as a site of racial privilege and exclusion by authors such as Frankenberg (1993, 1997), Dyer (1997) and Gabriel (1998). This general body of work has focused on sexuality but, curiously, has not as yet centred the family within its debates.

Giroux (1997) points out that white studies has emerged at the very moment when whiteness is being claimed as a racialised class consciousness among the white working class in the USA. Right-wing groups are using the discourse of white race to appease white working-class men mediated in reactionary TV talk shows, news magazines, the speeches of Republican politicians, and so on. Although the all-encompassing category of whiteness deals effectively with certain fundamental issues of racism in the United States, much of the American scholarship on 'whiteness' is culture-bound and treats it as an essential, pure and fixed racial and biological category that can only be distinguished by its opposition to blackness. Reducing ethnic identities to the binary factors of black and white, domination and subordination, makes it difficult for us to recognise the complex ways in which race and ethnicity are deployed to idealise nuclear familism and the ways in which both are being challenged or renegotiated in the search for non-hierarchical intimate relationships. The ways in which these issues are approached in Britain and the USA remain remarkably clumsy. As we have seen in relation to the sociological debates about race and family above, in the United States the term 'non-Hispanic white' is used alongside more loosely used terms such as 'Anglo-American', 'WASP (white Anglo-Saxon Protestant)', whilst in Britain the term 'Anglo-Saxon' is more commonly deployed. But there is a distinctive anglocentric bias woven into much research that infers an anglodominant discourse combining race with nation and culture to produce a naturalisation of a particular version of and disposition towards white ethnicity within dominant representations of familyness. This white family is class-bound as middle-class, aspirational, individualistic yet patriarchal and nuclear, and is emblematic in its figuring of the modern functional family ideal in western anglophone nations.

The white nuclear family remains a powerful ideological device for naturalising hierarchies of race, class, gender and sexuality, the historical foundations of which are discussed in Chapter 2. Throughout the twentieth century, familialism was used to mobilise anxieties about national, ethnic and sexual identities and deployed as a powerful myth for organising material reality across lived cultures in Britain by consolidating a biological and racially structured discourse about identity. As Kathleen Paul (1997: xii) states, the 1948 British Nationality Act, which generously granted the rights of citizenship to all members of the British Empire, was profoundly racialised, creating a fundamental contradiction between the formal definition of who was allowed to enter Britain and the informal idea of who could really *belong*.

During the 1980s, the British Conservative government promoted the myth of a fixed and unchanging nuclear familial type as essentially white Anglo-Saxon Protestant. This version of the family was represented as biologically and psychically natural, stable and universal, and yet also as vulnerable, in a state of crisis and under threat (Barrett and Macintosh, 1982; Gittins, 1993; Harwood, 1997). The 1981 British Nationality Act was conceived to confirm this. It was prompted by the public's *alleged*, but not proven, fear that Britain would be overwhelmed by people of a 'different culture and colour', thereby legitimating the idea that non-white migrants were a threat to British society. The law appealed to familialism for legitimacy. It placed more emphasis on *parentage* than on geography compared to the 1971 Act, thereby positioning the rulings within the larger post-war discourse of blood, family, kith and kin. The Conservative government gave up its imperialist pretensions by shifting to a domestic familial discourse of Britishness (Paul, 1997: 183). The 1981 Act reconstructed British nationality to fit preconceived notions of family and domestic community. It meant that white-skinned 'children of the Empire' gained entry to Britain while subjects of a different colour (meaning black and Asian) were excluded. This was exemplified by the contrasting treatment of the 'white' Falkland Islanders and the residents of 'colour' of Hong Kong.

ACADEMIC REINVENTIONS OF THE NUCLEAR IDEAL

Feminist debates about the family gained momentum in the academy from the 1960s onwards (Barrett and Macintosh, 1982; Friedan, 1981; Gavron, 1966; Oakley, 1974). The nuclear version of the family was exposed as culture-bound: that is, Anglo-American, white and middle class. And the disjunction between statistics on family life and functionalist representations of the ideal modern family was gradually being acknowledged. But these arguments only began to be incorporated in 'mainstream' sociology of the family debates from the late 1980s and 1990s. Ideas about a perceived shift towards a 'postmodern family' of diversity began to emerge, raising questions about the redundancy of the traditional nuclear family as a universal norm.

Evidence of the widespread nature of divorce, remarriage, post-divorce families, single parenthood, joint custody, abortion, cohabitation and two-career families could no longer be ignored. It began to dawn on the social sciences that this kind of 'dysfunctionality' was actually the norm, not only among ethnic minorities, migrants and the working class, who had always been treated as 'different' and dysfunctional, but even among the white middle classes on whom the functional version was modelled. In fact, there were so many problems with existing sociological concepts and theories of the family that feminists began asking whether 'the family' is a useful category of analysis any more and whether it ought perhaps to be dropped in favour of some other term such as 'household' (Barrett and Macintosh, 1982; Bernardes, 1997; Morgan, 1996). It raised questions about whether the modern 'functional' form was actually a figment of the imagination. Sociologically speaking it *was* fictitious; culturally speaking it was treated as the 'truth'.

One of postmodernism's most important undertakings is the recognition of diversity and difference. Yet, as Jo Van Every (1999: 166) states, sociological analysis has tended to treat diversity and difference as temporary problems that are solvable and less significant than meanings and structures of convergence. The 'family' has a history of being deployed as a discursive device for social and cultural convergence as a way of masking poverty and systems of social inequality: 'the family of man', 'one big happy family', 'the nation as family' and the 'commonwealth family of nations' (as I discuss in Chapter 2). Van Every undertook an analysis of all the key sociological journal articles about the family in the UK in 1993 and discovered that even by that date very little had been written on 'alternative' families 'of any sort'. In fact, 'sociologists were helping to construct a "normal" family which looked remarkably similar to that which an earlier generation of sociologists felt confident enough to define' (Van Every, 1999: 167). Van Every found that the kinds of families being defined as 'alternative' were those in which women were employed full-time or those that consisted of divorced or remarried couples. Households that consisted of familial arrangements and relationships that were *not* nuclear were treated as if they were transitional and somehow not worth studying. And immediate 'family' was treated as more important in the hierarchy of relationships than other close relationships such as friendships or relationships between siblings.

Sociological research tended to exclude, in its samples, households and families that did not resemble or fit the nuclear type. Many studies limited their samples of families to the nuclear form in case other types of families were to contaminate the findings for identifying factors that influence outcomes.[13] This nuclear-family-centric research bias implies that all households are, by definition, made up of heterosexual couples. Heterosexuality is often not even mentioned, but simply assumed. The fact that single-person households, single-parent households and same-sex households are the most rapidly expanding categories in western society is not reflected in the research, and the proportion of divorced or remarried couples or same-sex couples is not identified. Relatives, such as grandparents or close relationships, outside the conjugal couple rarely get included or mentioned as worthy of study for an understanding of significant emotional, material and caring support to the parents and couples who *are* under study. The concepts and categorisations of data invent the idea of the nuclear family as a relatively isolated unit, cut off from extended kinship networks and from the economic and public sphere. This 'isolated nuclear family' is privileged over members who live outside the household but contribute to its structure and meanings, such as siblings, parents and offspring.

Research on familial poverty still relies on the concept of the male 'head of household' through the assumption of a male breadwinner and female homemaker division of labour. And it often gets conducted with the assumption of gender-neutral language even though there is overwhelming evidence that women's part-time employment is frequently necessary to keep the household out of poverty. Van Every (1999: 174) points to examples such as the work of Callan et al. (1993). She argues that even though criticisms of nuclear familialism are numerous, 'modern' family sociology, as characterised by the structural-functionalist approach, persists in the USA and the UK because of a dominant idea that it somehow *should* be the ideal type under industrialism:

> The concentration on the relatively isolated nuclear family with a breadwinner-housewife division of labour was not due to the statistical predominance of this type of family in the post-war period in either the US or the UK. Rather it was theoretical considerations which highlighted this form as that most suited to the demands of modern industrial societies. Central to the 'modern' theoretical perspective is an emphasis on convergence rather than diversity. (Van Every, 1999: 175)

There is, then, overwhelming evidence that the modern nuclear family household is being reinvented, not only through political rhetoric and much popular imagery, but also, significantly, through academic research. Although functionalism, the main theoretical approach to the family of the 1950s and 1960s (outlined in Chapter 2), has been discredited, it lives on in dominant sociological research, and this contributes to the perpetuation of the idea of the nuclear family as the norm. Sociology is, as Van Every says, a 'textually mediated discourse' (to use a term made by Dorothy Smith [1988] and contributors to Roman et al., 1988) that influences the very social relations it analyses. By treating a particular type of household and unit as the norm, sociology reinforces the public discourse from the state. It is particularly worrying that welfare policies are based on the findings of this kind of family-centric research. The myth is still being reproduced, and even recent definitions and modes of research that acknowledge diversity often collude with the nuclear ideal by measuring their difference from a fictitious norm. So the use of categories such as 'divergent' and 'new' actually make the nuclear form seem normal (Van Every, 1999). If the nuclear form of the family is a myth, then the conceptual framework needs to be reworked rather than bolted onto it.

In her study of the shaping of policy in the United States, Judith Stacey (1999) outlines the impact that social scientists have on political debate. In turn, political debate has a powerful influence on the social sciences by creating the climate for funding certain types of research and censoring others. Family policy is strongly influenced by research agendas that get shaped by political agendas. A 'marketisation' of research has taken place in Britain and the USA in which researchers compete with one another to orient their research topics to a range of specific 'users' of research. How the research is carried out, disseminated and evaluated is decided by these users. The government is one of the largest funders of research on the family and therefore has a strong influence on the shaping of research agendas about the family. In Britain, for example, the most prominent policy debate is centred on fears about declining parental responsibility and the 'inadequate' socialisation of children resulting from high levels of 'family breakdown'. This has prompted a sharp increase in research on childhood but has, at the same time, shifted blame onto parents (particularly mothers) who fail to conform to the nuclear model, and has eclipsed other key factors that contribute to children's welfare, such as growing levels of child poverty (Brannen, 1999). So familial ideology has a profound impact on concepts, research processes and knowledge surrounding familial issues. Sociological discourses have thereby contributed to the connection made between familial breakdown and the breakdown of social cohesion.

The intellectual projects of feminism, anti-racism, post-colonial theory, queer theory and the politics of identity have shown that the traditional libertarian approaches of modernism are inadequate for an understanding of the complexities and diversity of lived relations (Van Every 1999: 179). As I outline in the chapters that follow, discourses on a white nuclear family ideal were constructed collaboratively, though not seamlessly, by the academy, the popular media and the state. 'Families of choice' and the new discourse on postmodern familialism have challenged traditional familial ideology and opened up inquiries about representations of nuclear, trans-nuclear and diverse family practices.

'TRANSFORMATIONS OF INTIMACY' AND THE 'NORMAL CHAOS OF LOVE'

Giddens (1992, 1999) and Beck and Beck-Gernsheim (1995) have recently identified and advocated a liberalising shift taking place in family meanings and structures as a consequence of globalisation and the individualisation of everyday life. The suggestion is that, within this new global era, there is now a democratisation of intimate relationships in which emotional communication and egalitarian ties are replacing traditional hierarchical ones. These theories of familial utopias claim that we, in western nations, are now beginning to accept a whole variety of relationships, such as lone-parent, step-family, and gay and lesbian relationships, as 'families'. The familial metaphor is being used to embrace living arrangements that deviate from the nuclear model.

Pure Relationships and Confluent Love

Within his work on the changing nature of the self and society called *The Transformation of Intimacy*, Giddens (1992) examines the significance of human agency and develops the idea of the reflexive self as a key characteristic of late modernity. The reflexive self has emerged out of the cultural and social conditions of late modernity but, at the same time, it has acted upon society and reshaped social life. In an increasingly complex world, biologistic discourses that once legitimised nuclear familial relations are collapsing. The concepts of the self and family are therefore being redefined. Individuals are now experimenting in new living arrangements in the absence of old certainties and binding values. Within the search for ontological security, individuals are producing narratives of the self in the spheres of intimacy and personal life. They do so in order to give meaning to the changes taking place in wider society as a consequence of massive social change such as globalisation, technologisation and secularisation.

Giddens does not refer to the term 'family' centrally in his analysis. As Smart and Neale (1999) point out in their important empirical study of post-divorce families, this is probably because the term carries a lot of baggage from which such an analysis needs to distance itself. As well as privileging one set of living arrangements over others, the term 'family' evokes ideas about a private sphere separated from the public sphere, and the idea of public and private 'selves'. Giddens attempts to transcend such divisions by referring to themes such as parent–child relationships, intimacy, and the body and sexuality. However, this creates a problem around the refusal to acknowledge the profound influence that the ideology of the family and the separate spheres have on human agency and the nature of society in late modernity. Giddens identifies a new form of intimacy that is composed of the notion of the 'pure relationship' and 'confluent love'. The pure relationship is defined as a social relationship developed by a couple for its own sake and continued 'only in so far as it is thought by both parties to deliver enough satisfactions for each individual to stay within it' (Giddens, 1992: 58). By confluent love he means an active, contingent love as opposed to the '"for-ever", "one-and-only" qualities of the romantic love complex' (Giddens, 1992: 61). The high levels of divorce are indicative of this shift from romantic to confluent love. It seems that a set of changes have taken place from the early nineteenth century, when individuals married for economic reasons or to bind two families within meanings about heritage and continuity, to the late nineteenth and early twentieth century, when people married for eternal love, to the present, when individuals accept that love is contingent and that commitment has been replaced by the idea that the relationship can be terminated and a more suitable one initiated if there is no longer any compatibility between partners.

The pure relationship is distinguishable from the traditional romantic marriage by the fact that it is founded on a negotiated normative framework in which collaboration and communication are paramount. The former marital ideal of romantic love was structured by inequality, dependence and the segregation of gender roles. But because it is being continuously revised and rethought, and is part of the 'project of the self' involving personal growth and change, the pure relationship tends to be unstable. As individuals' needs and desires are acknowledged to be changeable, the couple may become incompatible or the relationship becomes subject to renegotiation. So, in contrast to earlier sociological analyses of marriage and family, in which outside structures such as the economy impact on the family, Giddens sees individuals, especially women, as active agents impacting on wider social structures. Couples become conscious agents of change in the intimate sphere through the rise of the individual as a reflexive self. However, Giddens (1992: 131) also notes that 'men are largely unwilling to release their grip upon the reins of power', so the transformation of intimacy has not yet led to the dismantling of patriarchal power in the family.

Notwithstanding the continuing presence of gender inequalities, patriarchally structured relations are being undermined by the rise of the pure relationship. Giddens points to lesbian and gay relationships as a kind of vanguard for the rise of the pure relationship model precisely because they have been excluded from the norms that shape marital relations and exist outside conventional gendered relations of power in families. The pure relationship depends on democracy and equality and is therefore incompatible with the patriarchal structure of orthodox heterosexual marriage relationships. Giddens thinks it unlikely that the pure relationship will replace the old marital ideal of romantic love within heterosexual relationships. But, given that most couples enter marriage to have children, moves towards it will either take the form of a modern companionate marriage based on friendship and mutual sympathy but not much sexual involvement, or a form of co-residence in which the home is shared but there is no emotional relationship.

What is most important about Giddens' approach is that he sees the family as a site for the democratisation of intimate relationships and a platform on which debates about moralities and ethics are staged. There are problems with his argument concerning the lack of detail about the structural inequalities and differences of class, gender, race, first and third world. But he does claim to be aware of the differential access to the resources allowing 'lifestyle' choices upon which the project of the self and the construction of the democratic pure relationship depend. As Smart and Neale (1999: 12) state, 'it is important to understand how the pure relationship is mediated by religion, ethnic difference, wealth, employment status and so on'.

Giddens implies that confluent love and the pure relationship could be practised by all couples were it not for the fact that they are held back by the normative constraints of romantic love and patriarchal power, as if these barriers were merely temporary residual cultural forces. But this residual culture of nuclear familism is propped up by a number of powerful institutional structures, as Smart and Neale (1999: 12) observe, including pension provision, the privatisation of child care provision, a gender- and age-segregated labour market, the housing market, and so on, as well as the ways in which the educational system teaches about sex and family life. They also suggest that 'racism might in fact exert a push toward traditional marriage rather than away from it for some communities'. Smart (1997) has also claimed that the pure relationship, of moving from one long-term commitment to another, ignores the effect of children. Having children makes the move much more complicated for many couples at the financial as well as the emotional level. She points out that Giddens' model is essentially dyadic and needs to take into account the existence and active agency of children within triadic relationships. Moreover, this model precludes the significant trend of 'ongoing parenting after divorce' that Smart and Neale examine in their empirical and theoretical analysis of family practices in modern society. While sexual relationships may end, parenting carries on in one form or another.

22

Individualism and Chaotic Love

In his book entitled *Risk Society*, Beck (1992) describes the process of individualisation that emerges under conditions of late modernity. He emphasises that the traditional concept of class is no longer useful for understanding the kinds of social inequalities that structure human relations under conditions characterised by globalisation, individualisation, risks of unemployment and environmental damage. Beck highlights the *contradictions* experienced by women within the process of individualisation and erosion of traditional family life. While women attempt to move away from the old ascribed roles and try to combine marriage and career, they find that the process of individualisation is blocked for them by a myriad of barriers including the segregated labour market and the glass ceiling. They experience a lack of social protections against the burdens of domestic and child care work through the erosion of their labour marketability and pension provision during the phase of temporary full-time motherhood.

In *The Normal Chaos of Love*, Beck and Beck-Gernsheim (1995) examine the ways in which love has gained significance under modernity. In contrast to Giddens' carefully negotiated contingent love, Beck and Beck-Gernsheim's love includes the yearning love of children and is much more urgent and demanding. As a central part of the rise of individualism in late modernity, love has come to be the crucial way of finding meaning in life and yet it has become more fragile and precarious. The child provides new hope and becomes a guarantee of permanent love during the very moment when the adult relationship seems to be waning. Beck and Beck-Gernsheim point to the rise of an autonomous motherhood in which a woman has a child without a relationship with a man, and also to the fact that both parents want to keep the children after divorce, as examples of this need for children as a promise of greater fulfilment.

However, they claim that new conflicts come about between men and women at the moment of divorce as men start to reassess their affection for the children. Beck and Beck-Gernsheim suggest that men have begun envying women's closeness to children and their custody over them while divorced husbands traditionally have the reward of continuous employment. They observe that men think that women have it both ways: employment and children. This, they say, has led to men's bitterness over custody laws that seem to be stacked against them. Beck and Beck-Gernsheim claim that the increase in husbands' challenges to mothers' legal custody of children is a component of the individualisation process in which men seek a permanent bond of love through children. The growth of fathers' rights organisations in western societies is apparent evidence of this. This resentment is linked to the changing structures and meanings of work and to women's growing independence, and will be picked up in Chapter 4 in relation to representations of fatherhood in the popular media. Yet as Smart and Neale (1999: 18) point out, Beck and Beck-Gernsheim do not distinguish between men's perceptions of the child as server of unconditional love and actual parent–child relationships. Men also have an unrealistic perception of the structural disadvantages that women put up with in employment, earning 30 per cent less than men. The difficulties women have as mothers in bringing up and bonding with their children are well documented, demonstrating that children are not an uncomplicated and effortless guarantee of love. A critical issue is why men would view children in this way. It seems likely that it is associated with their lack of closeness to child care, as Smart and Neale suggest.

Beck and Beck-Gernsheim refer to the fragmentation of traditional modes of collective solidarity formed through class and community. This is the consequence of changing market forces and the ethos of self-improvement and self-absorption which characterise individualism. Yet the more individualistic people become, the more they desire closeness, security and connection with a loved one. Beck and Beck-Gernsheim claim that, ironically, as relationships become more fragile and vulnerable, people look more to relationships for fulfilment. They interpret these forces as push/pull factors. Women, in particular, are being pulled in two directions: towards conventional domestic roles, on the one hand, and towards independence, on the other. For women, these contradictions are all part of the difficulties of combining employment with child care. They lead to the desire to have financial freedom and they contribute to high divorce rates. However, unlike Giddens, Beck and Beck-Gernsheim see individuals not as reflexive and active agents, but as somehow caught up in outside forces beyond their control. They claim that the dangers of individualisation are counteracted by the ideology of love (Beck and Beck-Gernsheim, 1995: 181). They approach love as the new opiate of the masses, as an addiction to give meaning to people's alienated lives in a secularised society. It is not made clear why love comes to be such a crucial and destructive force as we become increasingly individualised, and the logic of this position has been questioned by Smart and Neale (1999), who challenge the idea that individualisation is a consuming self-interest associated with moral decline in the form of rising divorce rates. The ideology of love apparently involves self-sacrifice and promises fulfilment through altruistic commitment. Yet for Beck and Beck-Gernsheim, modern individualised love is a troubled form of love which can be demanding, selfish and therefore destructive.

Beck and Beck-Gernsheim do take children into account in their analysis, but they assume all couples to be heterosexual. Giddens' approach is a more useful one for exploring new modes of moral knowledge within intimate lifestyles, although both treat intimacy and love and family relationships as a narrow, isolated unit. Smart and Neale point to the work of David Morgan (1996), who focuses specifically on the family rather than a theory of modernity. Morgan examines care and caring and the negotiations involved in being responsive to the needs of others as both love and labour and involving skills and agency. He points out that the term 'family' is widely used and has, in fact, become radicalised through the idea of 'families of choice' (Weston, 1991). It would therefore be unhelpful to drop the term or replace it with the concept of 'household', given that 'family' implies an emotional commitment and form of caring not implied in the latter term. As lesbian and gay couples have adopted the term 'family', the meaning and value of the term shifts. Rather than seeing the family as an institution, Morgan uses the term 'family practices' to indicate the fluidity and diversity of family relationships. So a new post-nuclear, post-patriarchal familial model has been conceived and projected by sociological theory. However, within 'the messy improvisational patchwork bonds of postmodern family life', Judith Stacey (1999: 189) claims that contemporary changes in family values have led to normative instability. A feature of the postmodern condition seems to be the rise of a normative vacuum and definitional crisis for the 'postmodern family'.

THE FAMILY AS A DISCURSIVE CONSTRUCT AND REGULATORY IDEAL

The family functions as a sign within the politics of representation. In cultural studies, representations of the family are approached as cultural constructions and not simply as direct reflections of the real world. The range of meanings about 'family' depends on the narratives, groups of images and discourses that operate through a variety of texts and areas of knowledge. We have looked at one of these prominent discourses above, namely sociology, which represents the 'family' in particular ways. Within a constructionist approach, Foucault's (1978, 1980) work has contributed to an understanding of the ways in which knowledge and power operate through representation. He has focused not just on meaning, but also on the production of knowledge through 'discourse', as a significant approach to the problem of representation. He was more interested in relations of power than relations of meaning in his own work, and focused his attention on the various disciplines of knowledge within the human and social sciences. He found that these disciplines had claimed such a dominant and influential role in modern culture that they were regarded as truthful knowledge, which surpassed religious and other earlier forms of 'truth'.

By studying discourses as systems of representation as Foucault did, we can approach expert knowledges, such as sociology, as systems of representation that construct meanings of 'family'. Discourse constructs and regulates knowledge about the family. It works by defining and producing the topic of 'familyness' as an object of knowledge. It controls the way that the topic can be discussed and how ideas about the family get put into practice and used to regulate people's conduct. For example, the 'expert' knowledge of sexology, circulated in popular sex manuals of the late nineteenth and early twentieth century, was produced by medical discourses on sex and marriage that not only regulated the meanings and actions of married heterosexual couples but also regulated what was publicly defined as permissible or perverse sex (discussed in Chapter 3).

Foucault's study of subjectivity and sexuality in *The History of Sexuality* (1978) has been central to theories of representation. However, with the emphasis being more on the body as a site for the regulation of sexed subjects, less attention has been paid to 'the family' as such, even though they are intimately interrelated. Following Foucault, the family can be approached as a focal point for the exercise of power and the production of subjectivities. It is one of the key regulatory discourses through which our identities become gendered. So the family can be seen as a discursive construct. Political rhetoric, academic knowledge and popular media texts are all discourses that place limits and restrictions on ways of talking about the family as a topic. They also place limits and restrictions on ways of conducting ourselves in relation to the family. These discourses do not necessarily share the same style, strategy or actions. But they attempt to define acceptable ways of discussing, analysing, performing, experiencing, narrativising, memorialising, and symbolising 'the family'. When the same discourse appears across a range of texts, institutional sites and social practices, then they belong to the same discursive formation. As we shall see in the chapters that follow, at different historical and cultural contexts, these familial discourses often share the same discursive formation.

Given that the family has no fixed meaning and takes on meaning as an object of knowledge within discourses, it is unstable and continuously being reshaped within particular historical contexts. So we need to analyse the discourses to see how the family is evoked as meaning and knowledge. As Stuart Hall (1997: 55) has outlined, this can be done by studying the elements that make up discourses: *statements* made about the family; the *rules* that prescribe how we should talk about the family; the *subjects* who come to personify the discourse (the male breadwinner and full time housewife, the teenage mother, the single mother, the absent father, and so on); the acquisition of *authority and 'truth'* by this knowledge (through, for example, medical knowledge as 'truth'); *the practices in institutions* for dealing with and regulating subjects (family therapy and counselling, family law, welfare practices, and so on); and awareness that a different discourse will emerge, such as a radical notion of family through the idea of 'families of choice'.[14]

For Foucault, truth is not absolute. He looks at the way in which 'truth' is *produced as authority* to regulate the conduct of others through the combination of power and knowledge. He refers to 'regimes of truth' sustained by discursive formations. What we believe we know about the family influences our approach to it. If we conceive of it as only 'nuclear', then we are likely to regard it as in a state of decline, and attempt to regulate it accordingly through law, taxes, welfare policy. Hall (1997: 49) uses the example of single parents:

> ... it may not be true that single parenting inevitably leads to delinquency and crime. But if everyone believes it to be so, and punishes single parents accordingly, this will have real consequences for both parents and children and will become 'true' in terms of its real effect, even if in some absolute sense it has never been conclusively proven.

Rather than looking at representation through individual texts, Foucault analyses it through the discursive formations in which texts are located. For Foucault, the body is the key object over which power is applied, through techniques of regulation. In *The History of Sexuality* (1978), he examines how power is exerted over the body by sexualising it through sexual discourses produced by medical and psychiatric institutions. In various ways, then, the body gets classified, categorised, inscribed within regimes of power and truth. Professional discourses and power relations construct our knowledge about 'normal', 'perverse and 'deviant' sexual behaviour and identities. In this sense, the family is a discursive field that produces the body by inscribing particular and general meanings on it and giving it a familial identity, as legitimate or illegitimate member of society through naming, heritage, religion, belonging, claim to citizenship as nation and territory.

Family practices can be approached as 'socially scripted behaviour' (Gagnon and Simon, 1973: 262) to emphasise that in order for families to exist, as practice and meaning, they must be acted out through performed roles of sex, coupling, caring, parenting within intimate relationships confirmed publicly by specific codes of behaviour. Familial scripts are internalised by family members so as to reproduce continuously the essence of familyness. In this sense, there has to be a continuing dialogue between families themselves and the public representations of them in constructing the meanings of familyness. This idea of the family as something that has to be scripted, performed and treated as a staged spectacle is a theme that is taken up as a critical thread throughout this book. Here, Judith Butler's approach is useful.

Drawing on Foucault's social constructionist perspective, Judith Butler argues that discourse operates as a normative regulatory power that produces the subjects it controls. Discourse defines, constructs and produces bodies as objects of knowledge. As a discursive construct, the family is a site through which the sexed subject is produced, is familialised, as a 'sexed' and 'gendered' subject. Just as the category of sex is a normative category, so too the family is a regulatory ideal through which individuals are produced as sexed subjects. According to Butler, sex and gender are produced through

27

the enactment of discursive practice by citing, repeating and reiterating a set of norms.

Butler (1994) draws on a psychoanalytic approach to explain why all sexual norms are tenuous. She argues that since heterosexual sex has a sense of its own superficiality, so 'it has to ritualistically reproduce itself all over the place' (1994: 33). It is a repetitive performance that always fails. This is because it is a sexual *norm*. A sexual position has to be crafted, and as soon as *one* sexual position is recited, others have to be excluded, which 'always involves becoming haunted by what's excluded. And the more rigid the position, the greater the ghost, and the more threatening it is in some way' (1994: 33). This does not only apply to a heterosexual norm. It applies to all sexual norms. Sex is produced only as a citing or confirmation of hegemonic norms, and familyness is compelled by a regulatory apparatus of heterosexuality.

Within lesbian and gay politics, many people have interpreted Butler's *Gender Trouble* (1990) as an assertion that gender categories can be destabilised and de-centred by exploring different identities through transgressive performance. Butler sees performativity as something distinctive from performance. She sees it as re-signification, as a way of changing the meanings, the labels attached to identities. She says that 'performativity is that aspect of discourse that has the capacity to produce what it names' (Butler, 1994: 33). But what about the biological constraints on 'discourse'? After all, in the end, women have babies and men don't. In answer to this question about the limitations of discourse, and dominance of biology over the social and cultural, Butler says:

> Now it seems to me that, although women's bodies generally speaking are understood as capable of impregnation, the fact of the matter is that there are female infants and children who cannot be impregnated, there are older women who cannot be impregnated, there are women of all ages who cannot be impregnated, and even if they could ideally, that is not necessarily the salient feature of their bodies or even of their being women. What the question does is try to make the problematic of reproduction central to the sexing of the body. But I am not sure that is, or ought to be, what is absolutely salient or primary in the sexing of the body. If it is, I think it is the imposition of a norm, not a neutral description of biological constraints. (Butler, 1994: 34)

Butler therefore asks, under what discursive and institutional conditions do biological differences 'become the salient characteristics of sex'? In response, she says:

> It's a practical problem. If you are in your late twenties or early thirties and you can't get pregnant for biological reasons, or maybe you don't want to, for social reasons – whatever it is – you are struggling with a norm that is regulating your sex. It takes a pretty vigorous (and politically informed) community around you to alleviate the possible sense of failure, or loss, or impoverishment, or inadequacy – a collective struggle to rethink a dominant norm. (Butler, 1994: 34)

So when people ask whether biological differences govern the body, they are actually asking whether the social institution of reproduction should be the most dominant one for thinking about gender. The very preoccupation with such questions about biological destiny are proof that there is a discursive enforcement of such a norm.

Lesbian and gay 'families of choice' subvert the category of normal 'sexuality' by untying sexuality from gender. Following Butler (1990), we can say that it is through repeated performances 'that congeal over time' that 'gender' and 'sexuality' are produced. As such the family becomes an important site of performativity. Within Jeffrey Weeks et al.'s (1999) 'families of choice', subversive possibilities come to the fore, making 'gender trouble', undermining old binary restrictions. So Giddens is right to focus on lesbian and gay families of choice as the vanguard of change in meanings of familyness, as they have the greatest potential to disrupt and weaken dominant family discourse based on heterosexual/reproductive discourses. These problems are being publicly battled over in the UK around the vexed issue of sex education in schools, as addressed in Chapter 6.

A myriad of checks and balances that constrain our gendered and raced behaviour steer it towards or away from some kind of familialism – for example in the very naming and changing of surnames for women when they marry, in the expectations people have to marry, to have children, to have a gendered division of labour in the household, and so on. So the cultural need to perform family relationships implies an audience (Dunne, 1999). A myriad of public platforms are available on which the performance can be staged, such as in the context of family rituals from rites of passage, for example weddings and christenings, to family-based religious festivals and touring holidays. Family photography, the family album and home video are powerful ways in which these rituals are captured and framed so as to offer families an audience, a kind of private/public gaze that surveys and monitors the parameters and success of the performance. But family photographs and the way they are displayed in albums do much more than check whether individuals within family relationships measure up to the imaginary modern family. Chapter 3 takes up this theme and looks at the intriguing ways the family photograph album offers a powerful ideological device for the continuous reinvention and re-presentation of familyness.

FAULTY FAMILIES

The catalogue of familial failures around infidelity and parental irresponsibility being paraded within the public sphere through Hollywood films, television drama and, of course, press stories of politicians' and the British Royal Family members' infidelities seem to indicate profound public and private concerns about the 'proper' role of men and women within the search for a post-patriarchal, postmodern set of familial structures. 'Ideal' and 'dysfunctional' versions of familialism are being offset against one another. Lone mothers, working mothers, black, immigrant, gay and lesbian families have all been blamed, at different times, within political rhetoric and the news media for undermining the *proper* family. Until quite recently, the label of 'dysfunctionality' has been applied predominantly to Afro-Caribbean and other non-white families in Britain by stigmatising them as anarchic and perverse through both rhetoric and policy (Chamberlain, 1999). Today, however, white heterosexual parenthood is in the media spotlight. It is also being scrutinised and marked out as a key problem in the news media and official discourses in support of a particular moral agenda.

In my attempt to contribute to the positioning of 'the family' within cultural debates, the following chapters trace some relevant themes and issues surrounding western anglophone media representations of white nuclear familialism as they appear in academic discourses, political rhetoric, social and welfare policies and the popular media. And in doing so, they raise questions about tensions that are emerging between representations and lived experiences of 'family'. I offer some thoughts about the fluid cluster of meanings that surround familial ideology and contemporary popular media representations of familialism. I draw on the construction of a historical model of white familialism during the period of the nineteenth century as a theoretical standpoint and reference for certain subsequent cultural discourses. In Chapter 2, I refer to current critiques of family history to confirm the disjunction between actual living arrangements and ideas about kinship and household stretching from the nineteenth century in imperialist Britain. This section indicates that familialism played a central role at the level of ideals and values, rather than lived practices, in shaping identity through gendered and racialised relations of power.

Thereafter, I explore contemporary popular media and public discourses that are crystallising around three dominant, though by no means exhaustive, versions of the family: the 'ideal', modern nuclear family (Chapter 3), the 'dysfunctional' defective or perverse family (Chapter 4), and a 'hybrid', transformative, trans-nuclear family (Chapter 5). The empirical basis of the three categorisations is founded on three combined forms of evidence: the mass media, including television, film, photography and advertising; public discourses, including political rhetoric; and shifting academic debates within the sciences and social sciences, and among wider 'experts'. My interpretations are based on observable shifts in familial themes, values and characteristics in popular media representations and public discourses of 'the family' in Britain, the United States and Australia. This is combined with evidence drawn from related cultural debates and analyses of romance, sexual and familial identities represented in Hollywood films and other popular media. In Chapter 6, I trace the recent emergence of revisionist family-values discourse and attempts to recover a white nuclear family as a key feature of a trend towards a moral fundamentalism in western anglophone nations. This is seen as a reaction against the increasing public tolerance of gay and lesbian lifestyles and the rise of alternative 'new family' arrangements and representations. In Chapter 7, I inquire into the changes in familial relationships claimed by authors such as Giddens (1992) who have contributed to discussions about postmodern familialism. I address the implications of the ethnic and class status of the white family being represented in political and academic discourses, and the popular news media.

In these ways I wish to provide historical, conceptual and empirical popular media evidence of certain key processes through which a white, nuclear version of familialism has been mobilised and naturalised in western anglophone cultures. The aim is to construct a theoretical bridge between representations of family ideals and distinctive hierarchies of race, nation and gender within a given social order. Despite popular cultural and official tendencies to mediate and universalise a white nuclear version of family ideology, the point is that this version is neither a local or universal set of cultural experiences, nor a globally dominant set of representations. It is simply one version, one example, of a more general historical trend in familial ideology that, at the level of ideas, continues to have a profoundly pervasive influence on images, debates, policies, practices and identities.

NOTES

1. Aspects of the subject matter of this book have been published in an essay in the *European Journal of Cultural Studies*. See Chambers (2001).
2. *Observer*, 5 September 1999 'Blair's Moral Crusade' by Andrew Rawnsley, page 1. Teenage pregnancies in Britain are the highest in Europe with 7,700 under-16-year-old conceptions per year. Just under half of the mothers give birth, according to the School Standards Minister, Estelle Morris, quoted in the *Daily Mail*, 29 December 1999 by Tony Halpin, page 15. Also see the Social Exclusion Unit's report on *Teenage Pregnancy* (1999).
3. See, for example, Babb (1994), Campbell (1993) and Selman (1996) for discussions about evidence of the link between teenage pregnancies and economic deprivation, lack of employment and continuing educational opportunities for young women.
4. *Observer*, op. cit. 5 September 1999. Op. cit.
5. From 'In Baptist talk Clinton stresses moral themes', *New York Times*, 10 September 1994, quoted in Stacey (1999: 185).

6. From 'Quayle talks tough on fatherhood', *San Francisco Chronicle*, 9 September 1994, quoted in Stacey (1999: 185).
7. See, for example, Collier (1999) concerning debates about men, heterosexuality and the reconstruction of fatherhood in the law and social policy.
8. *The Guardian*, 1 October 1997.
9. For a linguistic analysis of Tony Blair's public speeches, see Fairclough (2000).
10. Peter Dobbie, 'Welcome the babies, but spare us the moral godfather', *Mail on Sunday*, 2 January 2000.
11. This strategy was demonstrably successful, as Michael Portillo was re-elected as Member of Parliament in a by-election and quickly made Shadow Chancellor by the leader of the Conservative opposition in February 2000.
12. 'Hegemonic masculinity' is a term used by Connell (1995) to refer to the privileging of a heterosexual mode of masculinity in society.
13. Van Every (1999: 172) states that 'Only two articles describe the sample as also containing single women but the analyses focus on marriage and the articles provide much more information about this household/family form.'
14. See Stuart Hall (1997) for an excellent introduction to Foucault's ideas and method.

CHAPTER 2

MYTHS OF FAMILIAL ORIGINS

The central, singular term 'the family' is privileged as an abstract notion, which makes it difficult to consider the ways in which familialism has been exploited as an ideology to domesticate the empire, and hierarchicalise relations of race, gender, generation and sex. The demand, by state and other official bodies and public discourses, to restructure the family according to a white, middle-class, patriarchal model was shaped by British imperial power and activated in the colonial context. During the nineteenth century, the family was transformed and fixed into a symbol of colonisation. The idea of 'family values' and the collapse of the modern family as an institution rely on a narrow set of assumptions about its historical and biological basis, and its universality. The family continues to be represented in official and popular discourses as *natural*. So there is a need to review and unravel some of the ways in which this process of naturalisation has operated historically to shape ideas about it today.

Meanings about the family and gender roles are essentialised and fixed not through a single site but through a range of discursive sites, including biological, scientific, psychological and historical codes of knowledge that attempt to universalise and dehistoricise the family. Yet the social investment in representing the practices of the ideal nuclear family as normal, natural and inevitable contradicts the perceived need to *train* and *teach* people – through family welfare policy, education, and medical care – to perform these 'natural' and instinctual roles in such ways as to censor other versions of being and living and performing cultural practices and meanings. This chapter approaches some of these contradictions by exploring examples of the kinds of discursive sites through which the family was constructed and represented in official and popular discourses as a *natural* entity. It looks at the way in which the family was deployed as a metaphor, from the nineteenth century to the mid-twentieth century, to support particular social hierarchies and perpetuate inequalities of race and gender. The aim here, then, is twofold: first to offer some sense of history, yet also to emphasise the contradictions that form the 'ideal family', perceived as both 'normal' and in need of training to reach this natural state; and second, to examine the ways this ideal white, nuclear family is anchored within 'nation' and the support of social hierarchies and inequalities of race and gender.

The explosion of political rhetoric and moralising about the family is premised on powerful myths that I refer to as *myths of familial origins*. Roland Barthes (1972) uses the term 'myth' to refer to signs that convey familiar and powerful systems of cultural beliefs in such a way as to naturalise them. The workings of the signs and codes in the cluster of signs that make up 'familyness' are hidden by myth. It often has traditional, historical acceptance in the sense that the meanings and values of the sign structures of 'familyness' seem to occur in a common-sense way, with universal applicability and relevance, across time and space. In fact, popular myths about the family have been so persistent that academic historians, anthropologists, economists and demographers, along with sociologists, have been active contributors to the construction and resurrection of unverified assumptions about the family as 'truth'. Even though many scholars have demonstrated that the popular narrative of the family is simplistic and wrong, several fundamental premises are still taken for granted (Davidoff et al., 1999: 16).

Davidoff et al. (1999: 4) refer to this set of myths as *a public story*, an unhelpful public story because it consistently foregrounds the nuclear family and denies the complexities of familial relationships that actually existed in our recent past. These myths also hold out the hope of the nuclear family unit as the means by which a golden age might be recovered in the future. So the myths and assumptions behind the golden age leading up to and including the 1950s need to be uncovered and challenged so as to shift the nuclear family from its central, idealised position and place it alongside other familial and social relationships.

The roots of social inequalities residing in modern family values lie in historical structures and changes during identifiable periods and institutions, including the impact of industrialisation, institutional life in nineteenth-century western anglophone nations, twentieth-century welfare and legislative reform, and in the range of state, social and medical policies that were framed by pre-existing familial ideals and practices. Many familial discourses that originated during the nineteenth century have remained in circulation and came to influence evolving popular media representations of the family in the following century.

The myths of family origins are appropriated within discourses that naturalise hierarchical social relations based on patriarchal, colonial, racist and heterosexist ideologies. These myths are situated within a set of codes that imply that the social order structured on male authority, and the inferiorisation of specific social groups such as women and non-white races, is natural, ahistorical and unchangeable. In these ways, the family, familial metaphors and familial practices have played a fundamental role in the imperial narratives of European nations and have constituted a crucial arena for forging a set of ethnicised identities by English-speaking settler nations such as the United States and Australia, within a set of colonial relations linked centrally to Britain and differentiated from other parts of Europe.

In this chapter I explore foundations to the myths of familial origins and examine the invention of the ideology of the family. The nineteenth-century origins of myths and definitions of 'family' and 'household', which continue to be in circulation today, were formed in this period. I identify the sources of public, academic and popular cultural representations of the white nuclear family as morally superior, as a 'functional family'. The mythologies of Victorian ethics obscured the power relations between the sexes, races and the public state within the structuring of a dominant version of the private, middle-class, white nuclear family. Postcolonial theory has exposed the colonial structures and meanings through which the white family has been constructed as a 'natural' site of racial privilege and gender hierarchy. The chapter refers to British imperialist roots of an anglophonic familial ideology anchored within the values and ideals of the extended white Victorian English-speaking family, which later gave way to the celebration of a white, middle-class nuclear family form in the desire to make families adapt to a Protestant, Anglo-Saxon work ethic and to the structures of capitalist societies. I draw upon the new research in social history that challenges familism through evidence of significant discrepancies between ideologies of the family, actual household types and kinship relations, and shifting meanings of family life. Sexology is taken as a case study to explore the ways in which medical discourses on sex were used to confine sex to heterosexual marital sex and reproduce patriarchal relations in the family. Talcott Parsons' twentieth-century post-war theory of the 'functional' family is outlined to show how the ideology of the family shaped sociological theories and encouraged the treatment of non-nuclear family forms as deviant and 'dysfunctional'.

THE MYTHS OF FAMILY ORIGINS

A pervasive assumption about familial origins in western societies is that the institution of the family underwent a dramatic and decisive change during industrialisation and that this change was part of the 'progress' of western societies in the shift from a traditional to a modern form. The myths of familial origins are white myths, located firmly in the white, British imperialist historical context of the nineteenth and early twentieth century. Within colonial discourses, there are various stages and layers of this popular narrative that take on crucial myths of racial, cultural and territorial conquest, and white settlement with frontier and outback metaphors associated with the related pioneering ethos, which I address below. As Davidoff et al. (1999) argue, the family story begins with the assumption that before industrialisation, families were extended with several generations of kin who were self-reliant with little outside interference. People were said to be knitted together by blood ties that gave them status, and these ties were cemented by timeless rituals associated with birth, marriage and death. But relationships in such families were somehow less emotionally intense than today.

This set of myths of familial origins is vague in its periodisation, claiming, rather suspiciously, that the modern family emerged just before living memory. Social historians and sociologists have conflated complexities of industrialisation to a brief transitional period with a distinct 'before' and 'after'. The decades of the 1780s to the 1840s have been centred on by historians, who broadly agree that it constitutes a key era of change and a standard period during which the so-called 'modern era' of familialism emerged. Davidoff et al. (1999: 20) observe that '[t]he search for a precise turning point is necessarily an elusive one, whether for the end of an idyllic past and the start of the modern nightmare, or for the beginning of progress from backward poverty to modern affluence.'

New research in social history challenges the persistent ideology of familism. It shows significant discrepancies between ideologies of the family, actual household types and kinship relations, and shifting meanings of family life (for example, Davidoff and Hall, 1988; Davidoff et al. 1999; Hall, 1992). Notions of a turning point in the history of the family determined by economic and social structural changes are now being questioned by many family historians. The mid-nineteenth century is now acknowledged as a key period of consolidation of discourses around 'family values' that disavow evidence – from a growing number of legal, literary and prescriptive sources – of the disjunction between the values and ideals, espoused on the one hand, and lived experiences and familial relations, on the other. For example, a feature of the period that is much more common than previously thought is that children were brought up by relatives other than their biological mother: by aunts, uncles and older sisters. Many household arrangements were contractual and not biological. Contemporary familial ideology appeals to a mythical heritage that was invented during the Victorian period of imperial arrogance yet has since been continuously reinvented and re-enacted on the popular media stage. Contemporary notions of belonging, lineage, naming and heritage, nation and the anglophone evolution of the idea of democratic nations that stand for the exclusive needs of implied white, English-speaking nuclear families were fused during this period.

NATIONHOOD, RACE AND FAMILIAL HERITAGES

Within the privileged power blocs of Anglo-America and Anglo-Celtic Australia a postmodern emphasis on the differences between nations, cultures and identities is important for uncovering and legitimising minority cultures. It can, however, result in white identities remaining unmarked. Their alliances and the nature of their interlocking power can remain unacknowledged (Spillman, 1997). So we need to revisit whiteness specifically in the frame of anglocentricity and examine what it means in terms of its privileging within analyses that normalise a particular version of the family, both in the context of 'white contact' with indigenous cultures and in the context of slavery. Intrinsically racialised familial ideals functioned as mechanisms of cultural control and were activated in British colonised territories to establish anglocentric national cultures. By the mid-nineteenth century in Britain, the concept of the family was perceived as nuclear, patriarchal and hierarchical, and its members were defined by their primary relationship to the conjugal couple (see Davidoff and Hall, 1988). Discrete family units, headed by a male breadwinner, became the hallmark of both civilised society and stability. Deviation from this family model (signified by overcrowding, illegitimacy and lone parenthood) was regarded as savagery. This model of the family assumed a normative role in mid-nineteenth-century British society and, by extension, within its colonies.

The origins of the white, anglophonic nuclear version of the family lie within a cluster of complex lived practices and a repertoire of powerful symbols shaped by discourses of empire, through the church and public and private institutions. From the nineteenth century to the early twentieth century, the state and various institutions within the education system, commerce and trade contributed to the construction of a whole mythology around race, gender and nation that converged on a distinctive and narrow set of discourses about the family. These myths consisted of hegemonic ideals that appealed to the 'natural order of things'. Together they constituted a set of universal standards by which actual living and childrearing arrangements throughout the British empire were to be judged, negotiated and struggled against.

Britain was perceived by the state as the 'mother country', as the ultimate arbiter of domesticity and bearer of a grand 'civilising' mission within a paternalistic discourse. Like politicians today, nineteenth-century colonial authorities were obsessed with 'domestic instability', which was categorised and measured by the low rates of marriage and high rates of illegitimacy. These factors were seen as serious threats to family formation, good citizenship and the moral and social progress of the nation. In response to the abolitionists' campaigns against slavery and racism, the pro-slavery lobby struck back and claimed blacks to be no more than animals: bestial, pagan imagery was used in which blacks were portrayed as licentious and depraved.

The official discourse of scientific racism and eugenics was central to the British empire in the Victorian period and popularised through images in the media. Cartoons in *The Times* and other publications began to circulate images of 'niggers' and the African character as an ulcer and a disease (see McClintock, 1995). Eugenic ideas of populating the British empire with the white British race expressed the Victorian revulsion for mixed races. During this era, a social hierarchy was devised to segregate blacks from British national identity because Britishness was defined as 'white'. Biological distinctions between blacks and whites were articulated in terms of racial characteristics. The eugenics movement was preoccupied with national purity, defined by racial purity and fitness, and drew on Darwinian ideas for its scientific legitimacy. During its heyday, in the 1920s, eugenics was used in Britain to dictate and control who could have children. Certain social groups who did not fit the ideal – such as blacks and people labelled as disabled and as mentally retarded – were forcibly sterilised (Davidoff et al., 1999 and Weeks, 1985). Eugenics philosophy and science culminated in the Nazi concentration camps of Germany under the leadership of Hitler. Today, eugenics is still alive, but being framed within a genetic discourse, and articulated through biogenetic technology.

In the West Indies, former slaves were viewed as savages and considered incapable of achieving the moral sensibilities of family life. They were regarded by evangelical missionaries who worked in the colonies as unstable, promiscuous, insensitive and ill suited to raising children with propriety or reproducing the patriarchal structure of the family (Chamberlain, 1999: 130). These kinds of attitudes also applied to Chinese and Indian labourers brought to the West Indies even after the abolition of slavery. Marriages that were not made under Christian rites and law were not recognised by the colonial authorities in the nineteenth century and so most children ended up being categorised as illegitimate, and most wives as concubines. Chamberlain (1999) observes that rebellions and riots such as the Morant Bay Rebellion in Jamaica in 1865 and the Federation Riots in Barbados in 1875 were blamed on domestic instability rather than on the racism and poverty experienced by the former slaves. She states: 'As in Britain, focus on the family as the cause of civil ills and poverty deflected attention away from economic and political inequality. Within the colonial imagination, the link between illegitimacy and good citizenship was inseparable' (Chamberlain, 1999: 130).

The colonial association of illegitimacy with the destabilisation of citizenship confirms a cultural process of the familialising of race and nationalism within the zones of imperial power. The Moyne Commission, which reported on widespread disturbances throughout the Caribbean in the 1930s, claimed that they were caused by the family structure of the former slaves. As Chamberlain (1999: 130) points out, the western European family as 'nuclear, patriarchal and with the conjugal union at its centre' was the norm against which all other living arrangements were measured. These attitudes have persisted, as exemplified by the fact that black British West Indian families who migrated to Britain in the 1950s and 1960s were labelled by the state as deviant and unstable.

Anne McClintock's (1995) work on race, gender and sexuality in the colonial context shows that nations are often figured through the iconography of familial and domestic space, and symbolised as domestic genealogies. She argues that under nineteenth-century British colonialism, the family trope naturalised national hierarchy as a unity of domestic interests, as in the 'Family of Nations', the British and Commonwealth 'Royal Family' and the United States' 'First Family', which are still used today. In this way, the family became an indispensable *metaphor* signifying a single historical genesis narrative for national history, but McClintock points out that as an *institution* it was dehistoricised into a symbol and excluded from national power. During this period, social difference was signified as a category of nature within both the family and the nation, thereby naturalising and universalising the subordination both of women and children in the domestic sphere, and of indigenous people of colonised territories such as Africa, who were referred to as 'the family of black children'. Changing aesthetics in photography functioned to erase the presence of First Peoples in colonised nations by representing native American and Australian Aborigines as living anachronisms.

As national bureaucracies gradually took over the social function of the great service families in the nineteenth century, the family came to be a metaphor for the naturalising of hierarchy, of race, gender, generation, nation: 'the "national family", the global "family of nations", the colony as a "family of black children ruled over by a white father"' (McClintock, 1995: 358). Women were only treated as members of the nation-state as dependants of men and the family in private and public law, not directly as citizens. By drawing on familial metaphors, the naturally superior 'adult' races were perceived by the white British to be domesticating, by example, the 'children' of 'primitive' races. The hierarchically gendered middle-class family was therefore centrally a symbol of white imperial nationalism, providing a sexual, gendered and racial justification for the white male control over colonial space. The Royal Family became the embodiment of all families, projecting a visual model of patriotism, patriarchy and pedigree. As a metaphor for unions and hierarchies of race, nation and gender, the family came to represent social and moral order.

The assimilation and reinscription of native Americans and Aboriginal Australians are specific instances of British attempts at cultural annihilation that were put into practice by appealing to biologically framed familial discourses. During the white colonisation of Australia, Aboriginal families and family community life were principal targets to be systematically broken down through culture, ethnic cleansing and eugenics. Racial cleansing was instigated precisely in the name of 'the family' – the 'white family of man'. In this way, the trope of the family was effectively used to destroy 'other' and non-white families and replace them with a single, specific British imperial version of the family. The assimilationist metaphors, debates and practices in the immigration history of such nations can be traced through the struggles and resistances to anglodominant immigrant values and institutions by both native Aboriginal peoples and non-white migrants. The political motives and cultural impact of the planned population of a white, English-speaking Australian commonwealth nation through scientific racism, eugenics policies and demographic policies are examples of British imperialist reactions to the perceived threat to racial homogeneity. The infamous White Australia policy was an immigration policy begun in 1901 to exclude non-European migrants and was not officially rejected until as recently as 1973.

The term 'white contact' has been used euphemistically by European scholars to refer to the invasion, massacre, dispossession and institutionalised oppression of Aborigines in Australia from 1788 (Williams and Jolly, 1992). Aboriginal children were systematically stolen from their own families and communities and placed in white families. This practice was led by missionaries and labelled 'adoption' by both the missionaries and the 'host' white families. So Aboriginal children were forced to be 'adopted' and 'assimilated' into white families. Today, they are officially referred to as the 'Stolen Generations'. With the onset of white colonisation, such policies were brutal in their attempts to erode and replace Aboriginal family and community units and ties with white anglocentric familial models. The white colonisers regarded the white race as culturally superior, and biologically at a higher stage of evolution than black races. Their effects continue to this day as many of the children who are now adults are speaking out publicly about their experiences of being abducted and severed from their families, their culture, and their subsequent search for their familial origins.

The use of the family as a symbol and tool with which to assert authority, rule and racial superiority placed pressure on white settler families, who came to be surveyed and controlled during the invasion and colonisation of territories such as the United States and Australia (Jebb and Haebich, 1992: 29). Aboriginal women who were engaged, either by force or by consent, in sexual relations with European men were denied full citizenship, showing the intersection of racism and sexism during the white colonisation of Australia.

A significant amount of archival material was written by European missionaries whose values were shaped by puritanical Christian ideals. Within their mission to 'civilise', missionaries held specific assumptions about Aboriginal gender relations. Tony Scanlon (1986: 89) points out that missionary objectives were targeted at women by systematically pathologising Aboriginal gender relations. Missionary intervention was legitimised by alarm at what was judged to be polygamy, infant brides taken by older men, male violence towards women, and sexual promiscuity. Missionary condemnation of the sexual mores of Aboriginal culture justified white intervention and was reinforced by male anthropologists. Such sexist- and racist-motivated beliefs only began to be questioned during the mid-1970s when feminist anthropology emerged (see Moore, 1988).

So *familism* acted as a discursive device deployed to naturalise an ideology of racialised belonging and support a myth of ethnic purity. It not only functioned to bind together intrinsically hybrid cultures into a racialised cultural unity, but ensured the hierarchical relationship between white and other races. The claim for white superiority was authenticated through shared culture, customs and trade and special relations between the nations of settled white emigrants within Britain, the British dominions and the USA. In this way, a set of anglocentric and familial discourses were combined to subvert the differences between ethnic groupings of the white anglophone races settled across the British empire and to appeal to and emphasise cultural links with Anglo-Celtic and Anglo-American identities.

THE REGULATION OF THE MODERN PATRIARCHAL MODEL OF THE FAMILY

The use of eugenics and Darwinian philosophy to frame definitions of the 'family' ensured that the family could be appealed to as a natural, biological unit founded on blood relations. It also ensured the inherent class bias, racism and sexism of familism and the ideology of the family, required to justify the colonial invasion and settlement of foreign territories in the context of national and racial fitness and purity. During the early twentieth century, the British government was alarmed at the fall in the nation's birth rate, particularly that of the middle classes. A decline in fertility was seen to be synonymous with the decline of the nation. A high infant mortality rate during the First World War meant fewer men available to fight for the nation during the Second World War. The government commissioned a series of reports on population growth rates, including the National Birth-Rate Commission of 1916, to find ways of resolving the 'problem'. Women were targeted as potential mothers. Their rights to control their own fertility, to paid employment and to independence were severely curtailed in the name of 'the family'. Being specifically preoccupied with racial fitness, the eugenics movement coincided with national concerns of military defence and the needs of British industry. As Davidoff et al. (1999: 188) state, 'Good specimens of British manhood were needed not simply as cannon fodder, but also to revive Britain's declining fortunes as an industrial nation, and to populate the Empire with the British race.'

In addition to the eugenic ideas of populating the British empire with the white British race, the Maternity and Child Welfare Act was passed in 1918 to set up local authority services in order to reduce infant mortality rates and improve the health of children (see Davidoff et al., 1999). Middle-class women were identified as models for good mothering. Various forms of pressure, including blocking women's access to education, well-paid jobs and career promotion, and reliable contraception, were all used to pressurise middle-class women to marry and produce children. Working-class women were treated with more ambivalence. Some authorities felt that the working classes should be encouraged to reduce the size of their families (see Davin, 1978). Yet, after the publication of Marie Stopes' highly popular *Married Love* in 1918, as part of the birth-control movement, contraception was made more accessible to middle-class women than it was to working-class women. Other public agencies were worried about this class bias and felt that working-class women should have equal right of access to contraceptive knowledge. They expressed religious and demographically founded concerns that a racial population imbalance between the classes would emerge that would be antithetical to the intention of fostering middle-class family values within the nation.

Eugenics ideas fed into projects[1] that gave working-class married family women healthy birth care in the 1930s and 1940s but systematically denied such support to single mothers and women who lived alone. This kind of exclusion was based on a rigid and narrow definition of 'proper' forms and contexts of childbirth and child care so as to ensure increases in childbirth but only within a particular type of 'normal' healthy family (Davidoff et al., 1999). It was a model of the family that not only had to be middle class in its values, aspirations and cultural practices, but that also was dictated as patriarchally structured and thus headed by a man.

The powerful concept of the male head of household as 'breadwinner' husband with dependent wife emerged as a model from liberal economic theory during the 1830s in Britain, coinciding with the practice of paying wages to individual workers rather than families, with men commanding higher wages than women and children. Although gendered divisions of labour were marked before the 1780s at every level, from the household to the community and the nation, the distinctive roles of wage-earner husband/ father and domestic housewife/mother began to appear by the 1850s among a wide range of social groups. This gives us one important indication of the connections between industrial and economic change and family life.

The Ideology of the Separate Spheres

The notion of a natural division between a feminine, private sphere of domestic unpaid labour and a masculine, public sphere of paid employment was supported by the ideology of the 'separate spheres' that reinforced women's exclusion from the public world during the nineteenth century. Catherine Hall (1992) points to the importance of an evangelical movement coinciding with the emergence of a new entrepreneurial and professional middle class, which placed an emphasis on the special and separate role of women as carriers of social and religious virtue. This feminine role could only be realised if women were shielded from the competitive and vicious public world of the market and masculinity. The effectiveness of this ideology could be gauged by the way in which certain places and activities were perceived to be tainted by the public world and were therefore increasingly barred to women, while the sacred duties of maintaining the home and raising children were increasingly elevated as virtuous and pure. The public world now ruled over the world of home and family, and women's mobility and ability to engage with that dominant world were restricted.

The ideology of the 'separate spheres' reinforced women's dependence on male relatives, yet many women were unable to sustain this dependence. Middle- as well as working-class women were obliged to earn a living for themselves and their families even with the limited employment options available (Davidoff et al., 1999: 28). The *idea* of separate spheres has masked the ways that male and female members of families have always crossed the boundaries between work and home in their daily lives. The redefinition of 'work' as 'paid employment' rather than 'labour' began to crystallise during this early modern period. Work was equated with the market and exchange value; thus unpaid labour situated firmly in the domestic sphere, had no value in capitalist production and was devalued, leading to a feminisation and devaluation of the caring role in society as a whole.

The patriarchal concept of the 'male breadwinner'[2] and 'head of household' was bound up with that of familial legitimacy. Paternity is pronounced in the context of identity, legality and inheritance and relies on external regulation by the law for its definition. In contrast to the immediacy of maternity, paternity is always mediated. It constitutes *social* legitimacy (Doane, 1987: 70) in the sense that it governs social relations and the terms of the transfer of culture. Until recently, a child's right to inherit property, to be a legitimate member of society, and to be a citizen was dependent on being able to take up the father's surname, which could be acquired only through parental marriage. Thus, the stigma of illegitimacy affected women and children, but not men. Single women were confronted with legal and cultural barriers to adopting or fostering children, whether friends or family. Those who did manage to adopt were unable to let the child call them 'mother' in case members of the local community thought the child was the illegitimate offspring of the foster mother (Davidoff et al., 1999: 206).[3]

SEXOLOGY AND THE REGULATION OF MARITAL HETEROSEXUALITY

A new discourse called 'sexology', the scientific study of sexuality, emerged at the end of the nineteenth century to identify and regulate 'perverse', 'abnormal' sexual practices and classify sexual pathologies. By speculating about sexual aberrations within a scientific discourse, this new subdiscipline was placed on an authoritative footing and further justified by the increasing popularity of Charles Darwin's theory of natural selection. In *The Descent of Man, and Selection in Relation to Sex* published in 1871, Darwin argued that survival of the species depended on sexual selection for reproduction. Using biological discourses to explain the differences between the sexes, it was drawn on to justify differential social and cultural treatment of men and women. In this way, heterosexuality came to be regulated and administered by a repertoire of cultural, religious, medical, scientific and legal codes that defined sexual practices outside marriage such as homosexuality, abortion, prostitution, pornography, adultery and divorce as immoral, obscene, perverse and unhealthy. As Jeffrey Weeks (1985) points out in his analysis of sexology, over a thousand publications on homosexuality emerged between 1898 and 1908. Sigmund Freud's work was simply one small part of a huge growth in sexual theory. During this period, homosexuality was defined as a sexual condition, which allowed the concept of heterosexuality to be invented in order to explain 'normality'. Sexology was therefore instrumental in defining, classifying and categorising heterosexual sex, gender and sexuality as a biological imperative (Weeks, 1985: 69). The sex act was permissible if it took place within marriage and was linked to reproduction. It coincided with eugenics ideas, thereby fusing together the biological justification for heterosexual hegemony, patriarchy and white supremacy, fixed within the patriarchal code of familism.

By the early twentieth century, the regulation of heterosexuality within marriage was articulated through the notion of 'pleasure' but was dependent on the eroticising of differences between men and women and the suppression of their similarities.[4] The conventional view held by historians was that these researchers not only modernised sex in the twentieth century but actually liberated women from Victorian sexual repression. Sexologists played a central role in the early twentieth century in constructing a model of sexuality that claimed to be scientific and objective but in fact reflected and promoted the interests of men and eroticised women's subordination within a patriarchal discourse. So although they created a space in which women's sexual pleasure could be located as a right, it existed on men's terms in order to promote male pleasure.

Havelock Ellis's role in establishing sexology as a 'science' dominated popular sex manuals from the 1920s right up to the post-war years. His work was influenced by anthropology, including the work of Malinowski (1932) and Westermarck (1921), who were involved in a global movement called the 'World League of Sexual Reform'. Malinowski, Westermarck and Ellis defined the family as a natural monogamous union of men and women that reflected the animal kingdom (Weeks, 1985: 283). Ellis (1946: 79) claimed that '[t]he substance of the family is biological but its forms are socially moulded'.

Sexology insisted on the naturalness of male dominance in heterosexual behaviour by promoting the institution of heterosexuality as inherently familial and patriarchal. Patriarchalists ignored anthropological evidence, from the mid-nineteenth century onwards, of the existence of societies that were not structured by patriarchal relations – whether matrilineal or matriarchal (see Moore, 1988) – and, instead, drew on Charles Darwin's (1871) evolutionary theory of patriarchal patterns in animal life to argue that patriarchy was a natural state of affairs. Professional beliefs of the early twentieth century centred on the idea that men had natural sexual urges over which they had little control.

The patriarchal standard of sexual morality was resisted, challenged and critiqued by a wave of feminist activities and struggles from the 1860s to the 1920s. Campaigns were organised on issues of male violence and the sexual exploitation of women, including wife beating and murder, rape in marriage, sexual abuse of children and other forms of sexual harassment. Feminists fought for a female sexual autonomy through which women would have the right to define and control their sexuality, free from male exploitation and coercion (Jackson, 1987). But the discourse of sexology undermined feminist attempts to develop alternative models of sexuality by constructing a 'scientific' model of sexuality that not only declared heterosexuality to be natural but also structured male selfishness and brutality into heterosexual relations. As Margaret Jackson (1987) points out in her insightful survey and analysis of marriage manuals and sex education literature in the early twentieth century, sexologists, biologists and anthropologists defended patriarchal power as normal by depoliticising sexuality and consigning it to the sphere of 'nature'. Drawing on Darwin's ideas about laws of natural selection in which he claims that the best males pass on their genes to the best females, Ellis (1946) claimed that the male sexual urge is to conquer the woman, while the female sexual urge is to be conquered. Using highly dubious 'evidence' from anthropology and criminology, he claimed that women naturally enjoy being raped, beaten and sexually humiliated. The close association made between male sexuality, power and violence was thereby legitimised as a biological necessity. This kind of model of heterosexuality, which presented male heterosexual sexual dominance as biology rather than as patriarchal power, undermined legal and other attempts to protect women from violent male sexual practices either in or out of marriage.

Prompted by the sexology discourse, a number of sex and marriage manuals were published in the early part of the twentieth century that circumscribed sexual practices and meanings within marriage and family. Post-war sexual manuals promoted Ellis's sexology, emphasising that women had to learn that male sexual demands were inevitable and that they could only achieve sexual pleasure by 'consenting' to be conquered (Jackson, 1987). Sex manuals were aimed at preventing and curing sexual malfunctions, which were identified as the cause of marital instability and therefore as a threat to the social order.

Drawing on the new disciplines of psychology, psychoanalysis and gynaecology, the medical profession became the new 'sex experts'. The profession emerged as the authoritative voice that influenced sexual relations by mediating between science and the lay public, and was central to the process of medicalising sex, reproduction and motherhood (Oakley, 1976). Sexual problems were treated as the root cause of all marital discord (Foucault, 1978). This legacy of enclosing dialogue about sex and sexuality within the narrow discourse of medicine and health persists as a dominant discourse today, exemplified by the teaching of sexual advice in the national curriculum in British secondary schools through classes on 'Personal, Social and Health Education' (see Chapter 6). Topics about the 'pleasures' of sex and sexual identities are framed within information about health risks such as AIDS and sexually transmitted diseases. Significantly, the foreword or preface to sex manuals of the first half of the twentieth century was typically written by a member of the clergy or magistrate adopting strong evangelical tones, by referring to sexual intercourse as a 'sacrament', revealing a significant collusion between religious and scientific discourses in the normalisation of patriarchal heterosexual relations and practices. Most of the manuals were written with a male readership in mind, treating men as educators of their wives' sexual pleasure. The same theme, of 'man the hunter by nature', drawing on metaphors of 'capture' and 'possession', was communicated in sex education classes for young girls (Jackson, 1987).

Van de Veldes' *Ideal Marriage: Its Philosophy and Techniques*, first published in 1928, was so popular that it was reprinted thirty-eight times, was still in circulation up to the 1970s, and 'taught a generation how to copulate'. He dealt at length with the topic of love and pain, claiming that women wish to be savagely and deeply penetrated and that some women cannot obtain an orgasm unless they are beaten and brutalised. Sex manuals written by socialist feminists, such as Stella Brown, who was involved in campaigns for birth control and abortion, were surprisingly uncritical of the male active and female passive model. Celibate spinsterhood was regarded as an unnatural state. The sexual ideology of women such as Marie Stopes, who drew on the work of Havelock Ellis in her book *Married Love* (1918), was quite contradictory in its views. Stopes was deeply committed to female sexual autonomy and highly critical of the medical profession yet she did not challenge the patriarchal, 'scientific' model of sexuality that denied female sexual independence. Stopes accepted the 'man the hunter' metaphors yet she was radical in other areas, demanding that control be passed from the man to the woman. She was opposed by male sex experts in her conviction that the sexual coercion of the wife constituted rape, and that men should adapt themselves to their wives' sexual needs (Jackson, 1987).

The ideal of the companionate marriage relied on the notion of sexual pleasure for both partners as the foundation of marital stability. Yet Jackson's (1987) analysis of sex education literature in the early twentieth century leads her to the conclusion that so-called 'sex reform' was not in women's interests. Although sex was now gradually being emphasised as a leisure activity as well as a procreation activity, as long as it was safely contained within the family, women were only allowed to have sexual desires and pleasures on men's terms. It is no accident, according to Jackson's thesis, that female sexuality was emphasised as passive, dependent and responsive to husbands' demands at the exact moment in history when women's political and economic emancipation was taking place. None of the sex experts queried the fact that something that is a natural instinct somehow has to be learned, and only by women. Jackson emphasises that this sexual ideology must be understood in relation to other dominant ideas of the inter-war years, such as attempts to push women out of the labour market, and the emphasis on full-time motherhood. Together, these dominant discourses and values formed a complex matrix of patriarchal ideology. Yet the heterosexual institution of the family was naturalised and essentialised through the social relations of sexology, and framed within the discourse of science, thereby divorcing it from the socio-political context of patriarchy.

The threat of extra-marital sex was not mentioned directly in women's magazines of the 1940 and 1950s yet it constituted a crucial subtext. Women were continually advised to be sexually attractive and available to their husbands to stop them from 'wandering off' (see Finch and Summerfield, 1991). The key ingredient of the ideal nuclear family model, heterosexual monogamy, was so effectively and rigorously enforced that other forms of intimacy and sexual relationships were not simply marginalised but largely criminalised or medically pathologised. Research conducted by authors such as Kinsey and Masters and Johnson was based on different methods but held many features in common. Kinsey et al.'s *Sexual Behavior in the Human Male* (1948) made astonishing claims that if men's sexual drives were denied 'legitimate', that is, familial, outlets, then they would search for satisfaction in illegitimate ones such as rape, abuse of girls and other sex crimes. A huge amount of secrecy surrounded people's everyday lives as marital relationships were identified as the legal site for sexual activity, with condemnation of sexual relationships outside marriage as deviant or illicit. Prosecutions for homosexual offences rose through the 1930s, so this secrecy was a necessity for men (Weeks, 1989). Female homosexuality was not officially recognised so no women were prosecuted.

Remarkably, this model continues to circulate as 'common sense' today. Masters and Johnson's research acted as a foundation for more recent popular sex manuals such as Alex Comfort's *The Joys of Sex* (1972), which describes the penis as the primary organ of sexual pleasure for both sexes.

The criteria for sexual impotence and female frigidity are failure to penetrate, which is a model of sexuality that gives primacy to the penis.

The meanings surrounding sexual citizenship relied, then, on a public/private dichotomy. Sexology contributed to the creation, by the public sphere, of a distinctive mode of sexual citizenship. Within its attempts to control the private sphere, the public sphere constructed the realm of the private as the sexualised sphere (Bell, 1995; Cooper, 1998: 68). The instability of this public/private dichotomy is revealed by the desire on the part of public institutions to control and shape the sexual discourses and practices of the private domain as a heterosexual and familial sphere. Sexology confirmed other authoritative public and scientific discourses in the heterosexualisation of public space as well as private, familial, domestic space. This heterosexualised public space, which declares itself to be 'asexual', continues to operate in an exclusionary way by treating citizens who do not conform to the heterosexual norms of marriage as 'sexual dissidents'. As Weeks (1998: 35) argues, sexual dissidents are not only individuals who engage in homosexual practices or identify themselves as gay or lesbian. Anybody who fails to conform to the traditional gendered sexual dichotomy framed within heterosexual familialism is treated as a sexual dissident. Not only is homosexuality pathologised and outlawed through these kinds of processes, but all individuals and households who do not conform to the heterosexual norms of marriage are treated as 'sexual dissidents', that is, medically, legally, culturally and in terms of welfare provision. Those whose status is derived from the private sphere – that is, women and children – are disenfranchised because their rights as citizens are often challenged in the public sphere, as are those of lone parents, gays, lesbians, transvestites, transsexuals and prostitutes. As an authoritative scientific discourse, sexology contributed both to the heterosexualisation of private familial space and the heterosexualisation of what was supposedly 'sexually neutral' public space. Foucault (1978) refers to 'regulatory fictions' organised around the polarities of heterosexual/homosexual that reinscribe masculine/feminine ideas of sex and gender. The field of sexology can be seen as an example of the ways in which the body is colonised by the apparatus of sexuality to normalise the containment of sex within marriage and normalise the subordination of women within the family.

The state desire to expand the population of western anglophone nations after the Second World War was translated into the need to rebuild 'the family'. This gave rise to a public re-emphasis on monogamous heterosexual love that was articulated within the medical and moral othering and pathologisation of homosexuality as well as prostitution. Familial identities have been regulated through the perversion of non-heterosexual practices, constructed as a threat not only to the heterosexual functions of biological reproduction but also to the moral fibre of the nation.

THE RISE OF THE MODERN 'FUNCTIONAL FAMILY'

The nineteenth-century appropriation of 'the family' as a site through which ideas about race, gender, nationhood and patriotism were mobilised, and through which people's dispositions and identities were regulated within a familial framework, was intensified during the twentieth century. It reached its peak around the 1950s, during which the white, middle-class, patriarchal, 'nuclear' version of the family emerged as the dominant model, referred to by experts as the modern functional family. Some of the principal foundations of the ideology of familialism prevalent in western anglophone nations today can be found within a functionalist model that became dominant during the mid-twentieth century. The social sciences were interlinked with sexology and the medical and natural sciences and public institutions, including the education system and the legal system, in privileging a white nuclear ideal that legitimised the male 'breadwinner' model within an asymmetrical patriarchal structure.

Within anthropology and sociology, scholars such as Malinowski (1913) and Talcott Parsons (1951) selected the white, nuclear family as an ideal type and claimed it to be a natural and inevitable form that evolved to adapt to industrial society. Talcott Parsons was an American sociologist who developed what became one of the most influential sociological paradigms for the family of advanced industrial capitalism in the 1940s and 1950s. He found a function for the modern white nuclear family: to fit the economic formation of capitalism. Parsons' functional model is a modernist theory in the sense that the unifying theme of the modern functional family model is the *rationalisation* of social life in western societies and is linked to accounts of the standardisation of the life course. As such, Parsons believed that modern nuclear families necessarily existed to meet the key basic needs in industrial society to regulate sexual behaviour, to reproduce the next generation, to provide child care and socialise children into the society's moral codes and rules, and to give psychological support to adults.

Parsons claimed that the 'modern family' was a product of urban-industrial society and had evolved from a pre-industrial, agrarian, 'multi-functional' extended family form. This past extended family performed social, political, religious and educational roles, as well as being central to production and economy. In contrast to the past extended family, the industrial modern nuclear family and in turn the economic system of industrial capitalism, are relatively unburdened by structural obligations to wider kin groups. Parsons claims that *affective* relationships characterise the modern nuclear family. Only the male breadwinner moves between home and work within this narrowly defined modern functional family. He is featured as a mobile labourer, flexible enough to adapt to the shifting patterns of the labour market. In this way Parsons invented a model of the family that would fit neatly the labour needs of post-war American society.

This structural model indicates the desire by social scientific experts of the mid-twentieth century to provide a theory that claims that the economic sphere of capitalism determines and shapes people's lives rather than the other way round or within an interactive and dialectical relationship. Human agency is thereby subordinated to abstract economic structures rather than approached and explored as a reciprocal and negotiable relationship in which the economic sphere is also shaped and constructed by familial forces. The regulation of sexual behaviour is a familial need based on sexology and constructed precisely to circumscribe and police sexual practices in order to locate them firmly within the heterosexual reproductive domain. The power of this academic discourse is so pervasive that many historians, as well as sociologists, continue to use a functionalist framework without acknowledging or questioning it. It promotes the vision of the family as a *single, undifferentiated unit* that has moved and adapted to wider changes. As Davidoff et al. (1999) point out, historians have typically examined intergenerational relationships in terms of *parents* and their children, often without acknowledging the different positions, roles and experiences of mothers and fathers, and the different sexes and ages of children.

The rigid functionalist categorisation of individuals into undifferentiated family units has typically obscured structural inequalities of race, class, gender and generation. Inequalities between men and women have not only been rendered invisible by the category of familyness but have been represented as natural, legitimate and even as positive features of it. 'Families' have been counted and classified at the expense of other social configurations of space, community, individuality, patterns and styles of consumption and other maps of everyday life. Their economic functions have been described and their responses to historical change traced as if 'the family' were a historical actor (whether dominant over or subordinated to other social forces such as the economy or culture). So the functionalist model denies not only the diversity of family forms but also the power relations that operate between family members *within* families. Moreover, it neglects the relations between family members and external authorities. Feminists have been particularly critical of the general lack of acknowledgement of the power relations in the family caused by the normalisation of patriarchal relations (see Barrett and Macintosh, 1982).[5]

The everyday practices associated with family life in the 1950s, including important activities such as domestic consumption, did *not* involve co-operation between family members as an undifferentiated family unit, but rather entailed the exercise of male power and female subordination (see Parsons and Bales, 1956).[6] Domestic consumption was neither communal nor egalitarian. It was structured by husbands' economic authority and wives' dependence, resting on husbands' ideological claim to breadwinner status.

Yet, to this day, households tend to be treated by governments and market surveys as homogeneous familial units (Jackson and Moores, 1995). Although the components of consumption and individualism were profoundly structured by gendered inequalities, they were *naturalised* through a nuclear familial narrative. Paradoxically, the perceived decline of the 'family's' role as a central informal welfare institution has been an ongoing process coinciding with this cultural emphasis on individualism and consumerism even though it was *women*, rather than 'families', who were, and continue to be, the principal unpaid and low-paid carers in society.

Parsons' main functions of the family not only ignored cultural variations across class, ethnicity and region but also pathologised constructions of families that lie outside the functionalist model. As such, the functionalist model is firmly culture-bound and dehistoricises the nuclear family as something fixed and unchanging. Research conducted to support functionalism has focused on those families that fit the model, such as studies of the emerging middle-class nuclear family, usually in an American context, or studies of working-class families responding to industrial change (for example, see Edgell, 1980; Willmott and Young, 1967). The multiplicity of family experiences and forms and the ways in which their members have survived difficult times during industrialisation, colonialism and war have been reduced to responses deemed 'successful' in fitting them to industrial capitalism (Davidoff et al., 1999). Deviation from, or alternatives to, the model are regarded simplistically as unorthodox and labelled 'dysfunctional' with little room for the study of how or why variation takes place.

We find that black, immigrant, single-parent, gay and lesbian families are the kinds of familial relationships that have been discredited as deviant. Parsons was writing about his narrow set of experiences in the United States, and argued that the cultural standard for American family life was that of the urban middle-class family (Cheale, 1999: 58). The modern middle-class family was declared as the standard, the 'normal American family'. Lower-class families, which included all non-white families and the white working classes, were treated as the exception and came to represent the prevalence of 'family disorganisation'. So, with the exception of the 'lower classes', Parsons claimed that the general trend of development in America was an upgrading of standards and the inclusion of more social groups within the modern nuclear model, thereby leading to a substantial homogenisation of patterns of life in the population (Parsons, 1971: 53, 63). Supporters of Parsons' theory, such as Gee (1986), have suggested that widespread improvements in the quality of life have led to an increasing standardisation of family forms towards the nuclear model. They argue that a decline in mortality levels, a rise in economic affluence, and so on, are said to lead to a rise in the 'predictability' of family life and the standardisation of marital status.

What certainly *did* become more standardised and homogenised was not individual families but, rather, public exposure to expert cultural definitions of 'correct' and appropriate family performance based on the standards set by the functionalist model. A huge investment was made by the state, in western anglophone nations, in supporting a model of the family that would ensure its 'fit' with capitalism, with the aim of reducing the reliance of families on the welfare state. Emphasising women's role as physical and emotional caretaker was therefore regarded as crucial. Major government efforts were made to teach women how to rear their children effectively and raise their standards of health and hygiene. For example, in America, Australia and Britain, between 1880 and the Second World War, the household chores of cooking and cleaning, traditionally taken on by women, were subjected to rational scientific management (Rieger, 1985, 1987).

Scientific management, in the form of Frederick Taylor's (1974) principles, was originally developed to organise the work tasks of factory and office workers and then applied to housework. It was directly linked to a regime of hygiene in the home. Schools began to teach about hygiene and schools of motherhood were set up (Davin, 1978; Forty, 1986). Through formal instruction, experts from the human services professions contributed to a redefinition of family life, which, in turn, led to a redefinition of mothering. This movement was profoundly middle class in approach and in values. But the working classes were taught differently from the middle classes. For the middle classes, hygiene and mothering were presented as something voluntary by associating them with relaxation and sport, whereas for the working classes they were associated with a reduction in death and disease and the improvement of the health of the labour force (Forty, 1986). So changes were not brought about so much by the adaptation of families to the modern economic structures as by a plethora of expert advice within a standardisation of values. These were translated into instructions, advice, recipes and tips illustrated and circulated within schools, advertisements, magazine stories, cook books and advice manuals on parenthood and marital sex. They were not, however, taken up by wives and mothers in a linear manner.

'BAD MOTHERING' AND THE REGULATION OF MATERNAL RESPONSIBILITY

Meanings surrounding motherhood were enclosed by biological discourses and regulated by academic discourses and government policies in early twentieth-century western anglophone nations. The importance of women's maternal duties, across classes, was highlighted by a swathe of experts, including health visitors, teachers, psychologists and child care advice writers. Single mothers were perceived to be a drain on welfare providers and much effort was therefore invested by the state, through a range of official discourses, in treating them as undeserving, self destructive sexual deviants. Many professionals believed that infant mortality between the wars was caused not by poverty, but by a failure of motherhood. Governments decided that a sense of maternal responsibility needed to be taught to working-class mothers. In the first decade of the twentieth century, 'schools for mothers' were set up in Britain by voluntary agencies to give advice and training to working-class mothers. Since the middle classes employed nannies and/or nursemaids and were not expected to take part in 'hands-on' childrearing, they were not targeted.

'Mothercraft' was placed on the school curriculum for working-class girls. Training manuals were published, such as Mabel Liddiard's *The Mothercraft Manual*, which ran twelve editions from 1923 to 1956 (cited in Davidoff et al., 1999: 208). It used a scientific discourse shaped by physicians such as Truby King who insisted that babies should be fed, toilet trained, sleep and even play by the clock. Health visitors, midwives and welfare workers were trained by the Truby King method and undermined informal networks of advisers such as grandmothers, extended kin and neighbours. During the post-war period, young mothers were being increasingly influenced by articles in women's magazines and child care books that began to adopt psychoanalytic approaches.

During the 1940s and 1950s psychoanalytic theories of professionals such as John Bowlby had become influential. Bowlby developed the maternal deprivation thesis in his book *Child Care and the Growth of Love* (1953), which complemented ideas about the functional nuclear family. Theories of maternal deprivation led to concerns about the maternal and emotional deprivation of children in day nurseries and prompted the rise of the child welfare movement. The emotional and psychological bonding between mother and child was emphasised, as were the adverse effects on the child of any separation from the mother. This approach underlined women's narrow status and role in the home and ignored and trivialised the role of fathers in the home, treating men's participation in child care as secondary (Davidoff et al., 1999: 210). Day-care provision was refused to women who were supplementing a family income on the grounds that it was wrong for babies to be separated from their mothers at any time. The lack of reliable child care caused serious problems for families in which women had no choice but to do paid work and who had no access to child care from their extended kin. Single and married Caribbean women who came to Britain in the 1950s had to work full-time to support themselves and their families. They suffered considerably from a lack of family support and the disapproval of their white neighbours.

By the 1950s an ideology of 'bad mothering' was firmly associated with working-class and non-white families and shaped the thoughts and theories of professionals involved in child care. The idea of bad mothering was articulated through a discourse of maternal deprivation, so that mothers who went out to work were 'bad', and their children condemned as 'latch-key children'. The maternal deprivation thesis, based as it was on middle-class values, conveniently neglected to condemn the middle-class practice of hiring nannies and sending their children to boarding school, as Davidoff et al. (1999) observe. In Britain, the number of working-class children forced into residential care rose sharply in the 1950s since, as a result of the Children's Act of 1948, local authorities were more concerned to remove children at risk from 'unfit parents' than to tackle the underlying structural problems of poverty that led to such deprivations. Even though adoption and fostering were regarded as a better solution, social policy dictated residential care, so that the number of institutionalised children rose sharply and was taken as proof of the decline of the family.

Middle-class values were inscribed in the theories of academic experts, which encouraged the fixing of negative meanings around working-class families who had 'low standards' of child care. Working-class, unemployed and single-parent families were marked through the use of categories such as 'families at risk', 'bad mothering', 'problem families' and 'undeserving poor' (as opposed to the 'respectable' working-class and the 'deserving poor'). Welfare services and voluntary organisations mushroomed in the post-war period to pinpoint and survey these families as 'deviant' and 'dysfunctional'. In Britain, a number of residential homes and rehabilitation centres were set up to cater for unmarried mothers, alcoholics, delinquent adolescents, and so on. Despite such support, the bulk of the care of the young and elderly was placed on both single and married women during and after the wars. Poverty was not only structured by class but also by gender. Women experienced poverty most severely, with or without dependants, since they were denied a breadwinner wage and barred from most avenues of employment.

The network of voluntary organisations that emerged in early twentieth-century western nations to support family life was concerned to regulate sexual behaviour, to conform to the model promoted by sexologists, so as to protect families and children from deviant and perverse sexual practices such as unmarried motherhood, prostitution and homosexuality. Yet, as Davidoff et al. (1999: 214) point out, domestic violence, sexual abuse and incest were ignored and their existence denied, particularly if they occurred in middle- and upper-class families. Reflecting the ideology of sexology, and the 'man the hunter' theme, domestic violence was dismissed as a private matter and the murder of women by husbands regarded as trivial. Male violence was condoned as a necessary part of the role of the male head of household, whose wife deserved to be beaten in order to ensure she fulfilled her duties as housewife. Violence was therefore accepted as a normal part of the division of gender roles to ensure its perpetuation as well as that of patriarchy, the subordination of women. In fact, the family was viewed as the arena that guaranteed the protection of women and children. Thus, the idea of companionate marriages in which men and women had complementary roles as a cornerstone of the egalitarian, democratic functional family remained a myth perpetuated by the textbook experts of the time. It not only concealed the diversity and differences in lived familial relations, it also legitimised the condemnation and deprivation of vast numbers of women and children in society.

The caring professions, law and psychology defined the mother and the raising of children as the essence of family life by appealing to biological and psychological criteria, even though, historically, it was fathers who 'made' families in the sense that their absence ensured the illegitimacy of mothers and their babies (Davidoff et al., 1999; Gillis, 1996). In 1920s and 1930s Britain, unmarried mothers were placed in mental asylums for life as an extreme punishment for their sexual sins. The institutionalisation of girls or women who had been sexually abused by a member of the family or male friend and became pregnant ensured the removal and silencing of the family's shame and avoided male punishment. Through the 1940s and 1950s female sexuality continued to be regulated. Adultery and illegitimate birth were stigmatised as deviant behaviour and so mothering an illegitimate child required secrecy. The law was intentionally punitive towards married mothers of illegitimate children and to unmarried mothers who wished to adopt their offspring (Davidoff et al., 1999: 250).

THE CONSTRUCTION AND INFERIORISATION OF 'NON-WHITE' FAMILIES

The negative stereotyping of working-class, lone-parent and non-white families and all households headed by women was perpetuated by academic and scientific discourse and articulated through public policy well into the twentieth century. In the United States, the current pathological approach to African American families has been shaped by the claims of E. Franklin Frazier (1932, 1939, 1949), who conducted research in the 1920s and 1930s to find a way of explaining the predicament of the black family. Frazier did not accept the common view of the time that high rates of illegitimate births, marital instability and family disorganisation among blacks were caused by biological abnormalities. Although he tried to refute previous research that presented the behaviour of all black families as uniformly disorganised, Frazier (1939) claimed that 'unstable' matriarchal black families were the norm and were the cause of black family disorganisation, which was linked back to slavery. He argued that the slave household was composed of a fatherless, matrifocal structure that was sustained across generations (Frazier, 1939, cited in Gutman, 1973). Frazier's study of the black family was about the impact of slavery on the black community rather than about race as such. Yet he focused on cultural pathology rather than social structure. Other scholars argued that racial inferiority was the cause of family breakdown among blacks. African Americans were depicted as sexually promiscuous animals who were condemned to lives of disorder and anarchy in the absence of any 'protection' from their masters. Blacks were perceived to be unable to develop monogamous relationships. They were seen to lack family values and marital traditions. Among the deeply held beliefs among white academics about the negative impact of the abolition of slavery, it was thought that without the protection of the slave owners, blacks were now victims of their own promiscuity and depravity (Gutman, 1973, 1976; Roschelle, 1997).

Social scientists held the view that those families not headed by a man were dysfunctional. Believing that the typical black family in the American rural and urban south between 1855 and 1880 was headed by a woman, Frazier (1939) came to the conclusion that the matriarchal family was a form of 'disorganisation' carried through family values. This (now discredited) theory of a self-generating cycle of fragmented, pathological interaction within lower-class black urban communities was labelled 'the culture of poverty', in which the black family was perceived to suffer from by unruliness and anarchy (Lewis, 1959). A cultural mythology of black matriarchy dominated academic ideas, as Roschelle (1997: 5) points out. Frazier's research on three-generation matriarchal black families was historically inaccurate. In fact, recent studies on nineteenth-century black families existing after the Civil War have shown that patterns of marriage, divorce, fertility and two-parent household rates were quite similar between blacks and whites. Regional variations, especially socio-economic conditions, accounted for most differences (Roschelle, 1997).

Even though there was no solid empirical evidence to support Frazier's claim that slavery made the black family pathological, the idea gained acceptance among policy makers and other social scientists. One of the most widespread myths was that of the black matriarchy, influenced by Daniel Patrick Moynihan's 1965 report for the Office of Policy Planning and Research of the US Department of Labor, entitled *The Negro Family: A Case for National Action* (see Roschelle, 1997). Moynihan depicted the black community as a matriarchal society in which the household is headed by a women, and is characterised by 'high rates of illegitimacy, divorce, matriarchy, economic dependence, unemployment, delinquency, crime and failure to pass armed forces entrance exams' (cited in Roschelle, 1997: 6). Moynihan drew on Frazier's work in his claim that unstable black families caused rampant pathology in the black community. He declared that the unstable nature of poor black families was caused by domineering women in female-headed, and therefore *dysfunctional*, households. So the blame for all the social and economic problems suffered by black families, including poverty, unemployment, low educational levels and what was labelled the 'dysfunctional personalities' of black children, was placed on the matriarchal structure of the families themselves. Rather than identifying economic disadvantage and discrimination as the causes of these social problems, they were attributed to the values, aspirations and psychological characteristics of the black families themselves. Moynihan (1965) rejected racism as a pivotal force in the perpetuation of poverty. In fact, his principal policy recommendation was to change the family form and make it conform to a white, middle-class, patriarchal model by forcing black women to give up their power over the black community (Roschelle, 1997: 7). Thus, familial 'dysfunctionality' was systematically structured by (white) racial and patriarchal codes.

CONCLUSION

The period between the late nineteenth century and the mid-twentieth century was a crucial one during which the physical embodiment of white, heterosexual, patriarchal, middle-class familial values and practices took place. Groups of 'experts' influenced the emergence and celebration of a particular version of the family that became established in the early twentieth century and acted as the foundation to the post-war ideology of familism in anglophone cultures. The church, the state and private business blocked women's equality in the labour force to uphold and defend an ideal family form in which women were socialised to be full-time housewives and caretakers of the physical and emotional needs of husbands and children. The medical profession engaged in the promotion of a particular form of family health, sexual behaviour and family planning by defining and attempting to gain control over sexed bodies as essentially heterosexual and reproductive. The education system and the media sanctioned a narrow and nuclear familial version of sexual and social relationships. Academic research pathologised the black family as unstable. These institutions set themselves up as authoritative knowledge on the family and conspired to undermine other versions of social interaction and identity, sexuality and community and experiences of other living arrangements.

Through these forms of social and cultural regulation 'the family' emerges as a coding of social meanings and values that represent larger cultural structures of thinking. By connoting powerful ideas, 'the family' disguises the distinctive social influences that underpin the codes and make them appear natural. The family becomes a complex cluster of meanings, of signs and connotations that appear 'normal' because they are presented as truthful, as factual, as a platform for beliefs that are universalised. Myth acts to transform the social signs of 'family' into facts so that 'the family' stands for something other than itself, something beyond itself. The concept of 'family' was fashioned into a powerful symbol to be exploited within colonial discourses of territorial claim, heritage, patriarchy, and cultural, religious and ethnic superiority that set parameters on the range of meanings, lived practices and identities within communities. The factors of gender and family are crucial for an understanding of the ideological construction of the separation of the worlds of work and of home and how the nuclear family came to be understood as the normative experience by the twentieth century (Davidoff et al., 1999).

By claiming the social practices, institutions and social structures of heterosexuality, patriarchy and white racial superiority to be natural, the modern nuclear family was built upon and placed under the control of an assemblage of expert knowledges from sexology to medical science. Assumptions about the shift from a 'traditional' to a modern 'functional' family form are therefore crucially tied to ideas around the male breadwinner and dependent wife. These were fused into a dominant model for family relationships and structures influenced by a wide range of public policies, including state support for maternity care, the rise of sexology and sex manuals, and the reinforcement of ideologies of the gendered division of labour and the separate spheres by the functional model of the family. These expert knowledges were critical to the emergence of a patriarchal and nuclear family form based on a middle-class, white model. Since it was only a model, which did not have a direct relationship to material and social structures and lived practices, it hid other values, experiences, practices and ideas that survived in modified forms from earlier societies and co-existed with the male breadwinner and female housewife 'functional' model that rose to dominance in the late nineteenth and early twentieth century.

NOTES

1. An example of this is the 'Peckham Experiment' described by Pearse (1945) and cited in Davidoff et al. (1999: 189). The project was influenced by eugenics principles in which health care was provided for working-class families in London during the 1930s and 1940s but was barred from single parent families and single women who lived alone.
2. In Britain, the male breadwinner model has been linked to political movements such as the Chartists and trade unions, and to the demand for an extension of citizenship by working-class men.
3. Yet a survey conducted by Margery Spring Rice in 1939 called *Working-Class Wives* revealed that many women were adopting the children of friends *not* of relatives. This seems to indicate, as Davidoff et al. (1999) point out, that it was good will and *not* simply family duty that prompted people to take in orphaned or abandoned children. In 1950, Parliament legislated for adopted children to belong to the new 'family unit' and lose contact with the natural parents and any

inheritance. However, adopted children were not permitted to inherit a title, as this was only passed on through a bloodline – thereby overdetermining the biological discourse (Davidoff et al., 1999: 206).

4. Twentieth-century sexology was represented by the work of Havelock Ellis (1946) between 1900 and the 1930s, Alfred Kinsey and colleagues (1948, 1953) between the Second World War and the 1950s, and then Masters and Johnson (1970) from the late 1960s onwards (see Jackson, 1987). Also, see Brunt (1982) for a discussion of Alex Comfort's manual *The Joys of Sex* in the 1970s.

5. David H.J. Morgan (1975) provides a comprehensive analysis of Parsons' ideas on the family.

6. Christine Delphy (1984) was one of the first to critique the notion of the family as an undifferentiated unit in the early 1970s.

CHAPTER 3

THE 'GOLDEN AGE' OF THE MODERN FAMILY?

In post-war western anglophone nations such as Britain, the United States and Australia, ideas about sexuality, intimate relationships, living arrangements, reproduction and the socialisation of children were shaped by key discourses that promoted a static, nuclear version of family. These discourses are identifiable in a range of 'expert' and popular accounts. They had a profound influence on ideas and values surrounding the construction and fixing of a twentieth-century white, English-speaking ideal, in terms of the correct way to 'be a family', to live and *perform familism* in respect of a whole range of everyday cultural practices. In a recent edition of the BBC's *Radio Times*, which celebrated the official 100th birthday of Britain's Queen Mother on 4 August 2000, it was declared in large type next to a photograph of her that: 'Elizabeth Bowes-Lyon turned the Royal Family into a happy family, giving the myth a human face.'[1]

So the themes traced in this chapter about the period during which the ideal, white modern family was contrived are addressed precisely because they form the bedrock of dominant, albeit contested, family values that are alive and prominent today. Interestingly, the Queen Mother figures as a powerful matriarch and thereby continues to evoke an extraordinary sense of stability and cohesion with regard to the British monarchy, despite the recent publicity surrounding its divorced members. Having lived through two world wars, she has come to represent both family and national durability and stability. Yet the title of 'Queen Mother' assigned to her is newly invented, in keeping with the myth. Moreover, echoing the themes of the last chapter, we find in this chapter that motherhood has been strongly policed, condemned as illegitimate, and marked out as pathological if practised outside the net of familial patriarchal power through the control of the biological father, and as such has led to the erasure of much family history. In being elevated to the status of an icon, motherhood becomes a vulnerable and precarious signifier of the nation's morality that must be surveyed, controlled and disciplined. The popular media in the United States, Britain and Australia contributed to the promotion of distinctive white nuclear and middle-class familial values that underpinned concepts of the nation, including national practices of childrearing and national ideas of suburban community cohesion. Radio and then television entered the home as crucial media of contact between the feminine, privatised and isolated world of the suburban family and the masculine, public world of politics and employment.

Drawing on research and debates in film studies and cultural studies, this chapter examines how these important structural and discursive changes were articulated. After discussing the rise of the concept of the 'companionate marriage' as a central feature of the nuclear marriage to combat the perceived rise of women's autonomy, I look at three themes that address important strands within processes of representing the family during the mid-twentieth century. First, Hollywood films of the 1930s and 1940s are approached to explore the dominant representations of motherhood circulating within the popular media in relation to dominant discourses of family and mothering. Second, this is followed by a brief discussion of television family melodrama and sitcom of the 1950s, and the rise of a distinctive familial consumerism. Third, I discuss the ways in which families themselves actively engaged in representing 'familyness' through a study of family photography. This case study maps the ways in which families experienced and engaged in the performance of familism through the exhibition and spectacularisation of families within the popular yet intimate and private cultural form of family photograph albums. In fact, this sense of 'exhibition' and 'spectacularisation' connects these three areas, as the family is seen as a 'performance' that is acted out by its members in the theatrical space of the home and staged on film, television and in family photograph albums. But in order for this performance to work, the conjugal couple have to learn their lines. And this requires advice on how to 'perform' the 'companionate marriage'.

REGULATING FEMININE INDIVIDUALISATION THROUGH THE 'COMPANIONATE MARRIAGE'

The idea of a 'companionate marriage' first emerged in the 1920s in North America and became a key feature of the modern functional family form. This model of marriage promoted the idea that husbands and wives had different roles that were, nevertheless, 'complementary'. It implied sexual pleasure and friendship based on equality and emphasised communication and joint decision-making by couples on issues such as family size. The companionate marriage model promoted the idea of a sexually intimate relationship between heterosexual partners based on romantic love and mutual interests, which should be fulfilling for both. Influential 'experts' argued that childless couples should have access to legal forms of birth control and should be permitted to divorce by mutual consent (Gittins, 1982).

Early twentieth-century ideals of the 'companionate marriage' implied egalitarian relationships between husbands and wives but were bolted on to a model of family that, as we have seen, required a male 'head' and was quintessentially patriarchal. The concept incorporated the seemingly opposi-tional characteristics of power and control as well as private, physical, sexual and emotional aspects of conjugal relationships. In fact, these ideas act as the foundation to Giddens' (1992) principle of the 'democratic pure relationship' within the contemporary postmodern familial framework, which shows how powerful the model is in acting as a standard by which marriage and family continue to be measured and judged (see Chapter 5). Importantly, during the early twentieth century, public acceptance of the ideal companionate marriage allowed the separation of reproduction from sex and the idea that marriage was not simply a means to having children, even though it was still seen as a key function. As discussed in Chapter 2, medical doctors and other professionals who set themselves up as advisers and counsellors on sex and marriage began to talk about sex as a vehicle for bonding, as a form of pleasure, as well as for reproduction.

Although in Talcott Parsons' model the modern family was treated as a unit that functioned for industrial capitalism, it became clear that the ideo-logy that produced this materialism contained the seeds of its own destruc-tion. Even by the 1950s there were fears that the values of individualism and consumerism that accompanied the rise of capitalism would lead to the break-up of the nuclear family. The ideology of companionship was devel-oped at this particular juncture out of these very concerns in order to secure a timeless model of conjugal friendship that would strengthen the family against an encroaching individualism. It was regarded as a necessary ingre-dient to married life that would shield the family from the dangers of rampant individualism, the break-up of older communities, and the rise of the more anti-social or asocial elements of urban-industrial living. For example, between the two world wars, Burgess and Locke (1945) argued that the model of the American family was shifting from that of an *institution* to one of *companionship*. They claimed that:

> 'In the past ... a stable and secure family life was guaranteed by external pres-sures of law, custom and public opinion. Those controls were reinforced inside the family by the authority of the male family head, the rigid discipline by parents over children, and elaborate public and private rituals. (quoted in Cheale, 1999: 74)

It is not made clear when this 'past' actually is, and the 'stability' and 'secu-rity' of the family is only guaranteed by those outside regulatory forces that legitimised patriarchal control over family members. This traditional system of control was said to be breaking down in early twentieth-century North America, prompted by key factors such as the decline of domestic production; the economic deprivation of the 'Great Depression'; rising 'individualism', allowing individuals greater freedom *from* families and *within* families; and a rising democratic ethos that loosened public controls over morality and over the internal authority of relationships (Cheale, 1999). The decline of an economic function to family life was accompanied by a growing emphasis on its social and cultural function. These major social changes were also connected with migration and the growth of cities and suburbs, and public exposure to new forms of behaviour through the mass media, leading American functionalists like Burgess (1973) to argue that such trends were encouraging 'family disorganisation'. This 'disorganisation' was apparently characterised by normative uncertainty, changes in social behaviour and the breakdown of relationships. The underlying fear, which was never stated directly, was that women were escaping the bonds of patriarchal family ties, and becoming more individualistic. Women's growing autonomy constituted a grave threat to the 'stability' of the nuclear family, which itself was formed to suit men's needs. The notion of the companionate marriage was a crucial ideology deployed to defuse feminine individualisation and evoke a new kind of egalitarian family, which, paradoxically, was already changing into something else.

Burgess and Locke (1945) claimed that traditional ties of duty that were publicly regulated were much more powerful than ties of affection. The socially isolated companionship family was therefore always going to be more susceptible to change. So modern family life had to be reconfigured on the basis of interpersonal relationships of mutual affection and understanding, framed within the 'companionship family'. But families themselves would not, apparently, be able to make this shift without the help of experts. Practical techniques developed by 'family experts' had to be communicated by a stream of social agencies such as child guidance clinics, marriage counselling centres, psychiatrists and clinical psychologists with the aim of treating the behavioural problems of children and adults. The groundwork had been laid, and a precedent set, by the nineteenth- and early twentieth-century sexologists and child care psychologists. Burgess assumed that the human service programmes – 'therapeutic agencies' – would inevitably be committed to the values of familism, that is, to the preservation of the modern nuclear family as a unit of interacting individual personalities (Cheale, 1999).

The 'companionate marriage' emerged as a way of conceding women's growing sense of independence associated with the rise of consumerism and individualism to ensure that the modern patriarchal family would remain intact. The idea of the companionate marriage was, according to Cheale (1999) in his discussion of Burgess and Locke, an important antidote to the encroaching values of individualism. But he blames human service practitioners for promoting the values of individualism and emancipation from social constraints. For evidence to support his claim, he points to the critical rethinking of social scientific theory and practice in relation to the abuse of women within their families. Cheale argues that this rethinking is part of a trend that is not conducive to reconstituting family life: 'Today, feminist therapists and workers in women's shelters often see it as their responsibility to provide women with personal resources with which to *leave* their families' (Cheale, 1999: 75, his emphasis).

Cheale comes close to implying that the cause of familial breakdown today is women. The kinds of physical abuse that women experience at the hands of violent husbands is not problematised in this argument, but women leaving 'the family' (meaning men) *is*. The problem is that the values of individualism can be deployed either way: either to bolster or condemn women's autonomy, or to reinforce or condemn a modernist masculine individuality, or to support or deny the rights of children. Debates about the rights of fathers, of mothers and the unborn child have demonstrated precisely these kinds of difficulties. While the theme of individualisation runs through much social theory, revolving around issues of agency, autonomy and personal identity, admitting that this process should also involve women has been so grudging and reluctant that women's individualisation alone has been blamed by many sociologists for the breakdown of the family. The containment of women, as wives and mothers, also proves to be a preoccupation of popular media representations of the family during this 'golden era', as discussed below.

THE RISE OF THE DYSFUNCTIONAL FAMILY

The post-war shift from an ideological emphasis on *extended* family to *nuclear* family relations was framed within the cultural promotion of leisure and consumption. In his classic text *Television, Technology and Cultural Form* (1974), Raymond Williams refers to the development of two contradictory tendencies that characterised the cultural and technological imperatives of the early twentieth-century phase of industrial capitalist society – social and geographical *mobility*; and *privatisation* within the private family home – which appeared to be self-contained and independent. He brings them together as 'mobile privatisation':

> Socially, this complex is characterised by two apparently paradoxical yet deeply connected tendencies of modern urban living: on the one hand mobility, on the other hand the more apparently self-sufficient family home. The earlier period of public technology, best exemplified by the railways and city lighting, was being replaced by a kind of technology for which no satisfactory name has yet been found: that which served an at once mobile and home-centred way of living: a form of *mobile privatisation*. (Williams, 1974: 26)

He goes on to say that these two effects, of mobility and privatisation, 'combined in a major emphasis on the improvement of the small family home.

Yet this privatisation, which was at once an effective achievement and a defensive response, carried, as a consequence, an imperative need for new kinds of contact.' The disintegration of the old small, traditional settlements leading to this new mode of spatial and social mobility created a need for new forms of social relations. This new social contact came in the form of mass media technology and the conferring of social status by consumer durable ownership, allowing the reintegration of the private home with the public world. And it gave public institutions access to the family by new communication technology, bringing news and entertainment into the home via broadcasting. The family was able to function as a mobile, nuclear and privatised unit but only through the intervention of mass communication designed for domestic reception.

The tendency, during this period, to approach families in their domestic context as passive consumers of popular culture fostered ideas of radio listening and television viewing as a 'pacifying, emasculating, and feminising activity' (Boddy, 1998: 137). The female homemaker became a symbol of passive consumption of daytime radio programming and later of television soap operas (Spigel, 1992). In North America, manufacturers of radio sets and operators of commercial radio stations were targeting their marketing and programming activities towards an 'imagined distracted housewife listening to a loudspeaker-equipped radio set located in the family parlour' (Boddy, 1998: 132). It was part of a wider tendency towards the gendering of mass culture as something inherently feminine and feminising, and the positioning of female audiences at the heart of a kind of cultural and moral crisis. The continuing emphasis on a non-interactive mode of mass communication and familial consumption has perpetuated the tradition of approaching the family in a narrow way as 'audience' and 'consumer'. Despite the fact that research in media and cultural studies is now predominantly ethnographic in its approach to overcome the idea of 'passive audience', the cultural study of the family has tended to be confined to the category of domestic 'audience', albeit now acknowledged as 'active' in its engagement with television texts.[2]

There are, then, certain key emphases emerging within the early twentieth century and early days of broadcasting that have made a profound impact on structures and representations of the family: first, the *privatisation* of the mobile urban and suburban family; second, the increasing *consumerisation* of a nuclearised version of family in which material possessions and television viewing became vital aspects of the new, individuated familial lifestyle; third, the promotion of the home as the work and leisure venue of the female homemaker; fourth, the *feminisation* of domestic popular culture, and, in particular, the notion of the pathology of a female soap 'audience'. These emphases were reinforced within television programmes of the period, but not just through simplistic celebratory representations of the modern nuclear family ideal. A further important emphasis detailed by

Lynn Spigel (1992, 1997), which I refer to below, is the popular representation of the home as *theatre*, and family members as *performers*.

Embedded within the sign of the privatised, consumerised, feminised and spectacularised ideal family lurks its 'other': the dysfunctional family form. The modern functional family cannot operate effectively as a regulatory ideal without inventing the idea of being under siege from deeply disruptive forces. The dysfunctional family, and its individual members, act as a counter-foil, as a permanent reminder of the need to fight for the preservation of the ideal as something more than a myth, as something that once existed and that must be recovered. This pathological form signifies the demise of the 1950s male breadwinner model and the rise of postmodern instability, diversity and deviation. The nuclear ideal is invented and reinvented, and kept alive in political rhetoric and fiction through endless mobilisation against the perils of dysfunctionality. The middle-class white nuclear family may be a figment of the public imagination, but it has come to stand for something beyond itself: moral purity and goodness. It has come to represent something that *ought* to exist.

The functionalist idealisation of nuclear family values and the concept of the companionate marriage acted as a regulatory yardstick by which familial roles and identities and everyday family problems were measured. It played a central role in fixing meanings about gender, sexuality and nation as 'familial' meanings. Popular and private cultural forms of the early and mid-twentieth century contributed to this fixing of familial meanings, including women's magazines, film and television, and even family photograph albums. Traditional notions of femininity and motherhood were reinforced rather than challenged. For example, between 1945 and 1953, the main themes of women's magazines were marriage, domesticity, motherhood and how to remain feminine, as Janice Winship (1984, 1987) demonstrates in her important classic work on women's magazines. Since functionalism was incapable of explaining why the majority of individuals, families and households did not conform to Parsons' functional ideal nuclear family, all individuals and familial groups that lay outside this model were labelled dysfunctional and either pathologised or demonised. Dysfunctionality developed, then, as a key theme in popular media narratives of everyday life in the form of humour and tragedy.

In her discussion of American representations of the early twentieth century home, Lynn Spigel (1997) argues that family life was portrayed in terms of spectacle and theatre. She states: 'Magazines and advertisements of the 1920s devised elaborate ways to depict the home as a showcase for glamorous commodity lifestyles, while manuals on architecture and interior decor adopted metaphors of theatricality when speaking about the home' (Spigel, 1997: 220). Not surprisingly, the theatricality of family life was played out across popular media forms from magazines to film, radio and television drama. Spigel points out that sociologists of the time were aware that family living was acted out like a play and that the home was treated as a theatrical stage. For example, Nelson Foote entitled his academic paper 'Family living as play' (1955). As Spigel (1997: 220) notes, he claims that family members are all performers: 'The husband may be an audience to the wife, or the wife to the husband, or the older child to both' (Nelson, 1955: 299). Importantly, the use of theatricality as a metaphor for family relations is central to the depiction of family life within the popular media of early Hollywood film and, later on, television.

The Ideology of Motherhood in Hollywood Melodrama

Dysfunctionality is a principal theme, used as a regulatory device, within tragedy for the exploration and condemnation of troubled figures picked out for moral scrutiny and who cause or come from profoundly troubled family relationships. An intriguing example is the way in which Hollywood women's films of the 1930s and 1940s became a cultural site for exploring the dilemmas of the maternal. The contradictory position of the mother in patriarchal society was played out as a key theme on the Hollywood screen. In fact the 'woman's film' is worth looking at more closely because it is an interesting and important illustration of a popular cultural form that sanctified the institution of motherhood yet devalued and undermined the power of the mother as a figure, in the form of a warning. It is no accident that the latter theme was located within a melodramatic genre. The term 'melodramatic' implies excess and the artifice of theatricality. In contrast to the masculine Western, the melodrama was a feminine form addressed to a female audience, characterised by the claustrophobic domestic settings of small-town, middle-class Middle America. The plot conventionally involved the desire for an unattainable object.

In her work on the women's film of the 1940s, Mary Ann Doane (1987) shows how the pathos of 1940s melodrama was articulated through the sacrifice and suffering of women and their children, both of whom signified powerlessness and misfortune. Mothering requires the physical presence of the mother, whereas paternal power can be manifested through absence. Certainly, in films aimed at a male audience, including Westerns, war films, crime thrillers, and so on, the male protagonist's status of fatherhood was taken for granted. Men's role within families was only problematised if their wives and children were under threat or curtailing their freedom. As Doane (1987) argues, what was melodramatic about maternal melodramas were narratives of separation or threatened separation and return, centred on the mother/child relationship. She points out that in 1930s films such as *Madame X* (1920, 1929), *Blonde Venus* (1932) and *Stella Dallas* (1937 remake by King Vidor), the maternal melodrama plot usually centred on the separation of the mother from her child, and her fall from social grace. The mother watches from a distance the child rise to respectability in a new adopted family, and she risks contaminating the child in her attempt to make contact. The mother's reputation is recuperated through a chance meeting and, often, 'a cathartic trial scene' (Viviani, 1980: 7).

Films such as *Stella Dallas* (1937) focused on the demand by society for the unmarried mother to give up her child to the social order, and the overwhelming desire of the mother to keep the child. Being forced to watch the child from a distance reinforces the idea of motherhood as a marginalised role, on the edge of culture because her emotional capacity to control is a source of resistance to the class-based nature of the patriarchal social order. Motherhood has the potential to transcend society so its power has to be condemned and punished in order to be contained. The child can only succeed if the mother sacrifices herself. In response, the mother is forced to take on the mantle of anonymity to allow her child to enter society and progress. The negation of her identity is the price to be paid for her child's life. The American version of the maternal melodrama incorporates the traditional English and European emphasis of 'moral sin' within a middle-class emphasis on 'social error' where the mother becomes an embarrassment in her obsession with her child and forgets the need for social aspirations and social mobility.

The reorganisation of sex roles thereafter, during the Second World War, led to an ambivalence about mothering that was represented in women's magazines and Hollywood films of the 1940s. American film producers of the early 1940s thought that cinemas would fill with female audiences because of the movement of men into the armed forces during the war. They wanted to attract a female audience by using female stars and addressing feminine issues in what became a feature of the film industry. The films of the 1940s were, then, produced during a period of intense ideological upheaval characterised by a reconstruction of gender roles and the reorganisation of family life. Melodrama is characterised by its positioning of the woman, as character and audience, within the centre of the narrative.

Family separation continued as a major theme in the 1940s films, but it was situated in the absence of the father, through separation of husband from wife and family. In films such as *Tender Comrade* (1943), *Since You Went Away* (1944) and *The Reckless Moment* (1949), the maternal was exploited for and associated with national patriotism. Mother and child figures became a united signifier representing the home front that was being fought over by the husband soldier. Women were given important roles in contributing to the war effort but ones which did not constitute a threat to the traditional patriarchal order of things (Doane, 1987: 79). In fact, as Doane points out, the symbolic role of motherhood was invested with such power that it eclipsed the potentially challenging nature of the roles offered to women in the public sphere of paid employment. The loss of husbands, fathers and sons, was constructed in films such as *Tender Comrade* by reminders of male presence in photographs and other domestic references around the home.

These 1940s maternal melodramas were quintessentially middle class and white. Racial issues were a key focus in which black servants were used to prop up the white nuclear family as relevant attachments that reinforced the inevitability of racial hierarchy. In *The Reckless Moment*, the black maid, Sybil, was not only used as a backdrop to emphasise the whiteness and middle-class nature of nuclear family but she was a vessel of maternal knowledge who came to stand for the primordial nature of the maternal. As Doane (1987: 81) states,

> Perceived as closer to the earth and to nature and more fully excluded from the social contract than the white woman, the black woman personifies more explicitly the situation of the mother, and her presence, on the margins of the text, is a significant component of many maternal melodramas.

The mother is often portrayed as having too much power over her son, by being too close to him emotionally. The maternal as excess is signified in a number of films such as *Tomorrow is For Ever* (1946) and *Watch on the Rhine* (1943). In fact, excessive mothering is condemned as a threat to patriarchy and the family in the same way as promiscuous sexuality. A maternal ideology is often linked to an anti-isolationist politics by portraying the mother's desire to stop her son from entering the social order, the real world of politics.

So within 1930s and 1940s maternal melodrama films, motherhood is not simply confined to the position of comfort and nostalgia, but treated as a potential site of danger for sons, husbands and society, as an unstable identity with pathological or demonic power that must be punished. Luce Irigaray (1981) expresses the maternal as a space that challenges paternal law as separation, division and differentiation through its overwhelming, engulfing power to suffocate (the daughter). Inadvertently, the mother almost destroys her daughter's identity through an over-invested desire for the child. This analysis has connections with Julia Kristeva's (1983) idea of the maternal as abject. The abject is both horrifying and fascinating and therefore marginalised by being subjected to taboos in order to control and regulate it. The maternal space threatens to destroy identity by collapsing the distinction between the subject and object, between mother and child. This collapsing of identities threatens paternal law, upon which differentiation is based. Doane suggests that this explains the reason why the genre of maternal melodrama exists. The pathos of such films is made possible by the creation of a narrative in which maternal love is signified as a form of female desire that is unachievable, that cannot be fulfilled, and in which the separation of mother and child is a permanent threat.

During the battle played out between Hollywood cinema and television in 1950s America, Hollywood responded to competition from television by trying to attract audiences through a number of strategies, including the resurgence of the family melodrama. As Laura Mulvey (1989: 39) points out, melodrama films of the 1950s explored the icon of the American home and the sacred figure of the mother as a way of attempting to lure audiences away from the home itself to the cinema. It was a genre that dealt with sexual repression and frustration and, as Mulvey says, 'its excitement comes from conflict, not between enemies, but between people tied by blood or love'. She emphasises

> the dizzy satisfaction in witnessing the way that sexual difference under patri-
> archy is fraught, explosive, and erupts dramatically into violence within its own
> private stamping-ground, the family. While the Western and the gangster film
> celebrate the ups and downs endured by men of action, the melodramas of
> Douglas Sirk, like the tragedies of Euripides, probing the pent-up emotion,
> bitterness and disillusion well known to women, act as a corrective.

The melodrama performs the ideological function of a safety valve, exposing and working ideological contradictions in the family by exploring those tensions in the family, and between the family and a patriarchal society, that undervalue the feminine and family values. But, unlike the conventions of masculine genres, melodrama fails to deliver satisfaction. The conflicts are reconciled in ways that confirm and reinforce women's role as solely family-based.

Mulvey analyses a central scene in the film *All That Heaven Allows*, directed by Douglas Sirk in 1955, in which the actor Jane Wyman plays a widow in her forties. She is given a television set as a Christmas present by her adult children and resolves to stay in and watch it, anchored in the safety and material security of the middle-class home, rather than go out into the world and awaken her sexuality through adventure. As Mulvey says, the television comes to stand for powerful positive meanings about motherhood, home, the middle-class interior and prosperity, but it also stands for repression. The figure of the mother becomes the 'signifier of censorship' in 1950s Hollywood family melodrama. This is transferred to the television and the home as a space. Within the outside/inside dichotomy that structures the sexual politics of popular entertainment, the home becomes a mythologised female space in which the television is a sign of containment of feminine desire. The family offers a

> ready-made *dramatis personae* of characters whose relations are by very
> definition overdetermined and overlaid with tension and contradiction, designed
> to act out Oedipal drama, generational conflict, sibling rivalry, the containment
> and repression of sexuality. The family is the socially acceptable road to respect-
> able normality, an icon of conformity, and at one and the same time, the source
> of deviance, psychosis and despair. In addition to these elements of
> dramatic material, the family provides a physical setting, the home, that can
> hold a drama in claustrophobic intensity and represent, with its highly connotive

architectural organisation, the passions and antagonisms that lie behind it. (Mulvey, 1989: 73–74)

Popular Culture's Dysfunctional Families

The 1950s marks a period in which a dominant ideology of maternal and wifely virtues was framed within the feminine domestic category of full-time motherhood. Interestingly, these representations contrast sharply with the 'working mother' category represented today in contemporary women's magazines and television dramas, and with the newly emerging contradictory and ambivalent figure of the 'independent mother' in magazines such as *She* (Woodward, 1997). Within television drama serials, the ideal white family was performed as a positive model with key members held up as paragons of virtue, as in the ideal and self-sacrificing mother and authoritative paternal father represented in the famous American 'Walton family'. Meanwhile, the 'dysfunctional' family was built around the genre of sitcom through a number of formulas. Hilarious family figures of fun were depicted breaking the rules of family values and family life in a number of sitcoms such as the *The Beverley Hillbillies*, and cartoons such as *The Flintstones*, in which the family members have to be morally 'rescued' by kin or wider members of the community. In other comic dramas, the inherently dysfunctional family members themselves come to stand for the silent majority of protesters by exposing the hypocrisy and prissiness of the bourgeois family in middle America, as shown more recently in *The Addams Family*, and in comedy animation *The Simpsons*, who have been named 'America's First Family' in the British *Times Magazine*, in which Nick Griffiths (2000: 25) declares, sentimentally: 'Dysfunctional and degenerate they may be, but after ten years the Simpsons have proved that a family that plays together stays together.' *The Simpsons* is shown in ninety-four countries and followed on the trail of American sitcoms such as *Married ... With Children* and *Roseanne* that turned their back on the pristine image of family life represented in *The Waltons*, with family members depicted as spiteful, selfish, pretentious, yelling at one another, and sneering at others' troubles. The cartoon format of *The Simpsons* somehow acted as a more comfortable distancing device that allowed a hilarious way of exploring dysfunctionality through characters such as the antisocial behaviour of the son, Bart; the clumsy stupidity of the father, Homer; and the family's social conscience played by daughter, Lisa. In fact, this entertainingly subversive cartoon was so influential that during his 1992 election campaign George Bush declared: 'We're going to keep on trying to strengthen the American family. To make them more like the Waltons and less like the Simpsons' (cited in Griffiths, 2000: 27).

Cartoon characters, class difference, and mock gothic horror have all been successfully used as dysfunctional frames with which to tease and taunt the ideal nuclear family from the post-war period onwards. But the absence of black families is, crucially, a constant factor throughout the 1950s. Like Britain, which imported many American television programmes, Middle America was depicted as all-white during a period when blackness continued to represent chaos, disorder and a threat to the moral purity of the white family.

Family sitcom television rose to prominence in 1950s America during the very moment that the modern family, simultaneously mocked and celebrated by the genre, was on the decline (Stacey, 1999). The 1950s was a crucial period of national ideological struggle in America during the Cold War with the former Soviet Union. Images of a triumphant family and nation were fused within the national nostalgia for a golden era of wholesome family values (see May, 1988; Spigel, 1992). As Judith Stacey (1999: 199) points out, in her discussion about the revival of traditional American family values:

> The 1950s was the originary moment of the fable of virtual family values. Those halcyon days of the modern nuclear family were also the years when television became a mass medium, indeed an obligatory new member of 'the family'. From its hallowed living room perch, the magic box broadcast the first generation of domestic sitcoms, emblazoning idealised portraits of middle-class family dynamics into the national unconscious.

Yet the humour in family sitcoms relied precisely on breaking the codes of the idealised family. The genre of the sitcoms acted as a barometer of family values *through* familial dysfunctionality. The first batch of television domestic sitcoms in 1950s America such as *The Adventures of Ozzie and Harriet*, *Amos and Andy* and *The Life of Riley* may have placed idealised portraits of white, middle-class family dynamics into the national unconscious, as Judith Stacey (1999) suggests. After all, the kind of family represented was dominantly white anglophone American with some significant allowances made for an, albeit white, continental European background. But the ideal family was rarely represented in a straightforward way – it was mediated through the plot by rupture and crisis either imposed by the quirky but cute personalities of the internal family members themselves (exemplified in *The Beverley Hillbillies*, *I Love Lucy*, *The Burns and Allen Show*, the cartoons of *Popeye* and *The Flintstones*), or by mobilising against intrusive outside forces.

The narrative resolution typically conveyed the sentiments of the ideal white family: of caring, commitment, loyalty, sacrifice and permanence. In this way, the vulnerability of the white, nuclear family could be alluded to in order to underline the need to 'work at' producing the ideal family 'for real'. The soap opera of today's western anglophone nations, fifty years on, has perfected the art of combining these two forces, that is, of *crisis* from outside and *rupture* from within (see Chapter 4). It operates by drawing on the dysfunctionality of individual family members' weaknesses – through infidelity, violence and alcoholism – as well as outside forces such as unemployment, illness, death or dangerous strangers in the community as a way of exploring, testing and scrutinising the morality of family values (for example, in *Dallas*, *EastEnders*, *Coronation Street*, *Neighbours*).

Spigel (1992) shows how the theatrical quality of everyday life becomes a crucial factor in the organisation of television genres such as sitcom and soaps. Family sitcoms emphasised the performative quality of middle-class family life in a self-reflexive way. The CBS *Burns and Allen Show*, which contained the George and Gracie routine, was one of the most self-reflexive. It exemplifies early television sitcom of 1950s America (with 239 programmes made between 1950 and 1958) in which the characters themselves exhibited disruptive features on which the humour pivoted. In fact, it was a real-life couple, the ex-vaudevillians George Burns and Gracie Allen, 'who played themselves playing themselves as real-life performers' (Spigel, 1997: 222). The domestic setting of the narratives and the series of misunderstandings generated by Gracie's lack of logic caused waves of confusion with characters outside the family such as neighbours, delivery boys, sales people, who were all related in some way to the domestic space and situation. George's wise-cracks and the chaotic situations caused by the misunderstandings were the central components of the comedy. *The Adventures of Ozzie and Harriet*, *I Love Lucy*, *The Danny Thomas Show* and *The Dick Van Dyke Show* were other examples of sitcoms of the 1950s that contained celebrity couples and exhibited this self-reflexive theatricality by appearing to live out their family lives on the screen and combining show-business careers with family life. The home setting was often transformed into a stage in suburban sitcoms such as *I Married Joan* and *The Ruggles* as well. So celebrity families performed their familyness in these popular representations in the home, which was a space signified as a theatre (Spigel, 1992). The theatricality of the home, emphasising the performativity of family life, is a seam running through sociological accounts that, nonetheless, fundamentally contradicts traditional media approaches to the family as (passive) 'audience'.

Echoing Mulvey, Mick Eaton's (1977) analysis of 1970s British sitcom comedy emphasises that the sitcom generally treats the family as an insular unit and sets it up as a signifier of an inside/outside structure. Examples that come to mind are British 1970s sitcoms such as *All in the Family*, *Happy Ever After*, and *Love Thy Neighbour*. The family is set up as a stable unit, borne out by the weekly repetition of drama, and the 'chaos' is something imposed on it from the outside world. As Eaton argues, the soap opera's narrative differs from sitcom because its structure relies on the broader parameters of a street (*Coronation Street*), a square (*EastEnders*) or some other housing community (*Brookside*) with interlocking families, neighbours and individuals rather than one main family unit. So while sitcom celebrates the white nuclear family through dysfunctionality within a public/private dichotomy that emphasises the outside/inside boundary of the family as a distinctive nuclearised unit, the soap opera promotes the sense of wider community that tracks and surveys the morals of a number of families as an ongoing morality tale. The daily rhythms of domestic life dramatised in soap opera act as a contrast to the formality of the public sphere (Modleski, 1984: 111). Tensions and distinctions between 'outside and inside' the family or between 'private and public' in sitcom, and between 'individuality and community' or the 'private and the social' in soap opera, indicate important preoccupations in wider society, from the 1950s, about how the individual, the family and the public world should interconnect with one another in the formation of gendered and sexed human subjects.

As major popular cultural arenas that drew on metaphors that presented domesticity as *theatre*, sitcom emphasised the performativity and artifice of suburban, nuclear family life (Spigel, 1997). Although rival ideas of sub-urban domesticity wrestled for cultural legitimacy in the 1950s and 1960s, this centring of the domestic sphere provided strong female characters. Soap opera continues to give women a high profile and portrays examples of con-tested maternal identities such as single or working mothers that can be explored in contrast to idealised images of femininity. Importantly, the dys-functional anxieties and disruptions to stable family values played out in soaps convey the possibilities of a negotiation and contestation of subordi-nated maternal and wifely identities for women.

From within the privacy and comfort of the home, families could perform on their domestic stage the role of family audience by watching other, celebrity families perform familyness on the television screen. In a bizarre twist, today in Britain we watch BBC's comedy, *The Royle Family*, in which the Royles perform working-class familyness as they slouch in their armchairs in front of the television, eating snacks, drinking, watching and squabbling about the television programmes. Within plots of seemingly little action, the intricacies of the family relationships unfold to produce an amusing specta-cle of couch potato-ness, in which we, as audience, are uncomfortably colluding as voyeurs. Is this the ultimate in family television theatricality: couch potatoes watching couch potatoes? Baby Brooklyn's entrance in the new series gives audiences the opportunity to laugh at the hopeless mothering skills of Denise, demonstrating that women's maternal identities continue to be problematised by their treatment as a joke in contemporary comedy alongside the ongoing demonisation of the mother-in-law.

There are, then, a number of factors that converge within modes of popu-lar culture during the early twentieth century that set the scene for future patterns of representation. These factors come together to produce a domi-nant set of discourses about the mobile, privatised, white, nuclear family as a ritualised performance of rigidly gendered roles, played out through

Hollywood melodrama, then sitcom and soap opera on the theatrical stage of the home. The narrative consists of the idealisation of the nuclear form through the invention and acting out of its dysfunctional 'other'. What we find below, in the example of family photography of the same period, is that this performance of nuclear familialism is so strong that it gets taken a step further through the manufacture of familyness *by* ordinary families themselves. Families collude in the reinvention of the ideology of the family through the production of their own visual representations of the myth of the 'happy family'.

REPRESENTATIONS OF THE FAMILY BY THE FAMILY: THE PHOTOGRAPH ALBUM

Since the introduction of family photography, families themselves have been remarkably active agents in the production of private representations of the ideal modern family, and not just as 'audiences'. Within the ongoing search for the perfect stable, loving and supportive family, family members have actively colluded in reproducing the perfect vision of familyness in representing their own families as nuclear ideals supported by external extended kin. Family photography and family albums are powerful tools of cultural representation enabling individual families to narrativise their sense of unity, heritage, intimacy and spatial belonging. As such, the humble family photograph album became a sophisticated ideological device. It authenticated and celebrated public discourses of familial heritage, blood ties, continuity and connection within a private cultural form that also articulates emotions of intimacy, security and belonging. It performed the crucial role of transforming the experience of nuclearised parenthood into a spectacle.

The family photograph album of the 1950s was an icon of conformity, in which the perfect family was over-determined through the careful selection and display of family photographs of unity, connectiveness and ritual. This popular cultural form displayed and surveyed heterosexual familial identities yet, as I discuss in Chapter 5, it is a cultural form that also offers frameworks for holding other complex, unregulated desires and transgressive memories. The family photograph album's messages were as much about absences, fragmentation and exclusion as they were about presences, unity and belonging. In these ways, it played a central role in promoting images and meanings that conform to the familial ideal.

The growth and consolidation of family photography as a social practice began with the professional recording of 'the family' and later shifted to an amateur social activity through which 'the family' recorded itself. Family albums consist of pictorial spectacles and visual memories in which the compilers of albums use distinctive conventions to authenticate families by familialising identities, social relationships, space and time. The family values and meanings narrated through photograph albums constitute a visual dialogue between private and public discourses of identity. Despite this, albums are only intended for private consumption among the exclusive group of extended and nuclear family and friends and never for the public domain, for publication. It is simultaneously a very private and yet rigidly standardised cultural form. It is a popular medium which has always been much more than just the documentation of celebrated domestic events as a photographic diary or record of the nuclear family.

Viewing albums requires a ritualised oral dialogue of description, story-telling, memory-making, nostalgia and celebration as well as denial, absences and secrecy. A high level of *familiarity* is needed for decoding the subject matter of family photograph albums. It presumes distinctive modes of viewing so the family album is embedded in a domestic and private oral tradition. Complex, and often contradictory, meanings encoded by the compiler are lost on non-family members. Drawing on the findings of a collaborative oral history research project of 1950s family photograph albums from the Australian suburbs, I have explored, ethnographically, some of the ways in which families have represented themselves within family albums.[3] I comment on the use and meanings of family albums compiled by women who were in their twenties during a crucial period of spatial transition which took place through the rapid suburbanisation of Western Sydney. In these ways, the family album is explored as a series of messages about the familialisation of identities.

Reinventing Family

Family photography gets treated both as an 'authentic' witness of the colonisation and domestication of space and as a cultural device for naturalising hierarchies of gender and race. It became an essential genre and social practice for recording and celebrating the connectedness of family during a crucial period of social upheaval, according to Susan Sontag (1977). At a critical moment, during the nineteenth century, when the extended white family form was beginning to disintegrate,

> Photography becomes a rite of family life just when, in the industrial countries of Europe and America, the very institution of the family starts undergoing radical surgery. As that claustrophobic unit, the nuclear family, was being carved out of a much larger family aggregate, photography came along to memorialise, to restate symbolically, the imperilled continuity and vanishing extendedness of family life. Those ghostly traces, photographs, supply the token presence of the dispersed relatives. A family's photograph album is generally about the extended family – and, often is all that remains of it. (Sontag, 1977: 8–9)

When a smaller privatised, geographically and socially mobile nuclear family starts to be held in the collective imagination, amateur photography and its display format of the family album come to the rescue to recover and mythologise a fixed version of it as something private and contained yet with a heritage and security through extended kin. Family photography records and reinvents something that no longer exists (see Sanders, 1980: 4).

Emphasising that family photographs are integral to the ideology of the modern family, Pierre Bourdieu (1990: 19) says that the practice of photography functions to solemnise and immortalise 'the high points of family life' and to reinforce 'the integration of the family group by reasserting the sense that it has both of itself and of its unity'. Significantly, the family photograph album has evolved as a predominantly feminine cultural form, as a visual medium for family genealogy and storytelling shaped by women. Echoing Bourdieu, Claire Grey (1991: 107) has stated, in a study of related generations of women in her own family albums, that women often take on the role of 'keepers of the past'. While women have been omitted from the public narratives of history, they have been present in private narratives: in the context of compiling albums as celebratory, memorialised and nostalgic representations of parenthood and childhood. During the early twentieth century, men tended to be the authors rather than the subjects of amateur family photographs, but women were strongly encouraged to participate in this activity by Kodak advertisements of the period aimed specifically at them.

Interestingly, the private narratives of family albums have been influenced by national narratives of the nineteenth century in Britain and its colonies. The family, as the 'feminine' realm, played a central role in the metaphoric projections of the imperial modern nation during this period. The Victorian invention of the Royal Family coincided with the rise of photography and provided the ideal and model image of a universal white family for the photographic representation of motherhood as a sign of moral rectitude and father as ruler and protector of wife and children (see, for example, Hobsbawm and Ranger, 1983; Ryan, 1997). The conventions of portrait painting among the nobility and merchant classes of Europe acted as a model for the professional recording of the family. Portrait photography exemplified the public and private surveillance of white family lineage as visual spectacle. The nineteenth-century treatment of women as male possessions and an artistic use of the female form as an expression of 'desiderata and virtues' (see Warner, 1985) and object of beauty shaped visual discourses of formal portraiture, which, in turn, influenced domestic photography.

The family album became an authentic witness and memorialiser of the white family's colonisation of suburbia. Yet these important social shifts involving mobility, privacy and the breakdown of extended families were profoundly structured by race. The 'white flight' to suburbia was a central component of post-war attempts to create a geographical and cultural distance between white and 'other', indigenous, black and Asian races. Suburbia ensured the reproduction of racial hierarchy and the ethnic privileging of whiteness through a domestication of space as white place. The desire to link the family with the public world was in evidence from the nineteenth century through the custom of collecting mass-produced *cartes de visite* portraits of eminent individuals such as royalty, statesmen and clergymen. *Cartes* portraits were exchanged among family and friends and arranged in personally compiled, but commercially manufactured, albums with window openings for cabinet-sized portraits. This visual 'who's who' involved a domestic celebration of public figures, and a commitment to their public authority. Portraits of the Royal Family, heads of state, politicians and clergymen were typically placed alongside images of the family.[4] The practice confirmed that familial identity was formed through family *connections* to the outside world of politics, power and pedigree. A cultural framework for shaping discourses of memory associated with space was also offered by postcards. The desire to connect one's family to celebrated symbols of nature and 'high culture' indicates the need to connect the private family to the wider community and to public institutions that represent national values: the pleasure of the countryside, the grandeur of public monuments, parades, festivals and the celebration of community.

There is such an intimate relationship between images of the family in the popular media such as advertisements for leisure products of the 1950s and images of the family in photograph albums in terms of subject matter, composition, poses and backdrop that it cannot be overlooked. It demonstrates the kinds of influences that public popular images had on the idea of the image of the perfect family at the level of 'how to perform familyness'. Advertisements were strongly targeted at white families during 1950s Australia, during an era when standardised products such as consumer durables were being aimed at a mass market categorised by the manufacturers and advertisers into family units.

Norman Rockwell's *Freedom From Want* (Figure 3.1) is an example of a genre that has strong associations with family photography. It evokes the deep sentiments of an anglophonic culture in America: the all-white American suburban family celebrating Thanksgiving. Rockwell was an illustrator for the *Saturday Evening Post* from 1916. He produced large-scale magazine colour illustrations of typical white Anglo-American life. By the end of the Depression, he became a household name and yet his paintings were only ever seen as reproductions. These images represented the quintessential Anglo-American ideal family values portrayed with the sharpness and realism reminiscent of photography, and crossing between the styles of advertising, family photography and television realism. They seemed to represent a utopian American suburbia in which the family was sacrosanct. The great social symbol, as in the family album, was *family stability*. In *Freedom From*

FIGURE 3.1 *Freedom From Want*, Norman Rockwell (1943),
oil on canvas (45¾ × 35½ cm.). (By permission of Thomas
Rockwell and Curtis Publishing Company, Indiana, USA.)

Want, the massive Thanksgiving turkey stands for family cohesion, continuity
and progress, and the positioning of the father at the head of table confirms
the normality of the patriarch. Norman Rockwell symbolised the wholesome
goodness of American family life at a time when the nation needed to confirm

79

its natural, unquestioned superiority: the 'Golden Era'. Yet even now, Norman Rockwell is regarded by many Americans as an artist whose work sums up the last century, in fact evokes 'The American Century'. So, for amateur family photographers, there were many popular cultural styles of imagery to imitate in the search for representations of the ideal family.

Scenic backdrops of the wilderness, holiday resorts and monuments are common themes in family albums. Many families and communities fragmented by geographical migration, whether through past quests to colonise other countries or more recent quests to colonise western nations' city suburbs, were reconnected through visual narratives of extended kinship. The family album represented genealogical and national heritage – it became a social and historical document of lineage and spatial belonging. The ritual of photographing members of the family beside monuments of nation and at national events reveals a familial desire to record the family's involvement in the creation of *domestic* images and meanings of nation. Picturing ideas of belonging to a nation and place were ways in which the album came to represent symbols of imagined community, of continuity, and connections to the past. The perfect nuclear family strove to locate itself within the wider world.

Photographs from my own family's albums suggest how the evolution of western consumerism influenced the celebratory theme of possession of consumer items in family photographs from the turn of the twentieth century onwards. From the 1930s to the 1950s, the family home and even possession of expensive consumer items such as cars became established as a common amateur photographic *mise-en-scène*. This theme echoed earlier rituals of family members posing for photographs, standing by their horse and buggies. I came across many examples of family albums of the 1950s containing photos of the family standing beside the 'family car', or the positioning of the car as a backdrop to family photos of leisure outings. Figure 3.2, 3.3, 3.4 and 3.5 are examples from my own family's albums that contain distinctive meanings for my parents about the pictorial celebration of domestic consumption and the familial colonisation and domestication of public, 'leisure' space in late 1950s American suburbia where they moved to from the East End of London. As an example of social mobility, my father experienced a significant rise from a job as a telephone engineer when, after marrying my mother, he joined the British Foreign Office in the early 1950s and was first posted to the British Embassy in Baghdad as a British diplomat.

Among our postings abroad when I was a child was Washington in 1956. Figure 3.2 photographically captures the family home in the suburbs of Washington, with my mother and me posing on the front doorstep. Figure 3.3 was taken by my mother from the interior of the family home. My father and I are in the front garden, framed by the white veranda, with the family car acting as a backdrop. In Figure 3.4 the mother and child feeding ducks

FIGURE 3.2 Mother and daughter on doorstep of home in the suburbs of Washington, DC. (Chambers family album, 1956.)

FIGURE 3.3 Father and daughter in front garden with family car in background, in the suburbs of Washington, DC. (Chambers family album, 1956.)

FIGURE 3.4 Mother and child feeding ducks in the park (Chambers family album, 1957.)

FIGURE 3.5 Father and child leaning against the car. (Chambers family album, 1956.)

in the park are balanced to one side of the frame with the family car clearly visible on the other side, again in the background. By December 1956, my parents had progressed to colour film, shown in Figure 3.5 (but not reproduced in colour here), which figures the family car as a prominent prop for father and child captured in the centre of the frame on a family outing to the countryside. In our family, the use of the camera was shared more equally between my mother and father than in it was in many albums at the time. So there are more photographs of 'father and child' in our family album than in many others of the period, as I discuss below.

At a time and place of intense social change, 1950s suburban domesticity was being mapped out and re-presented by family photographs as a secure space in which the home became a showcase for the consumerist, middle-class, white nuclear family (see Spigel, 1997). These photographs were not only designed for our own nuclear family album, but were also duplicated for sending copies 'back home' to the extended family of origin in London, so as to show off the nuclear family's new successful suburban, consumer lifestyle in the United States. The photographs were not captioned but each one was dated by the commercial processor on the front of the white border so as to emphasise the intended use of the image as a visual diary of family activities and events.

Most of the family's albums produced by my parents in the 1950s were destroyed when sea water leaked into the hold of the ship during a trip to an overseas posting in the early 1970s. We now have no record of my younger sister growing up, which, understandably, makes her feel 'invisible', and it often feels to me as if we have no 'family history'. This is because the albums in existence, from which some of these pictures are taken, have been compiled from the copies sent back home to other relatives. Family photographs are often encoded with peculiarly totemic and commemorative qualities, and given mystical and talismanic meanings and values. According to Celia Lury (1998: 81), the special status of family photographs is derived from their potential to capture the 'magical moments', of intimate contact. To emphasise the cultural significance of family photographs, she cites Don Slater (1995), who refers to the results of a market research survey in which 39 per cent of respondents claimed their family photos to be their most treasured possessions that 'they would least like to lose'.

The Meanings of 1950s Suburban Family Albums

Within the study of 1950s Australian albums ten Anglo-Celtic, white women, now aged between 60 and 75, were interviewed about their own family albums that they had compiled when they were in their twenties in the 1950s. We were particularly interested in the ways in which family albums produced during the crucial period of suburbanisation were negotiating the spatial changes going on around these families. The sample was not representative but constituted a small-scale, in-depth exploration and offers some clues about the range of meanings and values associated with the role of 1950s family albums in women's lives.

Initially, the most striking feature was the similarities, rather than the differences, between families' albums. Subject matter, poses, framing and sequencing were rigidly standardised. The desire to conform to public images of familyness must have been powerful. The albums were characterised by rigidly formalised, repetitive sequences and narratives. They contained photographs not only of a narrow range of events, but even of a narrow range of candid and action shots. But on reflection, these distinctive family album conventions framed meanings specific to each individual family within the private narratives of its albums. Of the ten women only one was unmarried. All the women interviewed regarded the albums they compiled as artefacts belonging to the whole of their family, with the exception of the unmarried woman, whose albums were mostly a record of her holidays with friends. All the married women interpreted their albums as 'a record' or 'diary' of married life and/or of children, emphasising the album's overwhelming function as 'truthful witness' of familial events (Berger, 1980). Most albums held a cross-section of portraits, landscapes and holiday photographs arranged in chronological order. Yet some were quite remarkable in their deviation from this norm.

With one exception, all the women were Australian-born. The family album of the one English woman who had moved to Australia as a young married mother consisted of a narration of settlement in the 'new country'. The rest of the albums involved a visual narration of suburban settlement in 1950s Western Sydney. Interestingly, the album owners were divided into two groups in terms of their photographic treatment of their spatial surroundings. The first group consisted of those families who lived in the traditional country towns of New South Wales, in Western Sydney, before these towns were suburbanised. They chose to ignore and deny the spatial changes around them. Country backdrops were selected when photographing families and friends so as to avoid images of the encroaching new suburbs. Being proud country-town folk, they did not claim the suburban dream as a positive part of their family's experience. It was seen as an intrusion.

The second group consisted of those families who had moved to the region of Western Sydney during the crucial period of suburban expansion in the 1950s. By contrast, they produced visual celebrations of their arrival in the promised land of suburbia with shots of cars, their homes and next-door neighbour's home in full view. Many of these albums' photographs showed the move to the suburbs to be a progressive gesture (see Chambers, 1997). The poor conditions of the inner city were forsaken for the Australian dream of fresh air, wide open spaces, home- and car-ownership. Suburbia was pictorially embraced as a utopian dream community. What all album owners and their families had in common, however, was a lack of interaction with members of the rural or urban Aboriginal communities. Spatial and cultural segregation between white and black was severe. Aborigines and Torres Strait Islanders were not treated as citizens at all, and were not enfranchised until the 1960s.

Photographs were taken regularly by these Anglo-Celtic families, and by the 1950s they were no longer associated only with special events. Yet a distinctly gendered use of the technology could be still be discerned. Wives typically owned a basic, cheap box Brownie, and husbands often owned the more expensive and sophisticated cameras and regarded themselves as the 'experts'. For example, Meg's husband took all the photos in her albums 'because he was a better photographer: He carried the camera!' Similarly, Pam's husband owned a British-made Ensign camera, which she gave him for his twenty-first birthday, followed by a German-made Voigtländer, both roll-film cameras. The latter cost the equivalent of about a hundred (Australian) dollars in the early 1950s: 'a good camera was a luxury'.

> Well, I always had a camera, but it was only just a Brownie type one, you know – a little plastic one – it wasn't the Box Brownie. So we always had cameras, and on our picnics we always took snapshots you know. I guess it was the men because they had the more complicated cameras.

Although there were detectable gender differences in the complexity of camera used, a gradual democratisation of camera use was taking place in 1950s western societies: photographs were now often being taken by both wives and husbands. Nearly half the married women album owners took their own photographs while the rest filled their albums with photographs taken almost exclusively by their husbands. So we found examples of albums that lacked a key member of the family: the father. For example, Pam's husband took the majority of the snaps contained in their family album. Those not taken by him were invariably taken by her father-in-law. Her husband was therefore absent from most outdoor event and holiday photos. These were albums recording only the activities of the mother and children. This 'absence of the father' theme, so common in narratives of family during war, was curiously being repeated but for quite different reasons. The father's presence as 'authority' over *his* family, as owned by him, was underlined by his control over the camera and the gaze. Yet, for this reason, Pam's whole album signified 'wife and children' because she was in control of the way the subject matter was placed in a book display form. The one case where both the photographer and album maker was the husband (Meg's family albums, discussed below) was the most unusual in terms of subject matter. It was an extraordinary visual, chronological document of family residences and family business, and contained few human subjects.

So the main purpose of most albums of the 1950s was to create a crucial record and celebration of children growing up, weddings, friends, relatives, holidays, picnics, Christmas, activities in the garden, and scenes around the house within the task of giving the family a history, a sense of origin and progress. Some albums were interspersed with other memorabilia such as letters, certificates, baby booklets and drawings. Within western anglophone nations, the 1950s constitutes a period of rapid urban change during which the family desperately needed to narrativise and authenticate itself.

Alison compiled her own albums to serve the role of pleasurable memory:

Yes. I was inspired in doing them by my mother who was, you know, in her eighties, and she'd had them all in boxes all her life. It took me for ever to sort hers out into categories and she loved them, and it was the only thing she ever looked at. She had them beside her chair when she was 88 – and she died at 88 – and everyone that came she said 'Have you seen these?' They got so sick of those albums. But it gave her a great deal of pleasure. So I thought well I'll do mine before I'm too old.

Albums were often taken out and looked at as a private and personal activity by the album owners but more often as a collective family activity at family gatherings of more than one generation. They were used as powerful devices for visually binding family members and generations together. The married women consistently defined their families' albums as a 'record of the children growing up' and as a 'marriage record.' Chronological ordering was regarded as an essential categorising device. When asked how she organised the albums, Pam said:

Well I've organised them as a marriage record actually, of [my husband's] Robert's and mine from 1946 to 1965 which are the only black and white ones we have. All the rest are on slides or colour prints. Then I've organised his family, his mother and father's from their marriage through 'till when he married. And also my own family, from my mother and father's marriage through to when I got married.

The birth of children was a key motivating factor for both taking the photographs and compiling the albums:

Oh, well as the children were little, you know, and that goes from 1946 right through the '50s, we took photographs of practically all their happenings and events. Special birthdays and things like that. Picnics always. You'll find lots of picnics in there [the album] and car trips. Oh, if we think the garden looks nice we go out there and take a picture of it. So that's the sort of things we do with the camera. (Pam)

When the children grew up, a shift in album subject matter from the celebration of children to the celebration of material possessions and consumption was common. Albums contained photos of the new family car, the house, friends and other relatives. Evidence of housework was systematically kept out of the picture by all album owners, as Barbara stated: 'No I was always fussy about having the washing taken off the line before we took any pictures [of the garden].' The recording of public events and witness of the family's presence at such events in public spaces was a strong theme of albums:

And [this] picture is the Queen's visit and we are at the Memorial Garden which was opened that day. We went down at about 7 o'clock in the morning and we got a seat. We carried a park bench up to where she was going to be and we sat there and we were about 3 feet away from them [Queen Elizabeth II and the Duke of Edinburgh]. (Barbara)

In these ways, the humble family album of the 1950s took on the vital role of spectacularising the experience of motherhood and fatherhood, of childhood and grandparenthood. The experience becomes fixed and transformed into desired memory so that, as Sanders (1989: 145) states, 'the image produces a form of memory that takes an ideological form: the way "one would like to be remembered"'. The version of 'me' to be remembered through the visual medium of album is the one anchored by familial identity. In this way, the album becomes a cultural tool that lies at the very heart of sexualised, genderised, aged, ethnic, religious and community identity.

In contrast to the married women's albums, the albums belonging to Celia, who was the only single woman, signified her independence. The subject matter of her albums was holiday trips taken with girlfriends. She did not specify her sexual identity. Clearly, for this narrator, photographs and albums signified leisure: 'Oh yes! Just to be feeling you're on holiday.' Each album was devoted to a single Australian trip and included postcards of the holiday scenes. Celia did not keep any family photographs in albums. As an unmarried woman, she had full control over the subject matter of the shots.

Only one woman, Meg, possessed family albums compiled by her husband. These albums turned out to be most unusual, so that the gender of the author of the photos as well as the albums are significant. In addition to the usual photos of weddings, children growing up, picnics, friends and witness of public events such as the Queen's visit to Australia in 1954, some albums took the concept of documentation extremely seriously. Twenty pages of the first album were almost completely devoid of people. It constituted a visual record of all the houses in which Meg and her husband had lived since their marriage. Every room in the house or flat was carefully recorded, often from different angles in strict chronological order: page after page of tidy homes with little to indicate who lived there. Without the benefit of an oral history approach, this collection would have meant absolutely nothing, in respect of 'family', to the outsider. The photos spoke for themselves and yet meant very little to anyone beyond the family:

Well [photo] 'A' is the bedroom, the bottom of the bed and the dressing-table. And we had like a bay window. [Photo] 'B' is the bedroom – it shows more. 'C', that is our dining room. That house was old when we went into it. 'D' is, now, that's the spare room. Well we called it – no – that's my bookcase. So we couldn't get all our bedroom furniture in that bedroom, so 'D' – I'm trying to think. That's our dining room and this was another room that went off the dining room near the … Oh my God, isn't this dreadful!

At one level the album was a record and celebration of interior domestic space as 'home'. Meg commented on a series of shots of the same room from several different angles: 'That really is a diary of the kitchen there.' Yet, at another level, this family album was a witness and celebration of family progress within a consumer discourse. The images pictured progression from the small flat, to a small house, then the husband's shop, then the vacant land they had purchased to build the house on, then the completed house, nearby workers' cottages, and then the grand finale: the family's new poultry farm. The symbol of success culminated in the visual record, not of 'home' but of the first battery chicken farm in New South Wales, shot from all dimensions, including an impressive aerial shot. The album contained photographs of the inside of the brand new shed, hens, the feeding system and egg packing plant.

This family album is a comment on the modern and the prosperous, albeit pre-organic, phase of Australian farming history. It was a record of the farming family, as a producing as well as consuming unit, but the album typically records images of growth and change as signifiers of material accumulation. Photographed surrounded by countryside, the final large house stands for 'dream home' indicating the ideal Australian lifestyle in an ideal setting: the colonisation and domestication of space. Influenced by the estate agents' visual discourses of property as spectacle, the aspirational features of albums as records of achievement are highlighted here. This example of album use for the purposes of documenting each domestic residence is fascinating as an exception to the norm. Albums were rarely used as a loyal document of home space as empty space. Yet that space was always present in the frame, contextualising and giving meaning to the performances of 'being family'. The narratives of albums are tied to cultural myths of collective memory expressed by documenting fulfilment in marriage and parenthood, the innocence and potential of childhood, and the realisation of familial aspirations through material success.

Interestingly, the use of slides, and now more popularly camcorders, for recording family life, has not replaced the talismanic qualities that framed and albumed photographs continue to have. Slides, video and computer images of the family demand particular modes of viewing within a cinematic or televisual style that treats the viewer as mass 'audience' for whom the pace of gazing is set, rather than as a reader, who both sets the pace of viewing and can touch the image. Slides and video images are less tactile, private and treasurable and therefore less precious.

Visual Dialogues about and between Public and Private Spaces

What is so fascinating about family albums produced during the 'golden era' of the nuclear family is the way in which families themselves colluded in the invention of this public image, by visually performing familyness. It shows how powerful the ideology of the family was, and yet still is, because those albums still mean so much to the same families today, as this research project revealed. Within public preoccupations with national and imperialist needs to make links and connections in terms of lineage, genealogy and belonging, family albums have been implicated as powerful devices in rescuing a vision of the family as intrinsically white, extended and patriarchal. By creating photographic images of events, people and places, the visually selective nature of domestic photography traditionally serves the purpose of constructing the family as myth, by capturing a preferred version of family life. These structures set the parameters within which agents create their visual family 'life stories'. The family photograph album becomes a visual narrative that structures and organises feelings by fixing meanings of 'family'. In fact, the conventions of family photography are so strong that they can be deployed to cement and give cultural legitimacy to relationships that have been banished from the traditional 'family'. Lesbian and gay identities are often legitimised by being framed in familial meanings through the use of family photography, as Simon Watney (1991) discusses in an autobiographical exploration of the role of family photography in his parents' and personal life.

Among the white Anglo-Celtic families of 1950s Western Sydney, photographs were taken by both men and women, but men typically took possession of more sophisticated cameras, and albums were mainly compiled by women. Albums came to represent a feminine motivation to reunite generations and geographies of isolated and dislocated familial units. Women's involvement in the construction of the white family photograph album produced a visual dialogue between the domestic values that shaped their private lives and the public world that invented these values. The early family album signified the feminine desire to re-historicise the marginalised and 'private' world of the family, to reconnect it to public history and public space as revealed by the use of *carte* portraits and postcards. Ideological segregations of the public and private could later be symbolically reconnected through photographs for family albums by using the camera to act as a witness of the family's outings and presence in public spaces and at public events and monuments. The family photograph album became a fundamental visual marker of each individual white family's fulfilment of middle-class aspirations, where mobility, in the form of movement to the suburbs, was a sign of achievement, through conformity to public definitions of 'family'. In this way, the album contributed to the family's articulation of its settlement of space as domestic and suburban space, of familial leisure space beyond the home, and of an imagined community of relatives.

This private yet very popular cultural form, as it existed in western anglophone nations up to the 1950s, may not have subverted dominant structures of power but it has some transformative potential in the way albums are used to highlight celebration of spaces occupied by the family, domestic space, as *feminine* space: parenthood, children, friendships as relationships of community and belonging. While women have been marginal to public narratives, they pose the possibility of symbolic struggles over representation in their role as compilers of their families' albums. The white family photograph album of the 1950s traditionally surveyed and displayed heterosexual, mono-racial familial identities. Its messages are therefore as much about absences, fragmentation and exclusion as about presences, unity and belonging. Yet family photography is such a powerful signifier of familyness that it can now be used to bind together relationships that were once excluded from its domain. Simon Watney's (1991) essay exemplifies the problems and issues involved in the use of family photography as a powerful and yet ambivalent tool for representing gay relationships as both familial yet distinctive from familyness. Chapter 5 looks at this theme further by investigating the use of family photography as a cultural device of inclusion in its ability to represent friends as 'family'.

Patricia Holland (1991: 11) refers to the work of Stuart Hall (1991) and Andrew Dewdney (1991), both in *Family Snaps: The Meanings of Domestic Photography*, in her discussion of analyses of the role of family albums in relation to fractures caused by (all) family identities structured by histories of colonialism and racism. She states that 'we find a series of judgements about who does and does not "belong" to the group. In families where a lighter skin is valued, members with a darker skin may be pushed to the margins.' She points out that contemporary workings of race and ethnicity in family photographs are manifested through foreign travel. The colonial gaze is re-enacted through a white tourist gaze in which locations such as the Caribbean and South East Asian nations are exoticised and their residents commodified into images of 'authenticity' for the benefit of the white western eye.

CONCLUSION

As we shall see in Chapter 6, family photography's extraordinarily powerful combination of qualities of uniqueness, privacy and yet standardisation and conformity actually makes it flexible enough to allow the medium to be extended beyond the rigid definition of the modern nuclear 'family' to embrace intimate relationships and contexts that were once excluded from the orthodox vision. Family photography is a popular visual medium so deeply saturated with and implicated in the celebration of family that it works to fix and de-historicise essentially fluid, dynamic and ever-changing meanings, practices and performances of 'family'. The family album is a powerful editing tool that can confer codes of normality (Slater, 1991;

Spence, 1991) on transgressive as well as conventional interpersonal relationships. Today, family albums contain narratives of sameness and difference: of ideal nuclear familism, on the one hand, and of negotiations with and resistances to that ideal, on the other. The aspiring white nuclear family was essentially middle class: aspiring to middle-class values that could be expressed through consumer possessions, the perfect family became 'embourgeoisified'. The middle-class basis of the nuclear family could be signified through education and consumption. It could invent itself through consumption, purchasing material success and cultural capital within a public celebration of competitive individualism. The hybridisation of anglodominant values and meanings by the influences of diaspora communities settled in English-speaking nations, and the political and cultural tensions that this produced, exposed the exclusion of non-white families.

Through selective examples, this chapter has identified and drawn together some of the major strands of social change that brought about the rise of the ideal nuclear family in the post-war period. It has shown how the emergence of the 'dysfunctional family' and the ideology of motherhood became central discursive devices for regulating family life around the ideal of the companionate marriage, by mobilising the notion of the family as a natural but precious unit that was somehow under siege and in need of protection against, for example, wayward mothers. Yet, at the same time, the artifice of family life was alluded to in the sitcoms of the 1950s, in which the family was perceived as something that could only be conceived through ritual and performance. The home was transformed into a stage and the family members were both players and audience. This sense of performance and artifice was taken up in family photography and albums wherein families themselves came to invent family cohesion, stability and normality, but *not* dysfunctionality, through powerful visual symbols of familyness. So the early to mid-twentieth century was, indeed, a golden era in which the white modern family was formed as an ideal. But it worked centrally at the level of ideology, as representation and meaning, and was predicated on exclusion and condemnation of individuals and groups who did not perform the ideal. And this was worked through by drawing on dysfunctionality, through popular cultural forms such as sitcom engaged in the performance of familyness, in order to police the boundaries and reinforce the meaning of the ideal, which was so cleverly reproduced and performed within the context of family photography.

NOTES

1. Special Royal Mail centre-page section, *Radio Times*, 29 July 2000.
2. For example, the ethnographic work on audiences undertaken by authors such as Marie Gillespie (1995), Dorothy Hobson (1982) and David Morley (1986).

3. 'The Family Photograph Album' research project was conducted with Carol Liston at the Women's Research Centre, University of Western Sydney, Nepean, and assisted by Summer Research Scholar Louise Denoon and Research Assistant Robyn Arrowsmith. The project was funded by a seed grant from the University of Western Sydney, Nepean, 1992. Taped discussions were held with ten women album owners, aged 60 and over, who were in their early twenties during the 1950s. The names of the women quoted from have been changed. I have avoided publishing photographs of the album owners interviewed in the interests of confidentiality. This section on family albums was first formed as an essay for a collection edited by James Ryan and Joan Schwartz (2001).

4. I wish to thank Joan Schwartz for providing me with the information about these *cartes de visite* and for identifying their significance.

CHAPTER 4

DYSFUNCTIONAL FAMILIES

Since the golden era of the modern family of the 1950s, during which the nuclear version became an icon of morality, the family has been represented as both stable and deeply vulnerable. It continues to be conveyed as biologically and psychically natural and, at the same time, as crisis-ridden and under siege (Barrett and Macintosh, 1982; Gittins, 1993; Harwood, 1997). Ideas about the family being under threat of extinction allow it to be used as an ideological platform. The 'sexual revolution' of the 1960s was an important cultural watershed when the rigid bonds between love and marriage, sexual pleasure and procreation were seriously questioned and, to some extent, uncoupled from one another. Sexual choices and lifestyles were being made and celebrated by the youth of western nations, who, for the first time, had gained some economic independence from their families of origin. The role and status of marriage and the hierarchical relations of gender and generation structured by marriage were being seriously challenged. At the same time, the dismantling of Parsonian functionalist theories and the effective critiques of modernisation theory by Marxist and feminist interventions in the 1960s and early 1970s led to a serious re-evaluation of familial ideology. For example, Betty Friedan, an important contributor to debates about the subordination of women and the patriarchal structure of the family, provided a scathing attack on the functionalist approach in her book *The Feminine Mystique* (1963).

However, looking back, the 'sexual revolution' was a short-lived interruption. By the early 1980s, its liberationist ideology was derailed by revelations of sexual exploitation and violence against vulnerable members of society, by the intensified commodification of sex, and by the flurry of moral panics surrounding sexually transmitted diseases and AIDS. Traditional values of 'commitment', 'intimacy' and the early twentieth-century rituals of courtship and romance rapidly regained credibility over the experimental sexual ethics of the previous decade. Yet the continuing rise in divorce, sexual infidelity, the 'post-divorce family', lone parenthood and absent fatherhood were all evidence of a lack of permanence in family life that contributed to a public sense of malaise. Nobody seemed to be able to live up to the ideal. Feelings of ambivalence and despair about family life were expressed in a number of different ways through media representations of the family.

This chapter looks at the way in which modern family values are either cherished or challenged through popular media representations by focusing first on ways in which the ideal white nuclear family continues to be reproduced and then moving on to talk about contemporary representations of a particular trend: the emergence of the dysfunctional father. Representations of a crisis in the performance of fatherhood and changing family practices are represented in the popular media as 'dysfunctional'. I wish to argue, however, that white fatherhood is being retrieved and reasserted and that this reassertion is *dependent* on the problematising of motherhood. In Chapter 6 I discuss ways in which non-nuclear versions of motherhood, such as lone mothers, are condemned in the news media. Representations of familial crisis are stretching beyond the pathologisation of non-white races and the problematising of a transgressive kind of motherhood. Today, these kinds of representations are also centrally about the authority of white masculinity and the crisis surrounding white fatherhood, which is being recuperated as a new nurturing paternal identity.

POPULAR MEDIA REPRESENTATIONS OF THE WHITE NUCLEAR IDEAL

Notwithstanding the fact that popular media representations constitute a rapidly shifting terrain, contemporary images and narratives appear to be crystallising around distinctive clusters of meaning. Three key constellations of familial meanings can be identified in popular media and public discourses that have important implications for factors of race, ethnicity and cultural identity. Race is being used to convey either good or evil yet always neutralised as 'normal', but it is an arbitrary and shifting cultural determinant. Intriguingly, an *ideal* nuclear model tends to be promoted in one set of popular and public cultural forms and in official discourses. In a second category, a defective and unstable family is being scrutinised and judged as *dysfunctional* through morality tales about the violent, perverse or sexually scandalous behaviour of its individual members. A trans-nuclear *hybridised* family is represented in a third category, which I explore in the following chapter.

Within the first, 'ideal' family category, a range of advertisements, home magazines and official discourses mythologise the white nuclear family as normal and universal: as a natural heterosexual biological entity, as a household type, a kinship arrangement and a leisure pursuit. Here, the whiteness of white families stands for positive aspirational qualities. As we have seen, the foundations of this set of discourses were laid in the mid-twentieth century. Within the second grouping of dysfunctional popular cultural images, horror and crime films and television dramas and the tabloid press are problematising or demonising the acts of individuals within defective familial relations or revelling in exposing the steamy, explosive and scandalous problems of family morality and sexual betrayal. Whiteness is often presented as fragmented, individualistic, selfish, aspirational. The central focus of this chapter is an exploration of the way this category is represented through images of crisis surrounding white fatherhood. The third hybrid category, which is the topic of the following chapter, is transgressive but still ideologically familialist in the sense that it is committed to the transformation of social relationships into familial ones by embracing alternatives to the ideal and thereby celebrating 'the family' in all its complex contemporary versions – gay and lesbian, working relations, black, single mother, unmarried, illegitimate, and so on – within a recognition of the myth of nuclear familism.

Popular media projections of the white, nuclear family as the functional norm through which to market consumer goods interlock seamlessly with the official discourses communicated within public policy. Within these cultural representations, whiteness stands for positive aspirational qualities. As Robyn Wiegman (1991: 312) points out, 'the popular media continue to reveal, for the most part, a disturbing reliance on narrative structures that foreground the white, bourgeois ideal as a symbol of racial egalitarianism'. A predominance of media images lock on to a narrow anglocentric, aspirational nuclear family discourse and celebrate it. Advertisements aimed at both men and women for a whole range of products – for pensions and life insurance, supermarkets, prepared 'family' foods, 'family' cars and 'family' holidays – come under this umbrella. They often use humour by first mocking the family's infuriating characteristics then, by way of resolution, saluting its captivating charm and 'naturally' good qualities of intimacy, affection, caring, efficiency, even its aesthetic qualities contributing to a 'style of living'. Children, as well as houses, interior design, cars and gardens, are powerfully signified as fashion accessories that give *personal* pleasure. There is a strong commercial impetus to use the white anglophone nuclear family as a trope for the communication of material aspirations: the potential of success, individual satisfaction and long-term fulfilment through the act of consumption.

In Figure 4.1 we have the contemporary version of the 1950s 'Kellogg's cornflakes' family. The family is always closely associated with food, so in a risk society (Beck, 1992) the white family is often depicted as somehow under siege and therefore in need of constant protection, in this case from germs and harmful foods. In this image, the father clasps his daughter and appears to be protecting the mother and son she is holding in what becomes a conventional pose of protection and ownership. Yet this kind of image is so familiar – the white but tanned ensemble – that it has become an icon of

So here to help you discover what is good for you and others in your family, and to steer clear of foods that are not – is this important book from Reader's Digest. FOODS THAT HARM, FOODS THAT HEAL is probably *the* most helpful, revealing and interesting book about the intricate links between diet and health that has ever been published.

FIGURE 4.1   Image of a nuclear family from the leaflet promoting *Foods That Harm, Foods That Heal: An A–Z Guide to Safe and Healthy Eating*, Reader's Digest. (By permission of The Reader's Digest Association Limited.)

the family that we hardly notice cropping up across hundreds of holiday and tourist brochures, consumer catalogues and magazine advertisements. For example, in Figure 4.2 the family are firmly locked into the luxury space of the stylishly crafted kitchen unit, which acts as the theatrical stage for the performance of happy familyness. The father is holding the child, showing the active role of fatherhood, while the mother looks on. In Figure 4.3, we see the family members interacting over breakfast in another sophisticated kitchen environment – a stage set with an obvious absence of untidy clutter. These images evoke aspirational stylish family living, signified as a white middle-class experience for white married couples and their children and friends. Fathers are prominently figured as authors of the family. These kinds of images rarely figure black or Asian families and, not surprisingly, never figure lesbian or gay 'new families', despite the recognised strength of the 'Pink Pound'. But these typical representations are derived from only one sphere of the popular media. We find that within sitcoms and soaps, identities beyond the narrow confines of the nuclear model *are* being portrayed, as the next chapter shows.

FIGURE 4.2 MFI advertisement for 'Marlow' design, Schreiber kitchens, from MFI Homeworks brochure *Your Kitchen*, 1999/2000. (By permission of MFI.)

Figure 4.3 MFI advertisement for 'Newark' design, Schreiber kitchens, from MFI Homeworks brochure *Your Kitchen*, 1999/2000. (By permission of MFI.)

FIGURE 4.4 The Princess of Wales lifting her son, Prince William,
at Kensington Palace, London PA News Photo. (By permission
of PA Photo Agency.)

Whiteness is often conveyed not simply as middle-class aspiration but as innocence and moral purity. Sentimental and romantic narratives celebrate and fix qualities of stability and continuity exemplified by mother and child

97

iconography not only in advertisements, such as that for Calvin Klein's 'Eternity' perfume, but also in powerful photographic images in newspapers and magazines of celebrities and royalty, such as Diana, Princess of Wales, and her son, Prince William (Figure 4.4). This is an example of the plethora of photographs of Diana that were shown in magazines and newspapers all over the world after her tragic death in September 1997. This kind of image is an icon of the moral purity of motherhood, evoking the joy of a mother's love for her child – the most pure love of all: permanent, stable, lasting. The photograph now conveys something rather different from its originally intended meaning. It first signified a national celebration of the birth of a son and heir to the throne by a young, modern Princess who was not afraid to transcend the conventional and staid 'Madonna and child' style of pose in which the baby is usually laid in the mother's arms with father standing behind to demonstrate patriarchal hierarchy and claim over mother and child (although, of course, there were several photographs taken of the royal couple and baby prince that way). In this photograph, the Princess of Wales lifts her baby son in the air, in a very dynamic movement. Yet the image signifies purity through the whiteness of the baby's clothing, and mother's sleeves and ribbon dangling down to her waist. This whiteness is echoed in the luxurious pale marbled fireplace of Kensington Palace in the background. Today, after public memories of Princess Diana's divorce and then fatal car accident, the image seems to evoke a more personal yet collective memory: the confirmation of a pure passion anchored within maternal affection, not romantic love. In stark contrast to the symbolism of Britain's Queen Mother, the image of Diana and her child seems to be transformed into an icon of the joys and sufferings of a new kind of motherhood in the era of postmodern familialism. It symbolises the authenticity of maternal fulfilment in the wake of marital breakdown, during a period when the Royal Family has transformed from one that stands for *all* families as moral guardian, into one that is dogged by the dysfunctionality of infidelity, divorce and media attention. And this dysfunctionality is now centred firmly not only on single mothers and teenage mothers, but also on the white male father in the form of Prince Charles, Bill Clinton and regular middle-class white men.

NEWS AND POPULAR MEDIA MORALITY TALES OF 'FAMILY MAN'

While the image of the perfect white middle-class nuclear family pervades consumer brochures, catalogues and magazine advertisements, the 'dysfunctional' family is portrayed as a menacing threat in other public contexts. Within Hollywood cinema, television drama and the tabloid press there is a persistent and often lurid fascination with the idea of the 'state of crisis' of the white anglo-nuclear family. Parenthood has become a crucial site of contention within public debates about morality and family values. A 'dysfunctional' family is being represented within horror and science fiction films, psychological thrillers, police dramas and through tabloid press exposures of sexual scandals. The term 'dysfunctional' is calculatedly pathologising. Adopted by pop psychology discourse such as co-dependency counselling, it perpetuates the myth of a 'functional', ideal family and therefore focuses the blame for the breakdown in family relations internally on families themselves rather than locating it within the context of wider structural problems of society.

Contemporary representations of the family are shaped by a perceived crisis in masculinity that is located in yet recuperated by a new emphasis on fatherhood, albeit in the context of post-divorce parenting. This preoccupation with a reassertion of white fatherhood is a theme reflected strongly in public rhetoric and informs public policy on the family. Motherhood, on the other hand, continues to act as a powerful icon. While it is celebrated as biologically natural, it is aggressively contained and stripped of power. Mothers are condemned either as a passive background presence or as a dark threat to patriarchy, that is, to 'the family', through their multiple roles and demands as worker, parent-carer, and seeker of leisure and pleasure as individual(istic) consumer and citizen. The absence of fatherhood in anthropological and historical studies of parenting, and the lack of its visual presence in popular representations during the 'golden era' of nuclear familialism in the mid-twentieth century, exemplifies a social taboo surrounding men's engagement in parental nurturing. The work of Bowlby (1953), Chodorow (1978) and other expert discourses consistently ignored fatherhood both as an experience and as an activity. Radhika Chopra (1999) asks 'How is father care constituted and inscribed', given the purity and fixity of biological nurturing as mother care? It seems that the link between men and nurturing, and the treatment of fatherhood as a form of care-giving is a profoundly difficult one for western anglophone societies to forge. It is not surprising that a crisis of representation of fatherhood is emerging at a time when there is a growing recognition, within the popular consciousness, of a crisis of masculine identity brought about by a series of structural changes, including the rise in post-divorce families and the increase in women's employment coupled with rising male unemployment resulting from the collapse of heavy industry male occupations such as the steel industry, coal mining and ship building.

As rising divorce rates expose the problems, anxieties and desires surrounding fatherhood, fathers' roles become highly visible. The growing public preoccupation with fatherhood is being expressed in official as well as popular media discourses, around two contradictory trends: that of divorced men being denied access to their children and being 'ripped off' for child maintenance by ex-wives, and of men shirking their paternal responsibility as 'head' of families.

We find that the 'fatherly' side of the male is now on display in a wide variety of popular narratives, generated by preoccupations about how to perform as a father in post-divorce families. Growing debates about fathers since the last two decades of the twentieth century have been centred around questions about the role of the father after divorce. Men are often conceived as a failure in fatherhood because they do not appear to adjust smoothly to the new role. Coinciding with fears about harmful effects of divorce on children much of the original academic research on which these concerns were based was North American and then taken up in the UK, contributing to a growing alarm over the perceived increase in under-achieving and delinquent children (Smart, 1999: 100). There has been a significant shift in political rhetoric, policy and media discussion from debates involving the harm caused to children by the poverty that divorced mothers with children endure, to debates about the lack of a 'proper' father. This is a shift from a socio-economic to a psychological argument in understanding the harms of divorce for children.[1]

Against this backdrop, I consider popular media representations of anxieties surrounding parenthood and the family by exploring representations of white fatherhood in Hollywood and Hollywood-style films that are highly successful in other western anglophone nations such as Britain and Australia, and central to familial discourses circulating in popular culture. Popular cultural forms such as Hollywood constitute a powerful platform on which debates about the family and gendered power relations are staged. The role of white men in relation to the family is a central theme being played out within an emerging 'heterosexual problematic' (Collier, 1999) as a consequence of the rise in post-divorce families, teenage pregnancies and single mothers.

Significantly, popular media representations of white paternity from the late 1990s onwards have been coinciding with political discourses within dominant struggles to reassert a new fatherhood at the centre of familialism. This is taking place at the same time that motherhood is being reinforced as *the* problem of our age, as the root cause of the proverbial 'crisis in family values' (see Chapter 6). There have been important historical shifts in representations of masculinity in which paternity has been used, often strategically, to reproduce and naturalise the authority of white males. This has been happening during a critical period when gender roles and characteristics are being *de-essentialised* and reassigned within struggles to assert post-patriarchal, post-feminist family values, as Jude Davies and Carol Smith (1997: 23) argue in their incisive analysis of identity politics in contemporary American film. 'Father films' constitute a distinctive genre that involves the recuperation of fathers who were once absent. By contrast, 'identity politics' films such as *Falling Down* (1993) explore and expose the white male as a figure who is no longer neutral. Davies and Smith (1997: 23) state that 'the "bourgeois ideal", seen as a dominant model of inclusiveness, has lost prestige, such that in many films it is represented as dysfunctional'.

The 'perverse' sexual activities of men in public office, members of the Royal Family of both sexes, and the husband of the American First Family during Bill Clinton's office confirm the moral parameters of the ideal. The blame for familial ruptures is extended from feminism, working and single mothers, the gay and lesbian community or migrants, to white fathers and husbands in the form of middle-class male sexual perversions and working-class unemployed failed breadwinners. On the surface, this category of popular representations seems to problematise the family in its ideal form. The dysfunctional family is a category that does not, however, appear to be actually challenging the ideal. Anticipating the lived reality of a more complex hybrid familial form, the news media seem to defend the myth by their very condemnation of exposed moral breaches. Yet masculinity is not ultimately condemned. It is precisely recovered and reasserted by sanctifying the paternal desire to bond emotionally with children in the absence of the mother.

Car advertisements exemplify anxieties, usually articulated as masculine ones, caused by the tension between the search for individualism and adventure and the search for family security. A typical example is a magazine advertisement for a Mitsubishi car called 'Colt Space Star' that reveals the tensions surrounding masculine familial identities.[2] It portrays the vehicle in a state of flight – with an angled snapshot image of the car flashing by, so that the image is no more than a blurred blue streak. But among the streaky, flighty imagery, the captions make interesting reading. In large bold red letters above the image of the car the caption reads: 'MARRIED WITH KIDS AND STILL EXPECT THE EARTH TO MOVE?' A smaller caption below commands: 'Identify Yourself'. The small print on a side panel of the advert, white on black says:

> The words 'family car' have become a bit of a turn off. Too often, they leave you wanting more. But before you nod off, consider the Mitsubishi Colt Space Star. It combines size, stamina and technique in one compact and agile body.

The ad is designed to interpolate men, not women. Significantly, women have not yet won the right to dream of an individuated freedom, to transgress. Advertisers are continually attempting to grapple with the dilemma of selling the idea of a 'family car' to men who really want to be turned on by the 'size, stamina and technique' of a sports car's body. The concept of the 'family car' needs to be projected to demonstrate its practical efficiency and yet marketing research shows that men are subliminally attracted to speed and power. The manufacturers resolve the dilemma of familyness as a turn-off for men in search of freedom and individuality by playing, knowingly, on the fact that the 'family' car is unsexy.

Even the name of the vehicle, 'Colt Space Star', exposes a tension by combining the word 'colt' – signifying young horse – with the somewhat clumsy space age metaphors of 'space' and 'star', thereby drawing together the high tech/space age-ness with the cowboy/animal organic-ness in the idea of the wanderer as driver/horse rider/pilot of rocket. So while family values campaigners insist that 'The way a male becomes a man is by supporting his children...', as Dan Quayle declared,[3] advertisements for consumer goods, like cars, continue to acknowledge the deep contradictions that lie within representations of masculine familial identities: between individualism and the desire for flight, on one hand, and familism and the desire for a patriarchal stake in procreation and intimacy, on the other. Family man can fantasise about freedom and flight while at the same time being responsible and dependable. In fact, men are expected to combine both and are habitually forgiven for doing so while society's grudge continues to be borne against 'family' women even if they manage to avoid being teenage or lone mothers. In fact, the term 'family woman' sounds positively bizarre compared to 'family man'. Woman *is* family. She is already familialised by being domesticated – by man.

The problematising of men's roles in families is a theme being echoed by the preoccupation with sleaze in the western anglophone news media. A morality narrative is being communicated characterised by the surveillance and exposure of the defective sexual morality of the husband of the American First Family during Bill Clinton's office and individual men in public office, not to mention the Royal Family. This trend in news reporting is not simply a symptom of the trivialisation of news and rise of info-tainment or 'newszak' in a deregulated and highly competitive market (Franklin, 1997). It is now also a regular feature of broadsheet journalism. Press laws in other parts of Europe prevent this form of exposure of 'privacy'. The dominance of so-called 'bonk journalism' is a symptom of the desire to express outrage and indignation, to pass judgement on the moral standards of individuals in power in order to define sharp boundaries between ideal – interpreted precisely as 'normal' – family values and the perversions of individual members of 'dysfunctional' families. Scandalous meanings can only be signified by presenting them as threatening to an agreed moral norm. White Anglo-Saxon husbands are being targeted as the problem. Yet 'husbands' as a category are not seen as a threat to familism, only individual men. Furthermore, this pattern of reporting sexual scandals cannot fix the meanings and conclusions drawn by audiences. There is even a transformative potential to the scandalous reporting, so that media saturation inadvertently translates certain social and sexual practices from the perverse to the norm. For example, Prince Charles and Camilla Parker-Bowles can now be photographed together in public and Clinton's popularity ratings challenged the impeachment hearings. Male sexual adventurousness is tolerated and celebrated as a central component of western attitudes to masculinity (Giddens, 1999).

The news media exposure of the sexual infidelities of men in high public office has become so repetitive that these events were not only being referred to as moral witch-hunts but were perceived, in the case of President Clinton and the American nation, to be part of the shift from anti-communism witch-hunts to sexual morality witch-hunts. Continuities were therefore seen to exist between the 'McCarthy and Hoover' era and the 'Kenneth Starr' era.

Drawing on examples such as *Fatal Attraction* (1987) and *Total Recall* (1990), Sarah Harwood (1997) claims that although 1980s Hollywood cinema brought the 'new man' figure to the screen, fathers were contradictory figures. They occupied traditional feminine spaces such as the domestic arena and adopted 'feminine' nurturing, affective qualities. But this transformation was highly paradoxical. The father invested in maintaining the nuclear family and domestic bliss yet it was he who most frequently posed or introduced a threat to it. The paternal role was represented as unstable, jeopardising familial stability. Harwood (1997: 73) states that the father 'failed in his project to fix the family as a sustaining power base from which to maintain his social role'. Fathers simultaneously posed a threat to the family and yet defused the threat in attempts to mythologise a temporary institution into a fixed and permanent system of power and dependence. Texts were rarely narrated from a female viewpoint and the maternal role was frequently absent. The figure of the father, as central to the narrative, was problematised, treated as a paternal failure. According to Harwood (1997), two core tensions were central to this paternal failure: patriarchal succession and individuation.

Back to the Future (1985) and *Total Recall* (1990) are films in which the stability of the family is undermined by issues of succession of the father by the son. The former involves travel through time and the latter involves travel through space. Both deal with paternal anxieties through the eradication of the father by the son. So, the inadequate father is unknowingly undermined by the innocent son, using the trope of travel. In films such as *Rocky IV* (1985) assertion of fatherliness is based on the father's aspirational capacity, which in turn is dependent on the motivating factor of the father's relationship with his son. Using a psychoanalytic approach, Harwood identifies five types of father: the absent father, the failed father, the failed patriarch, the failed male and the betrayer. Curiously, Harwood does not query the racial and ethnic constructions of the key characters and narratives of the films even though they are all dominantly white, anglophone American characters. Yet the continued focus on crisis-ridden WASPs indicates a crisis of white anglophone familialism. In the 1990s, mainstream and Hollywood films have focused on the responsibilities of parenthood as burdensome and a threat to personal independence. These themes have been deployed as high drama but, importantly, from the father's perspective.

REPRESENTATIONS OF WHITE FATHERHOOD IN MAINSTREAM FILMS

The last two decades of twentieth-century mainstream western anglophone cinema witnessed a distinctive shift to the exploration and representation of a more sensitive kind of masculinity. Hollywood films have moved their focus from the responsibilities of paternity as a burden and a threat to personal independence, to a celebration of the liberating or transformational experiences and virtues of fatherhood. This change is indicative of a shift from late 1980s Reaganite/Thatcherite masculine ideology to the early 1990s search for a 'caring, sharing society'. The capitalist myth of the Reagan and Thatcher boom period is one in which hard, autonomous, white male agents are free from social ties to gain success through their careers of financial speculation. Men are represented turning away from parental responsibilities towards the arena of finance and trade. This image is contrasted with the caring, sensitive and responsible white fathers of the 1990s, who emerge, battered and dissatisfied from the public sphere of work after the economic depression that discredited the success stories of the boom of deregulated, laissez-faire capitalism (Davies and Smith, 1997).

These differing representations of fatherhood are being heralded in at least four key ways: 'male transformation' films, 'buddy-buddy fatherly' films, 'white father' films and 'crisis of white masculinity' films. They are categories drawn from analyses of cinematic representations of masculinity within key debates on identity politics (Davies and Smith, 1997; Jeffords, 1993; Lupton and Barclay, 1997; Modleski, 1991). I shall comment on all these categories but, in particular, focus on the last two, which exemplify some key shifts in popular debates about the role of fatherhood in contemporary society. The first, a genre of the late 1980s and early 1990s, which Susan Jeffords (1993) calls 'male transformation movies', is one in which the image of the sensitive man functions to reproduce privilege. These films involve the domestication of the white male action hero through his conversion into a sensitive, caring person. Films of the 1990s project a more introspective form of masculinity, not embarrassed to voice its traumas, burdens and other preoccupations. Jeffords cites films such as *Regarding Henry* (1991) and *Terminator 2: Judgement Day* (1991) as examples. Various strategies are used to give authority to the sensitive and domesticated action hero such as the trope of the avuncular father-figure. In *Terminator 2: Judgement Day*, Arnold Schwarzenegger's muscular body is somehow softened through his role as protector. Similarly, Fred Pfeil (1995) has identified what he calls 'sensitive guy' movies, in which sensitivity is exploited by male characters to defend patriarchal power by using it carefully and compassionately. The hero of *On Deadly Ground* (1994) appeals to eco-consciousness, and the *Die Hard* series (1988–1995) contains romantic scenes and foregrounds the hero's wife as a feature of the genre, as Davies and Smith (1997) point out. In a second category, the classic buddy-buddy action film has been reworked in comedies such as *Twins* (1988), *Kindergarten Cop* (1990) and *Junior* (1994) as Davies and Smith (1997: 25) demonstrate. These films involve the explicit feminisation of the white male action heroes by their sensitivity and the responsibility of caring for children, which, in *Junior*, even extends as far as the Schwarzenegger character, Arnie, going through a pregnancy as the central plot.

A third category can be identified consisting of films about fatherhood and the family, which Tania Modleski (1991) refers to as 'white father' films. She argues that feminine attributes and positions are being appropriated in new and ambiguous representations of masculinity. The 'fatherly' side of the male is now on display in a wider variety of films, such as *Three Men and a Baby* (1987) and its sequel, *Three Men and a Little Lady* (1990), *Look Who's Talking* series (1989–93), the *Father of the Bride* remake and its sequel (1991 and 1995) or *Mighty Aphrodite* (1995). Modleski shows that far from destabilising former dominant identities, this is part of a recuperative strategy to support yet disavow the existence of patriarchal and colonialist power. The rise in representations of 'white father' films from the late 1980s is a new strategy for maintaining the universality and progressiveness of white patriarchal hegemony by appropriating personal qualities traditionally coded as feminine – qualities of sensitivity, sacrifice, nurturing and nostalgia. In all three categories of film, the sensitive white man is the site of privilege.

The repositioning of the father back into the centre of the family is played out as a key theme but always solely from the viewpoint of the father. As Elizabeth Traube (1992) argues, female characters are forced to choose between the two spheres of career and parenthood, and the family is always seen to suffer if women choose their career. The mother is systematically demonised for daring to desire both career and motherhood while the father is praised for being able to do both. Male protagonists, on the other hand, are portrayed as succeeding in both career and as devoted and nurturing fathers. So, in *Parenthood* (1989), the 'new father' Gil can juggle both sets of commitments yet the women have to sacrifice one or the other (Davies and Smith, 1997). While men can enter a feminine domain, women are denied access to cross-gendered roles and status. Although the rigid gender specificity of the separate spheres is broken down in such films, only men are allowed to occupy both spaces successfully. Curiously, the application of Gil's skills in the domestic sphere is never shown in *Parenthood*, since only women are seen situated in the kitchen and doing the cleaning, as Traube points out. Such is the depth of stereotyped gender roles.

The American comedy *Nine Months* (1995) is an example of a 'white father' film that signifies the deep ambivalence surrounding the responsibilities of fatherhood for middle-class white men. Samuel, played by Hugh Grant, is a successful child psychologist with affluent lifestyle, sports car and attractive girlfriend, Rebecca, played by Julianne Moore. Rebecca is keen to get married; Samuel is reluctant to. When Rebecca announces her unplanned pregnancy, Samuel is horrified and we witness him grappling with his terror of commitment in a series of events that seem to indicate that fatherhood will destroy his freedom. Samuel's fears are expressed in hallucinatory nightmares in which Rebecca turns into a praying mantis, lying in bed next to him about to eat him up after making love. Woman as potent mother is conceived as excessive and monstrous.[4]

Samuel has a sudden change of feeling about impending fatherhood and starts to see it in a positive light when his bachelor friend, Sean, confesses that he was unhappy at the prospect of 'facing a life alone without a family' and would give anything to get his ex-wife back, and even reveals his desire to be a father. Arriving so late for an appointment to accompany Rebecca to the doctor's that she has been and gone, Samuel's feeling of joy is reinforced at a critical moment when the sex of the baby is revealed by the doctor to be a boy. Its maleness is a crucial factor underlining the bonding between father and future son. In his Hugh Grant-ish bumbling and excited manner, Samuel asks the obstetrician if the baby's penis is the right size. The black, female obstetrician hands him a video of the ultrasound image of his son in the womb and warns Samuel that the mother needs his full support. After his having missed the appointment, the last straw in a long line of events that have revealed his ambivalent feeling about her and the baby, Rebecca decides to leave Samuel. Afterwards, he watches the video of the ultrasound image, which becomes a significant point, with the sound of the heartbeat as a spiritual and profound moment for the prospective father. Samuel's eyes fill with tears of joy.

We witness Samuel and Rebecca, in their separate beds, leafing through birth and child care manuals, indicating that Samuel is now transformed into an enthusiastically responsible father. He even replaces the sports car with a family car. Samuel apologises for having been so selfish and admits he was scared, had been a coward and thought he was going to lose his youth through impending fatherhood. He asks her to marry him and hands her a diamond ring to the background sound of the 1960s song 'Baby I Love You'. The last shot of the film is of the baby crying in its bedroom nursery, and Samuel gets up to attend to him. He puts soft music on the hi-fi, a romantic ballad we heard at the start of the film. Rebecca also gets out of bed and stands in the doorway watching father soothing and cradling his son in his arms. Through her satisfied gaze, the image of father holding son, like a Madonna and child, becomes an icon that echoes the mother/child one. Father care is discovered in the making. The familial theme is emphasised in the credits with family photographs of babies as a backdrop to the names. The images of the two black women in the film contain ambiguous meanings. They are backdrops, no longer as servants but as nurses and even doctors but whose individual biographies are rendered irrelevant. They are treated as messengers, advisers or servants of the white family. They can be seen to act as a counterfoil to the whiteness of the couple yet also reinforce the primordial earth mother meaning of black women and, as such, they legitimise the couple's transition to parenthood, echoing the role of Sybil, the black maid in the 1940s maternal melodrama *The Reckless Moment*.

Mrs Doubtfire (1993) is an example of a comedy in which the father is given the opportunity to develop a strong affection for his children after he and his wife divorce. The mother needs a nanny to protect her successful career from the intrusion of the children. The father dresses in drag and takes on the role of the nanny so as to bond with his children. In the British film *Jack and Sarah* (1995) the mother dies in childbirth, which allows an exploration of ways for the father, Jack, to bond with his baby daughter. He has a high-powered career as a lawyer in London and employs a nanny to help him care for his daughter, Sarah. He is able to devote himself to his important job, develops a romantic relationship with the nanny and bonds with his baby daughter. These kinds of films rely on the marginalising or absenting of the mother through divorce or death, and the placement of the burden of child care on the father in order to provide him with the status of hero. Fatherhood is played out as both crisis and fulfilment. The father is empowered – he finds himself – through his discovery of deep affection for his child after the absence of the mother. So men no longer need to be individualistic in their aims and pursuits to prove their heroism as male protagonists as they did in the traditional male adventure films (Lupton and Barclay, 1997).

It seems that white paternity is being used as a device to reproduce and universalise the authority of white males. This is taking place at a crucial moment when the legitimacy of the patriarchal family is being undermined by individualism and ideas about the creation of non-hierarchical, 'pure relationships' within a 'transformation of intimacy' (Giddens, 1992). Hollywood is producing powerful representations of heroic, sensitive white middle-class men as good, nurturing fathers whose authority is reinforced by their successful professional careers. Yet white working-class and black fathers are treated in a very different way: as dysfunctional. The British *The Full Monty* (1997) is an example of the ways in which the decline of heavy industry and the rise of male manual unemployment are associated with fading fatherhood. Gaz's failure as a breadwinner is linked to his failure as a father. His ex-wife is seen as a bourgeois and materialistic working wife. The power relations between father and son are reversed in the sense that Gaz is portrayed as funny, irresponsible, laddish and infantile compared to his more responsible son. He is forced to go ahead with the absurd idea of a male strip show in order to sustain the relationship with his son and gain his son's approval. In the context of queer identity, another theme of paternal anxiety is explored in Australia's 1994 camp film *The Adventures of Priscilla, Queen of the Desert*. The character of Tick 'finds himself' through fatherhood after fearing his son's disapproval of his sexual identity. Queer identity and unemployed working-class status are played out as deep problems facing paternal identities.[5]

In all these contexts mothers are not sympathetically portrayed. The male body has become a space of multiple interrogations and there is a narrative centralising of fathering in performative representations that places paternity within homosocial bonding. Children are being treated as moral barometers of adult behaviour. They are used to convey hope and innocence, thereby revealing a utopian belief in the desirability, even the ideological necessity, of having a happy ending in new family romance. But these are deeply genderised categories because it is sons, not daughters, who act as a moral gauge of fathers' condemned behaviour (Harwood, 1997). The reclamation of paternity can be identified as something crucial not only to sons and fathers but also to the modernisation of masculinity. These themes of paternal crisis are not peculiar to one nation but somehow anglocentrically inclusive, implicitly claimed as transferable across western anglophone nations that struggle to cope with the huge disjunction between the mediated ideal nuclear family and real, complex, hybrid families and relationships.

The fourth category of films about the 'crisis of white masculinity' remains dominant in mainstream films, as demonstrated by the success and popularity of *American Beauty* (1999) which explores, in an ironic and parodic way, the mid life crisis of the white American family man, Lester Burnham played by Kevin Spacey. Lester loses his job as an ad man, is loathed by an aspirational wife and held in contempt by his teenage daughter who is disgusted by the fact that her father lusts after her attractive best friend. The bigotry and shallowness of American suburban life is exposed during Lester's search for some positive changes in his life.

This category of 'crisis of white masculinity' became established from the late 1980s, exemplified by a series of films that Michael Douglas starred in. These films located representations of white masculinity within discourses of political identity, as Davies and Smith (1997) show in their close analysis of this theme.

Michael Douglas has acted in a series of films, which Davies and Smith (1997) have examined in depth, that have located representations of white masculinity within discourses of political identity. In *Fatal Attraction* (1987) and *Basic Instinct* (1992), the authority of the male protagonist is determined by his role as head of family in the former and by his police career in the latter, both of which are threatened by his erotic desire for a sexually active woman. In *Fatal Attraction*, the Douglas character's authority as head of the nuclear family is threatened by his adulterous relationship. Significantly, it is the mistress, played by Glenn Close, who is figured as the threat to Douglas's family, not his own infidelity. The guilt of his adultery and the danger in which he places his own family are disavowed by a misogynistic narrative that demonises the sexually demanding, single, middle-aged career woman. Thus, the white father figure is privileged as patriarch, threatened by the menacing single woman who has been interpreted as a representation of feminism as a danger to the (patriarchal) family (Harwood, 1997). This remains in the third, 'white father' film category. Interestingly, reactions to this film in reviews centred on gender roles and ignored issues concerning race and ethnicity, as Davies and Smith point out.

THE DYSFUNCTIONAL WHITE MALE

Hollywood films have traditionally constructed white male American identities as definitive of universal, white patriarchal power. Film critics are now focusing on the strategies being used to privilege and naturalise dominant categories such as white, 'Anglo', European, patriarchal and heterosexual. Richard Dyer's (1997) study of the representation of whiteness in western visual culture provides important pointers. Classical Hollywood produces whiteness as racially and ethnically 'blank'. Dyer also demonstrates that, for example, white women provide a spectacle of moral suffering for the loss of empire in fictions about the Indian Raj such as the British *The Jewel in the Crown* (Granada Television, 1984), which is echoed in the image of Diana, Princess of Wales, discussed above.

Whiteness has moved from its treatment as a universal and 'blank' category to that of a discrete racial and ethnic category in certain liberal films such as *Grand Canyon* (1991). However, as Henry Giroux (1993) emphasises, the specificity of this whiteness, which recognises the significance of race and ethnic identity in others, is anchored within a privileged status that refuses to relinquish its power. This is being played out within the theme of white fatherhood, which is situated within the codes of nationality, class and sexuality. In a number of genres such as romances, comedies, action films and thrillers, domesticated, feminised and paternal white males have been represented within a revisionist masculinity that transcends past codes of phallic masculinity involving individuated competition, the military, heterosexual masculinity, patriotism and race – exemplified by films such as *Top Gun* (1986) and *Rambo: First Blood Part II* (1985) (Davies and Smith, 1997).

A range of films were produced in the late 1980s and early 1990s which engage with debates about identity politics, around issues of multiculturalism, gender and ethnicity. Films such as *Falling Down* (1993), *Disclosure* (1994) and *Malcolm X* (1992) have been called contemporary 'talkies' because they have been marketed as deliberately controversial. Although a 'coherent and normalised' identity is used in many films, 'recent Hollywood movies also court ambiguous and incomplete audience identifications, so as to appeal to several audiences simultaneously and to engage with individual audience members in multiple ways' (Davies and Smith, 1997: 5). The middle-class, white male is no longer being signified as neutral. White male protagonists are now taking on more marginalised identities, as Michael Douglas exemplifies in *Falling Down* and *Disclosure*. Powerful white males have also been portrayed as crisis-ridden.

A 'crisis of white masculinity' is being claimed from different quarters to signal a questioning of specific gendered and ethnicised characteristics linked to the undermining of the power and privilege of white males in western anglophone nations. This crisis is tied up with the prominence of white father-figures in late 1980s films. It refers to a range of identities such as the disempowered and disaffected Midwestern American 'angry white males'. Conversely it also refers to the idea that white masculinity is no longer viable as a universal set of codes within the unmasking of its white patriarchal and imperialist racial and ethnic representational foundations (Davies and Smith, 1997).

So while there have been crucial shifts in representations of the family in which white paternity has been used as a device to reproduce and universalise the authority of white males, a fourth type of 1980s and 1990s film can be categorised, as film critics such as Wiegman (1991), Davies and Smith (1997) and Dyer (1997) point out. This 'crisis of white masculinity' film is one in which the 'bourgeois ideal', usually understood as a dominant model of inclusiveness, has actually lost prestige to the extent that it is represented as permanently dysfunctional, that is, as incapable of recuperation.

Falling Down (1993) engages centrally in issues concerning race and ethnicity. An unemployed white man snaps into an angry rage and abandons his car in the middle of an urban traffic jam. The Douglas character, referred to by the number plates of his car as D-FENS, gets entangled in a series of confrontations in a desperate attempt to get back 'home' to his ex-wife and daughter. The film addresses discourses of identity by portraying the pro-tagonist as economically and culturally disenfranchised and involved in a desperate search for an identity politics for heterosexual white males (Davies and Smith 1997). Dyer's (1997: 222) convincing analysis of the film shows that the articulation of a white masculinity under threat is an emer-gent discourse of the 1990s.

D-FENS has a number of conflictual encounters with people of various ethnic identities, from a Korean shopkeeper, to members of a Latino gang, a white neo-Nazi owner of an Army Surplus store and a white, retired ama-teur golfer who orders him off his land. He tries to identify with the plight of an African American man picketing outside a bank that appears to have rejected his loan request. On his placard are written the words 'Not Economically Viable'. The black man says 'Don't forget me' to D-FENS as they exchange glances while the former is bundled into a police car. Liam

Kennedy (1996) argues that, through this scene, the historical specificity of African American identity is colonised by the white protagonist and thereby idealised and appropriated by the white imperialist agenda.

In their important analysis of *Falling Down*, Davies and Smith (1997: 33) suggest that D-FENS is actually denied access to a civil right protest position because of his whiteness and that, in fact, he finds that his whiteness lacks a history that he can position himself within precisely because of its universality. Despite being unemployed and divorced from his wife and separated from his child, D-FENS is trapped within a privileged white masculine identity and cannot occupy a space that could offer the authenticity of marginality and victimhood. The film draws on vigilante codes in the genre of Westerns yet also represents America as a deeply divided society in which white patriarchy cannot be guaranteed as a privileged identity. Davies and Smith emphasise that the political issues encoded in the film are unstable and that the crisis of white masculinity theme is open to right-wing readings as well as readable as a statement about identity politics, and as a film about economic power. The role of the family is, however, central to these issues about identity politics.

The dysfunctionality of D-FENS' biography is not only about attempts at staking out a position of victimhood for unemployed white American men. It is a discourse profoundly located within the family as the arena from which the failed man is excluded. The importance of the family to white male identity is confirmed at the crucial moment when the husband of the family loses his job, is disempowered, and can no longer claim his position as 'head of family'. The crisis of identity imposed by banishing the white male from the family is clearly linked to the loss of his role as breadwinner, as in *The Full Monty*. But the wife and child have been fearing for their safety for quite some time during which D-FENS has sought the sanctuary and comfort of his mother's home, which he also abuses. His anger and aggression are inflicted on his family as well as outsiders. The series of conflicts he encounters are all *en route* to his destination to his estranged wife and child on the day of his daughter's birthday. The fear felt by his family is communicated by his ex-wife having secured legal protection against him coming within a certain distance of her and their child. His crisis as a man is deeply located within the threat he poses to his own female family members but it is only through his encounter with other ethnic groups within the public sphere that we are informed that the factor of his masculine whiteness is the dysfunctional element of his identity. Thus, the exclusion of D-FENS from his family has violent consequences.

Davies and Smith (1997: 28) refer to *Wall Street* (1987) as an example of a film in which the patriarchal American family structure, 'purged of female members', is used as the framework for the relationship between three white men. Gordon Gekko, played by Michael Douglas, is a wealthy asset-stripper, Carl Fox (Martin Sheen) is an aircraft mechanic and union leader, and Carl's son, Bud Fox (Charlie Sheen), is a Wall Street broker. Gekko, representing the amoral 'bad father-figure' who engages in predatory financial practices, competes with Fox, the moralistic 'good father-figure', for his son's allegiance. Nurturing familial relations are often used to provide a caring, sensitive front with which to gloss over capitalist exploitation. The all-male family becomes the model for good capitalism and allows the fusion of patriarchy and capitalism as natural structures through the conflict over paternity that humanises 'Reaganomics'. Importantly, father–son relations and the exploration of homosocial bonding act as a cover for homoerotic desires, as Davies and Smith point out (see also Sedgwick, 1985). Gekko is the bad capitalist who seduces and tricks the younger man. Davies and Smith (1997: 31) argue not only that the themes of capitalism, paternity, the family and homosexuality are intrinsically linked but also that a homoerotic subtext is used to underline the badness of Reaganite capitalism and Gekko's version of fatherhood:

> More about gambling than about greed, the real problem with Reagonomics (in *Wall Street* as in *Pretty Woman*) is that it fails to produce things. It does not take much interpretative pressure to detect a master-coding behind this whereby productive and non-productive capitalisms are screened via the dichotomy between a paternal/filial familial relationship on the one hand, and a sublimated erotic relation between men on the other; a dichotomy predicated on the distinction between the all-male family based on reproduction (whose processes remain absent since Bud's mother is dead), and a sexuality assumed to be sterile.

Within this distinctive range of films, the white anglophone nuclear family is under threat from external forces. These external forces are disguised as female independence, sexually aggressive career women, homosexuality, and the lack of a discourse of identity politics for unemployed white males. The underlying problems are about the anxieties surrounding capitalism and economic performance for white men, which threaten their roles as husbands and fathers (Davies and Smith, 1997). In a number of ways, the family is used as a platform on which to stage anxieties about national, gendered, sexual and racialised identity and as a means by which these conflicting identities are resolved by naturalising social hierarchies and capitalism. The family is appropriated to authorise America's white patriarchal structures, past and present, by creating a fusion between paternity and national identity in films such as *The American President* (1995), in which Douglas plays the widowed father character, and in *Forrest Gump* (1994), which narrativises American history through a narrative of romance and marriage, as Davies and Smith argue (1997: 47). Although these master codes can be read against the grain, their significance lies in the persistent demonisation of women in order to exploit them as a threat to nuclear familial fatherhood as white paternity. As Santaolla (1998: 165) points out, films which explore fatherhood turn women into types 'rather than full-bodied counterparts', and serve to alleviate the threat to male heterosexual identity. They reveal that the fathers are intimidated by the idea of dominant female sexuality.[6]

CONCLUSION

The collapse of the old certainties of white male employment and of the sacredness of the kind of family that once functioned to legitimise patriarchy have given rise to major preoccupations with the status of fatherhood that are played out both in political speeches and in Hollywood films. Familialism is being appropriated as a powerful ideological device to re-instate patriarchal values within the recovery of an alarmingly widespread moral fundamentalism. It is being inscribed and reasserted across a range of public discourses, through government policy, political rhetoric and popular media narratives. Despite a significant public tolerance of 'unorthodox', diverse intimate relationships and living arrangements, women continue to be used as scapegoats, and to be pathologised as problem mothers in political rhetoric that is translated into policy by categorising them as 'dysfunctional' familial forms. Meanwhile fathers – whether divorced, adulterous or absent – are being hailed, valorised and recuperated within public and popular discourses so long as they are white, middle-class, heterosexual and aspirational. In Hollywood and other western anglophone films fatherhood is idealised and valorised either in the absence of, or by rendering invisible, a suspect mother. She is either killed off, divorces her husband, or chooses her career over her family in order for the husband to 'find himself' as a sensitive, caring, nurturing father. Men can have both career and family; women are condemned for their cheek in demanding both. This trend signifies deep anxieties surrounding the threat to the traditional family of fading fatherhood in western anglophone nations. The separation of men from the sphere of the familial as a result of rising divorce rates has led to the perceived need for a reassertion of the authority of fatherhood within a traditional nuclear family structure.

The 'crisis of white masculinity' films, such as *Falling Down*, show that such anxieties are now so strong as to be exposed and explored directly as a new, albeit tentative, trend within mainstream Hollywood films. The crisis of fatherhood is a symptom of the combined crises of the welfare state, individualisation and the loss of the legitimacy but not the material domination of patriarchy. The search for a post-patriarchal model of the family, defined by an individualisation and defamilialisation of rights, is a feature of the shift from a welfare state of citizens to a market state of consumers. Significantly, the modern nuclearised version of the family appears to be undermined as the source of male privilege within fixed gender and heterosexual identities at the same moment that the modern state and the modern male appear to be losing sovereignty.

Preoccupations with fatherhood tap into broader cultural anxieties. These are centred on perceptions of women's assertiveness and their disaffection with marriage in the context of the loss of men's monopoly on the role of breadwinner (Lees, 1999). As Santaolla (1998: 165) suggests, it may be a specific cause of the present-day urge to display heterosexual men's infidelity that explains why the news media are obsessed with exposing it – and wives' publicly exposed attempts to cope with it. The motivation for 'white father' films and political rhetoric about moral crusades is linked to a profound fear of the disruptive power on traditional family values of female and deviant sexuality. These discourses of white paternity and dysfunctional motherhood – from its pre-teenage version to the career mother – act as strategic attempts to remove the most threatening elements of shifts in gender relations towards the legitimating of a non-hierarchical 'post-patriarchal' familialism.

NOTES

---

1. See Carol Smart (1999) for an analysis of the growing debate about fatherhood and divorce in relation to the Children Act 1989 in Britain.
2. Shown in the British television magazine *Radio Times,* 2–8 October 1999.
3. The Dan Quayle speech is quoted in Chapter 1.
4. See Barbara Creed's (1993) work on *The Monstrous-Feminine.*
5. See Tincknell and Chambers (1998) for a discussion of representations of fatherhood in *The Full Monty* and *The Adventures of Priscilla, Queen of the Desert.*
6. Michelle Wallace (1992: 127) makes this point, and is quoted by Santaolla.

CHAPTER 5

HYBRID FAMILIES AND CELEBRATIONS OF DIFFERENCE

The white nuclear ideal is increasingly irreconcilable with observable evidence of diversity. Postmodern images of family life are now routinely appearing in the popular media, from soap opera to documentary programmes, depicting, as we have seen, an array of 'dysfunctional families'. In recognition of this growing detectability of family diversity, a shift took place in family theory from the early 1980s that led to a material, representational and moral crisis in public debates about the politics of family life. But, at the same time, it has given rise to a new social pluralism and led to a questioning of orthodox representations of family life. During the 1960s, the questioning of traditional family forms led to a search for alternatives *to* the family, whereas today there is a tendency to speak of 'alternative families' (Weeks et al., 1999: 83).

The 'postmodern family condition' is a term now being widely used but often in an untheorised way (Stacey, 1999). Knowing more about how this postmodern familial 'condition' is being represented in terms of the encoding and circulation of meanings may contribute towards an understanding of the complexities of ideals and values involved in these changes. This chapter asks whether there have indeed been changes in public and popular representations, and if so whether they are indicative of a reassessment and reshaping of familial meanings and values. In the last two decades a new set of discourses seem to have emerged, with an emphasis on changing relationships, friendships, experiences of intimacy, homosexual parenting as well as partnership rights and marriage. In fact, this period is said to be characterised by the development of a 'relationship paradigm' in western anglophone nations.

The postmodern era is characterised by the continuous production of instability, not only in knowledge in the form of science, art and literature but also in lifestyles and family relationships. The modernist assumption of a convergence towards an equilibrium advocated by Talcott Parsons is exposed by postmodernism as a myth. The traditional concept of a family can no longer be applied to the postmodern situation. The new 'postmodern family' is situated outside the modern paradigm of universal reason and progress, and as such is shaped by the experiences of pluralism, disorder and fragmentation within contemporary culture. By the 1980s, academics such as Norman Denzin (1987) were declaring that the modern nuclear family was no longer the norm in America. Within a bleak assessment, Denzin represents the moral panic surrounding the demise of the modern, nuclear family form in his image of the newly emerging, postmodern type of family: '[I]t is a single-parent family, headed by a teenage mother, who may be drawn to drug abuse and alcoholism. She and her children live in a household that is prone to violence' (Denzin, 1987: 33). Typically, the person causing the violence is rendered invisible in this statement. The problematic status and actions of the man are masked. And, clearly, the modern family's demise is interpreted as a fall in moral values rather than in terms of poverty and other forms of social exclusion.

The postmodern family condition is being argued over and negotiated in a very public arena through the popular media. A *spectacularisation* of postmodern family values and practices is taking place and being projected globally. But is there evidence, within popular media and 'expert' discourses, of an authentication of the postmodern family, and the overturning of the modern family-values orthodoxy? While this chapter looks at media responses to and positive celebrations of a new postmodern familism, the following chapter looks at negative responses, including the backlash and moral panic of the New Right that surrounds the demise of the modern nuclear family within public policy and public debate.

I refer to these postmodern popular cultural representations as 'hybridised familialism', thereby highlighting their re-evaluation or transgression of biological connotations of blood ties. However, they do not necessarily undermine modern family-values discourse even though they may be transcending such values. On the contrary, they seem to run parallel to, as well as being in tension with, white nuclear family-values discourse. Within news and fictional genres, a public dialogue is taking place between the modern and the postmodern sides of the debate and it is being staged within the print media, and in television drama, film, radio, books and magazines. I argue that, within this surge of interest in postmodern familialism, these alternatives to the modern white middle-class family are not necessarily leading to an erosion of family values as such. In fact, a recuperation of familial meanings is happening, albeit by way of an authentication of non-biological ties of friendship in societies that have hitherto overemphasised the importance of blood ties over *other* forms of emotional bonding. Fewer than 60 per cent of children in the USA lived with both biological parents in the early 1990s. But almost all children continue to live in households that *call themselves* families (Coltrane, 1998). So these representations do constitute a significant reassessment of the orthodoxies surrounding modernist family values, but they still cling to the ideology of familism to shield and legitimise their difference and 'otherness'. It is in this sense that they are hybridised rather than 'post-nuclear' or 'post-familial' in terms which suggest an overturning and replacement of familism by qualitatively different *ideas*.

PERFORMING FAMILIES OF CHOICE

By the mid-1980s, some social theorists were arguing that the family and family values were in a state of flux, indicative of a societal transition to something that could be characterised as 'postmodernity'. As mentioned in Chapter 1, sociologists such as Beck and Beck-Gernsheim (1995) and Giddens (1992, 1999) claim that the key changes which characterise a breakdown of former ties and traditional narratives in modern societies have led to the collapse of discourses that once authenticated nuclear familial meanings and commitment based on biology. Individuals are now obliged to explore new styles of living within an increasingly complex and rapidly changing world. According to Anthony Giddens (1992, 1999), emotional communication and intimacy are replacing traditional hierarchical ties that structured people's private and personal lives into sexual and gendered relations, parent–child relations and friendships. He argues that sexual and emotional commitment is now being negotiated and forged on a non-hierarchical, 'pure relationship', and is now dependent on 'trust' and 'self-disclosure'. In contrast to the dynamics of traditional social ties, this pure relationship is implicitly democratic and egalitarian. It is a relationship that conforms to the values of democratic politics with mutual respect and the assignment of equality of rights and responsibilities. In this way, Giddens (1999) makes claims for the emergence of a 'democracy of the emotions in everyday life'.

Popular cultural representations of hybridised familialism would seem to support this argument. Weeks et al. (1999) draw on Giddens' ideas with their suggestion that new families of choice are being created by gay and lesbian couples within a narrative of self-invention to produce what they call 'queer construct families'. The idea of a 'chosen' family based on negotiated modes of friendship, commitment and responsibility, rather than biological kin relations, prioritises the assertion of personal values over biological ties and thereby has the potential to undermine claims to racial and ethnic purity. The acknowledgement of a severance of sexuality from reproduction in popular consciousness means that the possibility of shaping and moulding sexuality is culturally legitimised, and increases the social tolerance for gay identities as familial (Giddens, 1999). It acts as a basis for the notion of the pure relationship, in which intimacy is valued as the main bond between couples and between parents and children. Giddens emphasises this pure relationship as an important feature of contemporary values surrounding the family. Active trust and self-disclosure are the basis for a mode of intimacy that is implicitly democratic. For Giddens, then, this democratising of intimate relationships, as a feature of postmodern familism, is a manifestation of the demand for public democracy within the public sphere. The family constitutes the platform for a democracy of emotions in everyday life, creating a basis for mutual obligations. However, the public sphere is the context in which political rhetoric is expressed and policy formulated to place severe constraints on the hybridised, trans-nuclear representations and meanings of familialism, so the notion of public democracy evoked by Giddens must remain an ideal.

Lesbians and gays have, and are creating, sophisticated cohabiting sexual relationships that contain the kinds of characteristics of intimacy and continuity normally associated with the orthodox family. Weeks et al. (1999) describe these relationships as 'families of choice'. Being able to live openly a lesbian or gay relationship has created new spaces for everyday life (Bell and Valentine, 1995; Weeks, 1995) and allowed the shaping of new narratives that affirm the distinctiveness of the homosexual experience (Plummer, 1995). A concept of a distinctive lesbian and gay community has emerged as a crucial social movement and led to a growing assertion of difference as a whole style of life (Weeks, 1996). These debates about transformations in family life contribute to an understanding of some important shifts in attitudes towards familial relations and experiments in the *performance of familialism*.

An interesting example of the way in which these kinds of shifts in familial meanings and values are being played out and represented in the news media is a news story in Britain's tabloid newspaper the *Mail on Sunday*, 5 September 1999, which was reported during the same week as the launch of Blair's 'moral crusade'. It contained a headline that declared: 'DEBTS AND DOUBTS OF GAY MILLIONAIRES WHO ARE EXPECTING SURROGATE TWINS'. The story was about a 'well-groomed' middle-class and independently wealthy gay couple, Barrie Drewitt and Tony Barlow, who paid £200,000 for a surrogate mother to have their twins, 'to make their dreams of fatherhood become a reality'. The parentage of the twins is complex. A boy and girl were conceived using donor eggs from one woman, and sperm from one of the gay partners, and then carried by a second woman. They are the first surrogate babies fathered by a British gay couple.

The image in Figure 5.1. was printed in the *Daily Telegraph* next to the headline: 'BABIES TO HAVE TWO GAY FATHERS BY LAW'. Cultural as opposed to biological claim to the unborn twins is evoked here by the prominent gesture, by Drewitt and Barlow, of the placing of their hands on the stomach of pregnant surrogate mother Rosalind Bellamy. This conforms to the other images shown earlier of family members assembled together (Figure 1.1 of the Blair family; and Figure 4.1 of the Readers' Digest family), where the father places his arm around family members to signify his claim to them. In this

FIGURE 5.1   'Barry Drewitt and Tony Barlow, of Essex, with surrogate mother
Rosalind Bellamy', shown in the *Daily Telegraph*, 28 October 1999.
Woman's Own Rex Features. (By permission of Rex Features.)

case, the claim is even more profoundly necessary because convention
dictates that the mother's biological link to the baby is natural and unquestioned (unless, that is, she is a teenager or lone mother) while the father's
link is cultural and social and has to be worked at. But in this case, the status
of 'mother' must be eclipsed because it is later to be relinquished and denied

in order that the status of two gay fathers can be successfully declared as the only legitimate claims.

The gay couple made an adoption application in Britain in 1995 that was refused by the social services, who apparently had serious misgivings, not about their sexuality but about their private lives, and felt that they would not make good parents. Drewitt and Barlow approached a surrogacy agency in California to gain biological fatherhood, and joined their surnames by deed poll in a double-barrelled name so as to make a legal bid for fatherhood on the babies' birth certificates, even though they know which partner is the biological father. A ground-breaking US Supreme Court ruling allowed the gay couple to be named as the children's parents on the twins' birth certificates. According to the report, the couple stated,

> 'We have received letters of support from local people but have also been warned that when the honeymoon period is over to expect some criticism. ... But, at the end of the day why shouldn't we have children? We have been together for 11 years and are in a secure, loving relationship'.[1]

Not only does science step in to help those who can financially pay to experiment with new familial arrangements so that gay couples can gain access to *biological* parenthood, but also, significantly, an appeal is made to the stable, long-term and loving intimate relationship as evidence of a right to fatherhood. It legitimises, along with social class, the biological claim at a moral level.

The continuous slippage from the political use of the term 'family' to the construction of a normative standard of family living is a prominent feature of political rhetoric on family values. Yet, as Silva and Smart (1999) and Fox Harding (1996) argue, government rhetoric about 'the family' and government policies on the family are often curiously out of step with one another, and, moreover, government policies on families are often deeply contradictory in their effect. Fox Harding points out that, in Britain, the Children Act 1989 prioritises parenthood over marriage while immigration law prioritises legal marriage. Gay and lesbian couples are allowed to become parents through adoption but the British laws that regulate assisted reproduction deny them parenthood. Silva and Smart (1999: 4) argue that the diversity apparently allowed in some quarters at policy level is given far less tolerance at the rhetorical level.

The gay couple who fathered surrogate twins experienced this very problem first-hand. Accompanied by the two gay men and two nannies on a flight to London in December 1999, the Californian-born three-week-old babies were refused official entry into the UK. The twins had American passports that were confiscated after they arrived at London's Heathrow Airport. The British Home Office decided that the babies did not have an automatic right to live with the gay couple in the UK and were only granted a month's temporary stay in Britain while their legal status was being established. Drewitt and Barlow were interviewed by immigration officers, who 'were asking who the parents of the children were, and Tony and I said, "We are". They could not get their heads round that at all.'[2] The two men were advised by an immigration expert that under British law, British citizenship can only be passed through a father if the father is married to the mother. What is ironic in this case is that if one of the men had adopted the twins, they would have been given British citizenship automatically. Mr Drewitt said that it appeared 'to be a clear case of discrimination against the children of gay couples. We'll take this right to the European Court of Human Rights if we have to.'[3] However, later the same month, Drewitt and Barlow were informed by the Home Secretary, Jack Straw, that the children could stay in Britain indefinitely.

Political campaigns are extending beyond equal rights issues and legal protection to include questions about sexual relationships such as legal recognition of same-sex marriages, adoption rights and partnership rights (Sullivan, 1995). The increasing social embeddedness of the lesbian and gay community as a sexual community (Weeks, 1996) is evidence of a growing pluralisation of society. These changes have also been interpreted as part of an opening up of all social identities in western societies, and what Giddens (1992) calls the 'transformation of intimacy'. The post-structural and post-modernist challenges to social theory have stressed the fluid, negotiable, and contingent nature of all social identities, including sexual identities (Weeks, 1995). It is increasingly being recognised that identities are not pre-given. They have to be articulated in more and more complex social and cultural circumstances. Lesbian and gay assertions of identity are only one aspect of a wider construction of identities. As they become more contingent and changeable, so it becomes important to understand how identities emerge, stabilise and are mediated through the popular and news media.

Giddens (1992) suggests that gays and lesbians are in the vanguard of change which has influenced transformations in the nature of marriage to reflect a greater emphasis on the couple relationship as a source of fulfilment rather than social, economic or sexual convenience. He comments that their location in society may resemble more recent developments towards the 'risk society'. According to Beck and Beck-Gernsheim (1995), people are no longer defining themselves centrally by their adoption of traditional male and female role models, and are less likely to follow set biographies or perform normative tasks. These kinds of ideas challenge conventional research on the family by accounting for diversity and change in the normative expectations of everyday living in households.

Another example of the way issues about such changes are represented was on the front page of the *Sunday Express* on 14 February 1999, which carried the headline 'LESBIANS CAN MAKE BETTER PARENTS: Family groups attack Cambridge study'. The article reported that:

The study, which is certain to upset family traditionalists, claims that two gay women will spend more quality time with their children than heterosexual parents would. It adds that heterosexual parents could learn good parenting skills from lesbians. But the research – written by Cambridge University sociology professor Dr Gill Dunne – has angered family groups, who say it undermines the role of men in bringing up children.

The report took a particular angle: the problem of the undermining of fatherhood, as the key emphasis and the fact that government funds worth £150,000 are being spent on the research project. The director of Family and Youth Concern, Valerie Richards, was quoted as saying: 'This is a ridiculous assertion that is yet another blow to family life. It is suggesting that men have no valuable part to play in child care and that is outrageous.' Interestingly no similar charge was made, about the lack of a mothering role, against the two gay men who have decided to father the twins. The article quoted Dunne's remarks about how lesbian partners share housework and child care tasks more equally, and spend more time planning child care time and being with the children (see Dunne, 1999). The majority of the women in the study had children conceived by do-it-yourself artificial insemination using sperm donated by gay friends. This information was juxtaposed with a comment by Conservative Member of Parliament Ann Winterton: 'It is my belief, and other research proves, that children do best with a mother and a father. They do better academically in terms of health and in many other ways.' A spokesman from the pressure group Families Need Fathers, Trevor Berry, claimed that the study ignored research that showed that families need male role models. A further story placed above this report was entitled: 'LESBIANS WHO YEARN FOR A BABY', which stated that actress Sophie Ward and her girlfriend wanted a baby, and that the comedienne Sandi Toksvig brought up her three children with her lesbian lover after having conceived them 'with the help of a close male friend'. Such comments confirm the dominance of the pro-family discourse of the Moral Right, which is discussed in the next chapter.

However, within the opinion section in the centre pages of the same newspaper, a positive comment was made on Dunne's research, pointing out that it is providing a valuable lesson to all parents that

> lesbian parents are more likely to devote equal time to their children than heterosexual couples, finding it easier to distribute domestic and parenting tasks fairly between the partners. The children of lesbians are therefore more likely to enjoy an extended support group to provide them with a variety of positive role models. This is not to deny the need for a father in an ideal upbringing and certainly this newspaper does not support the contention that lesbian parents are any 'better' than traditional families.[4] (*The Sunday Express*, 14 February 1999, p. 34).

These kinds of reports illustrate the changes taking place in public attitudes. On the one hand, there is continuing alarm at the apparent rising redundancy of fatherhood resulting from the rise of the new lesbian family. On the other hand, the example of lesbian parenting is used to press for equality in parenting within *traditional*-style families. The opinion column ends with the comment:

> The government and businesses should work towards freeing employees of either sex to participate more fully in family life, through increased use of part time work, flexible hours and job shares. It would be better for all Britain's children. It might even make parents happier too.

HYBRID FAMILIALISM AND CELEBRATIONS OF DIFFERENCE

Images and narratives of a hybrid family extend the label 'family' to encompass alternative and extended family forms in internationally screened soaps such as *EastEnders*, gay sitcoms such as *Ellen* and sitcoms of black families such as *The Cosby Show*. There are three sets of characteristics that are significant in the media dramatisation of families and that ensure media acceptance of 'difference': the morality tale; family as a tolerant and inclusive community; and (black) family as middle-class, successful and ultimately chic. The Australian soaps *Neighbours* and *Home and Away* depict the lives of dominantly white teenagers in the Australian middle-class suburbs, typically starring actors who are 'model WASPS', thereby confirming the universality of white anglo-ethnic familial relations. Aboriginal characters have been slow to feature in exported Australian soaps, showing that the demands of international marketing coupled with local ethnic struggles prevent the exploration of local issues of identity. Yet the extended family, adopted children and foster children have been an important feature of these soaps. Their 'communalising' quality is crucial for the celebration of a mythical community of families and, indeed, nation of families, denying the other story and other set of experiences: of racism, fragmentation, privatisation and isolation of suburban nuclearised familism today.

Important clues about modes of reception are provided by studies such as Gillespie's (1993, 1995) ethnography of South London Punjabi teenagers' use of *Neighbours*, which details the way such serials are used to negotiate relations between parents and peer cultures. Much of the teenagers' knowledge of white society derives from television. Gillespie shows that for Punjabi youth the Australianness of the programme is not as relevant as the fact that it is about English-speaking whites. The conflicting pressures of kinship duty, family honour and peer group acceptance for teenagers in *Neighbours* mirror the real-life relationships of the Punjabi youth that Gillespie researched and allowed the viewers to compare and explore these themes. Many Indian parents claimed that their own values are being undermined by their children's viewing of 'western' soaps such as *Neighbours*.

The 'family' is not only drawn upon as a textual device to celebrate both diversity and difference but is the quintessential trope for the 'morality tale' themes of soaps, acting as an arbiter of moral standards. The policing of moral values takes place within the domain, language and discourse of familism. In *EastEnders*, Irish, black and Asian, single-parent, extended, and stepfamilies are all carefully woven into the narrative. Nevertheless, the highly conventional 'blood is thicker than water' theme that runs through *EastEnders* remains the fundamental device used to confirm highly traditional family values, even though non-nuclear, hybridised versions of familial relations are sympathetically explored and embraced. Importantly, this diverse community of families, friendships and feuds is necessarily anglocentrically framed by the pivotal role of the dominantly white anglo-ethnic family values of the Mitchells, Butchers, Jacksons and Fowlers.

The case of the American sitcom *Ellen* is linked to the increased public recognition and inclusion of conservative and 'respectable' gay organisations and issues within mainstream politics and media. Such inclusion is, however, conditional upon the mirroring of white heterosexual monogamy and anglodominant middle-class family ties in homosexual relationships. These relationships are expressed and articulated by drawing upon familial ideology employed as a set of strategies in the 'coming out' episodes of *Ellen*. The sexuality and belonging of the character Ellen hinge on a 'family of friends'. *Ellen* can be read as a conflictual response to an American right-wing family-values campaign that reinscribes patriarchal family values and that has been a component of the anglodominant political discourse in the United States. It demonstrates that marginal identities can be sympathetically portrayed within popular cultural texts by drawing upon conventional family values and meanings as a textual device. Rather than labelling lesbianism as a threat to the family, the family is used to support a conservative lesbian-movement position of centring the family. The linking of lesbianism with familial ideology allows the incorporation of alternative versions into the hegemonic model. These kinds of white anglocentric versions of homosexual identity present the family as inclusive and sexually 'tolerant'.[5] However, the sitcom collapsed after the coming out scene as there was little else to say. In the UK on BBC2, a new sitcom has emerged around lesbian identity called *Rhona*, whose starting point, rather than ending, is the character Rhona's lesbian identity. Rhona Cameron is a stand-up comedian who has moved into sitcom. She plays the leading character of a neurotic lesbian but her neurosis is not due to her lesbian sexual identity. The difference between *Rhona* and *Ellen* is that Rhona has no hang-ups about her sexual identity. The plots are, however, centred around romantic relationships within a bold production.

In the United States, the high incidence of fatherless families in the contemporary African American community led to the public expression of anxieties, ranging from sociology to film narratives, about the plight of the black man during the 1980s (see Blount and Cunningham, 1996; Santaolla, 1998). Meanwhile, exposing the threads of representations of separatism and inclusiveness, the internationally screened American situation comedy *The Cosby Show* exemplifies the incorporation of a non-white family sitcom saga into a white American ideal. The African American Cosby family is marked by a class position and by cultural capital that is notably Anglo-American within a hegemonic normalising of middle-class and anglo-nuclear family values. The Cosbys are upper middle class and 'cultured', not simply in the sense of being 'educated' but educated in an anglophone tradition.[6] This family's cultural legitimacy is produced through their embrace of anglo-ethnic culture as an acceptable norm within their lived experiences, values and style of living. They inhabit a nuclear family in which other relatives come and go from time to time but the kind of culture and lifestyle that black American extended families experience is not represented here. It is a family in which patriarchal authority is firmly vested in the secure avuncular figure of Bill Cosby as gynaecologist Cliff Huxtable.

The success of *The Cosby Show* is due in part to the idealisation of a black American family in anglocentric terms to support the myth of the American dream (Lewis, 1991). As affluent blacks, the Huxtables sustain the 'myth of social mobility' among blacks, yet as Justin Lewis (1991: 94) states, the programme offers comfort to a nation which is 'still emerging from a system of apartheid'. America comes across as raceless, classless, thus with dissolving boundaries. Discourses of identity politics are being used in certain popular texts to defuse the conflictual, multiple modes of identity of individuals in everyday life through the use of liberal values of inclusiveness. Liberal mainstream films and television drama up to the 1980s were devoted to a model of integration and harmony that concealed, denied or ignored racial difference and that led to the reassertion of white patriarchal power (Davies and Smith, 1997).

President Bill Clinton deliberately attempted to woo middle-class blacks as part of a strategy to transform African American politics, triggering in the process a backlash among white working-class voters who perceived themselves to be neglected (see Davies and Smith, 1997: 8). The demand to make black faces, yet not black culture, more visible is a woefully inadequate goal. It fails to tackle the politics of racial representations. But the rise of African American filmmakers since the late 1980s has led to some important changes in mainstream films. An interest has been initiated in representing the kinds of shifting and fragmented postmodern identities in Hollywood productions that were previously banished to the sidelines of mainstream representations (Davies and Smith 1997: 9) While films and television dramas of the 1980s tried to harmonise and fuse racial difference, many popular narratives of the 1990s actually explored and exposed conflictual identities, multiple codes of identity, and problematised whiteness, as *Falling Down* etc. show (see Chapter 4, above).

In January 1999 the glossy international photography and design magazine *i-D*, which describes itself as 'a follower of style and fashion from the street to the designer catwalks', launched a photographic exhibition of family photographs called 'Family Future Positive' at Proud gallery in London. The event confirms the contemporary desire to hybridise the family and familialise working relationships and friendships. Famous participants such as Ralph Lauren, Alexander McQueen and Helmut Lang were among the designers, models, photographers, journalists, editors, TV producers, artists, stylists, and pop stars connected to the magazine and invited to contribute their own photographs, projections and drawings within a 'celebration of family life'. The *i-D* editorial team regard themselves as an extended 'family', related not by blood, but by the shared experiences of collaborating in the founding of the magazine. The editor, Avril Mair, states in the Introduction to the special celebratory edition magazine of Family Future Positive:

> When I first arrived here [at *i-D*] some six years ago, it was apparent that I hadn't just acquired a job but had instead been adopted into an extended family that spanned cultures and continents, a talented multigenerational tribe united by a love of life and each other. That *i-D* family is now scattered to the corners of the earth, its global importance defying its humble origins....
> (*i-D*, 1998: 5)

Most of the exhibited photographs are accompanied by short or long written messages that anchor their meanings. In keeping with the conventions of the family photograph genre, these messages are remarkably conventional and sentimental about the love and affection felt for their biological families. Almost half are images of friends and work colleagues, not relatives. Friends and close work-mates are claimed as 'family' through intimacy and shared commitments, goals and experiences. Despite the dominance of images of white familial groups, which establishes the racial norm of the whole range, there is a strong multi-racial feel to the exhibition. The photos that contain multi-racial groupings are clearly friendship- and work-based groups rather than blood relative families. South African filmmaker Bolofo Koto sent in formal posed portrait photographs of members of South African black tribes that were part of an archival collection he found in an antique shop in South Africa. These photos contribute to the idea of celebrating and preserving the cultural rights of indigenous people as a familial issue, although a faint undertone of white civilisation versus black exoticness is detectable. This theme is underlined by photos sent in by the Save the Children charity towards their 1999 campaign 'Save the Children from Violence' to stop the participation of child soldiers in war and to trace children's families and reunite them. Powerful images of children standing in groups in the streets of Belfast, on a tank in Kandahar City, Afghanistan and Honduras convey visually the meaning of the written text, 'Children are the future of our global family'. *i-D* are planning exhibitions on the theme of the family in Paris, Milan and New York as well as London.

This popular cultural form provides a crucial framework for presenting the self as intrinsically familial: *the familial self*. Co-opting family photography as a vehicle for the exploration of new family meanings is crucial. It is a cultural form already inscribed with the codes for communicating powerful meanings about family ties in which memory as nostalgia is embedded and celebrated. As an icon of the ideal family, family photography becomes a powerful signifier of stability, security and permanence, as we have seen in Chapter 3. As a genre, family photography reasserts and confirms the metaphor of bonds of affection and commitment, and frames the meanings of all the various types of relationships, from friends to colleagues, *within* the familial frame.

A hybridised family is publicly recognised as a metaphor for friendship, community and work. In a documentary television programme (*Omnibus*, BBC 1, 4 October 1999) called 'Blondie Beneath the Bleach', about the New York pop band Blondie fronted by singer Deborah Harry in the late 1970s and early 1980s, and who reformed in 1999, the focus was on the relationships between band members. One *member* remarked emphatically, at the end of the documentary: 'We *are* a family, even though it's a dysfunctional family.' Within the ideological constraints that reproduce racial hierarchies, a hybridised family is publicly recognised as a metaphor encompassing friendship, community and work. These kinds of 'unconventional' images and meanings of family are clearly striking a chord with audiences and readers because they bear a stronger relationship to lived experiences of familialism than the mythical nuclear version and its dysfunctional fall-out. In Britain, an ICM poll conducted for the *Observer* newspaper just before the government publication of the Green Paper, Supporting Families, showed that there is significant public tolerance of what are referred to as 'unorthodox', diverse relationships and living arrangements.[7] Eighty per cent of people interviewed disagreed that unmarried couples make worse parents, while 68 per cent felt that single parents were as capable of bringing up their children effectively. The survey concluded that there is general acknowledgement that 'the family' is not in a vulnerable and declining state today but in fact is surviving and flourishing by changing and adapting to take on a variety of different forms. Only 8 per cent of the sample believed that Ministers 'can be trusted to talk a lot of sense on family matters – agony aunts and unmarried priests score more highly'.[8]

Significantly, inside the January/February 1999 issue of the *i-D* magazine is one of those ubiquitous double-page Benetton advertisement photographs, this one of a pretty white child, holding up in both arms a black baby. Both are naked. The text simply says 'WE WANT YOU', and underneath, 'United

Colors of 1999'. This bold image of contrasting naked white and black children's bodies, with the white child cradling a black child in his (?) arms, is clearly intended to be provocative and impertinent through the commercial use of race and children's naked bodies to sell knitwear. This posed image is both innocent and guilty. Being set within the pages of a fashion magazine that celebrates 'the family' indicates the nature of the relationship between familial ideology and global capitalism. The marketing of 'difference' is a feature of global capital. It is not seriously in tension with the image of ideal, white nuclear familialism as it performs the role of the chic, exotic and exceptional. Advertisers have now woken up to the importance of wooing black and Asian consumers, using the term the 'Black Pound' in a similar way to the 'Pink Pound' and the 'Grey Pound', which recognize the buying power of the lesbian and gay community and of senior citizens.

INTIMATE RELATIONSHIPS AND THE CRISIS OF MORAL COMMITMENT

The temporary nature of all relationships is being recognised as a key feature of the postmodern family. Related to the discussion in Chapter 3 about the concept of the 'companionate marriage', social theorists are speculating that the diversification of family forms during the postmodern turn is linked in some kind of causal way to an increasing individualisation of values and meanings in western society. We have, here, a sense of *déjà vu*. The theme of individualisation running through postmodern social theory concerns the issues of autonomy, personhood, choice and identity as key features of the disruption of functionalist familial ideals. But by contrast, the modernist family's unifying theme was the *rationalisation* of social life to fit the economic demands of western industrial societies. It was based on a grand vision of life-course management under conditions of material improvement and institutional bureaucratisation. These assumptions have been severely disrupted in the last two decades. The emphasis within discourses of the postmodern, hybridised family is on human agency rather than duty. Not only has there been a recent recognition of alternative lifestyles, but various 'experts' and analysts are also becoming less blinkered about the fact that perhaps this had been happening all along. Hence, along with the rise of a postmodern approach to the families there has been a re-evaluation of previous familial and life-course narratives in the light of a new celebration of change, of 'alternativeness'. Rather than interpreting these changes simply as hiccups, as short-term interruptions to the secular trend of western modernisation, some social theorists began to view them as a cultural transformation that made classical sociological theories of the social order redundant.

However, within certain versions of the postmodern debates about new, diverse family forms lurk functionalist assumptions and prejudices. The new postmodern family is, in many quarters, being reluctantly tolerated rather than embraced or celebrated. The labels 'post-patriarchal' and 'post-feminist' being attached to new, diverse family forms are part of determined attempts to conceal the hierarchical nature of familial structures of power that still continue to operate in society, and they contain deeply entrenched patriarchal familial values. For example, as we have seen, Cheale (1999) argues that the de-standardisation of the modern family into some sort of 'postmodern' entity, associated with a growing emphasis on individualisation, is about the growth of individual freedoms and the erosion of a sense of duty and tradition that bound individuals together in sex/gender roles in the functional family within the project of 'staying together', bringing up the children, and caring for age-ing parents. He suggests that contemporary family relations take the form of a moral individualism because of the 'increased indeterminacy of cultural codes under conditions of social pluralism' (Cheale, 1999: 66).

Within this shift towards an exploration of a postmodern familial diversity lies a troubling undercurrent of gender bias expressed through the condemnation of women's desire for equality of individualism. The whole notion of 'individualisation' seems to hinge on the specific idea that it is *women* who are being disruptive by demanding some kind of freedom and equality as citizens. Men's rights to freedom, as husbands and fathers, are taken for granted in this kind of argument as part of an essentially patriarchal enlightenment project, but women's search for freedom and individuality is marked and problematised because it is female emancipation that is blamed for the breakdown of modern family values, thus denying the patriarchal nature of those values. In this way, traditional, patriarchal modern family-values discourse remains intact within a grudging acceptance of the existence of a postmodern rupture.

A moral panic has also erupted around the sexual promiscuity of today's urban young women in their search for pleasure, exemplified by headlines such as 'WOMEN BEHAVING DISGRACEFULLY' *The Sunday Times*, October 1999. This particular headline was followed by the statement: 'Women, not men, are driving a collapse in moral values that is undermining the family and ultimately themselves', and was penned by commentator Melanie Phillips.[9] Her comments on masculinity exemplify the populist end of the New Right and Ethical Socialist strands of thinking in public debates about changing family values when she writes that:

> It is a truth universally acknowledged that one of the most significant problems of modern western society is the male of the species. Without a job, without a role, outsmarted and outstripped by women, men are said to be reverting to their natural proclivities for rape and pillage. They truant from schools, abuse alcohol and drugs, commit crime and father children by serial girlfriends. They are innately promiscuous, heartless and unreliable.

A strong unease is detectable within the news media about a breakdown of family values and the erosion of stable marriages through the emergence of a new sexual order characterised by the spread of sexual relationships outside marriage. While the sexual infidelities of men are excusable because they are thought to 'have a powerful sex drive' coupled with a 'strong homing instinct which marriage brings together in harmony', 'female laddishness' is now identified as a new danger, as one of the fundamental causes of a wave of sexual promiscuity that is undermining the familial values of settled love and commitment and driving away the father from the family unit. Phillips (2000) typifies the moral panic in her claims that women are the traditional upholders of family values, and that their laddish behaviour is causing the breakdown of marriage in society. She goes on to say that 'women now openly boast about their involvement in adultery' and that 'the conventions of commitment, fidelity and duty which once restrained the sexual appetites of women have broken down. Women feel licensed to behave with the sexual opportunism that was once considered the particular characteristic of men. The family gamekeeper has turned poacher'. This moral indignation surrounding young women's sexual freedom and pleasure is closely connected to the moral panic about teenage pregnancy, within the public debates about family values, commitment and sexual equality for women.

The Crisis of Moral Commitment

The post-war notion of the companionate marriage, central to the functional family model, has been kept alive but in a revised version within the shift to a postmodern discourse. Indeed, by the 1980s, scholars such as Luhmann (1986) claimed, in a style that echoed the functionalist discourse, that love should be understood as a generalised medium of communication for the 'management of intimate relationships', rather than as a natural feeling. He argued that the code of love relies on the internalisation of another person's view of the world and becomes a crucial mode of interpersonal communication. Interestingly, the diverse postmodern family of today advocated by social theorists such as Giddens (1992) has many parallels with the modern functional family. Companionship, trust, self-disclosure and notions of democracy within relations between equal adults – whether they be heterosexual, gay or lesbian, – are values that can mask the patriarchal, racial, generational structures of power that continue to operate within both material and signifying practices of the family.

Of course, postmodern approaches do part company from modernist perspectives within their emphasis that 'family' has come to signify subjective meanings of intimate connection rather than formal blood or marriage ties.

Hybridised representations of familyness underline and celebrate these postmodern values. Recognising families as relational entities that play a fundamental part in intimate life, postmodern social scholars of the family talk of 'doing family' and distinguish this kind of family, with its central emphasis on performativity, from a bygone type that was shaped by biological discourses (Bernardes, 1987; Finch and Mason, 1993; Morgan 1996). As the fate of cultural representations of romantic love is intrinsically linked with a project of the self, the crisis of moral commitment looms large.

A resurgence of a discourse on the crisis of moral commitment has taken place as a response to the pressures brought about by the urgently contested contradictory trends of individualism versus familialism. The challenge posed by the debate about the postmodern, hybridised family is that it exposes the provisional nature of commitment between all couples. Yet governments are placing their emphasis, with regard to families, on policies founded on the assumption of long-term commitment in parenting. The state, if not mothers themselves, looks to men to back mothers up in parenting. So parenting and commitment have been forced together through welfare policy. Yet, during this era of trans-nuclear postmodern familism, this idea of 'commitment' is still being struggled over in terms of its meanings and how it is to be understood, performed and negotiated. These postmodern familial scenarios express the fear that fatherhood is being marginalised and should become a more central concept to encourage enduring commitment from men in relationships. Arguments about the crisis of commitment seem, then, to be centring on the ways in which men's role in the family has been problematised, as fatherhood is identified as a central cause of a crisis of masculinity. It is linked to the problems of male unemployment and the crisis around representations of men as fathers and husbands in post-divorce families, which are increasingly being exposed in the news media in relation to representations of the infidelity of male politicians. This is picked up in Chapter 6 in relation to the moral panic around lone mothers.

Since marriage is now centrally founded on the precarious notion of love and commitment rather than continuity and heritage, the postmodern crisis of family values is exposing this crisis around commitment within a scenario in which marriage is no longer guaranteed to last or seen as privileged above other kinds of sexual and intimate relationships. Given the contingent nature of confluent love, making a commitment is now riskier than ever. As we have seen, even members of the Royal Family are seemingly defenceless against shattering of the illusion of traditional romance. This is summed up as a national icon of familial dysfunctionality for Britain, in the sad example of the marriage of Prince Charles and Lady Diana ending in divorce. Public images of the wedding, such as the one shown in Figure 5.2, signified a kind of magic in which an old-fashioned fairy-tale romance was recuperated and brought alive again. Later, during the mourning of the death of Diana in 1997, the divorced princess had somehow been transformed into

Figure 5.2   The Royal Wedding, 1981. By Lionel Cherruault.
(By permission of Camera Press.)

an icon of feminine victimhood and survival, as mentioned in Chapter 4. Given that the crisis of moral commitment is not peculiar to commoners these days, we see its ramifications splashed across the press and even fought out by couples through the media, as the individual television interviews with the divorced Diana, Princess of Wales, and then Prince Charles, demonstrated.

Given that moral commitment has broken down in the world of work too, as Ray Pahl (1999) observes in pointing to the rise of a 'contract culture', it is not surprising that this is increasingly being reflected in the sphere of intimacy so that the strategies used to sort out disagreements in work careers are echoed in individuals' personal careers. Indeed, love contracts are now being drawn up and used in employment contexts as a way of dealing with increasing fears of sexual harassment cases arising from sexual relationships that form at work.

Pahl (1999) argues that the rise of this contract culture may be a positive move because it is based on ideas of equality between the partners. But he claims that it creates problems because the commitment has to be based on negotiation in a context in which the 'male breadwinner' identity is being discredited, and men do not yet have the confidence to know how to deal with it. He states that 'men may now be learning to envy women who appear more able to balance home, work and family. Men cannot manage to be fathers or grandfathers as effectively as women can be mothers and grandmothers.' (Pahl, 1995: 190). The idea of a 'contract culture' is anchored firmly within the historically patriarchally framed context of work, so it is no wonder that men are finding it difficult to operate on equal terms with women. Therefore it seems unlikely that this move will benefit women either. Echoing Beck and Beck-Gernsheim's (1995) observations about men's increasing resentment over women's closeness to children and anger over custody laws, Penny Mansfield (1999) points out that there is a growing fear, on the part of men, that women are 'rearranging the agenda in marriage', meaning that the postmodern family is centrally disrupting the patriarchal structures of family life. With rising unemployment among working-class men and increasing redundancies among professional and managerial middle-class men, there is a sense that what men now have to offer the family amounts to very little, as Pahl (1999) comments.

Two ways of dealing with the anxieties associated with the risks of commitment are being articulated in the news media. On the one hand, with the renewed stress on individualism, future society is being conceived as a 'singles society' in which singlehood is represented as a more attractive prospect than marriage or cohabitation. Young people are no longer feeling forced to have to choose between doing things as an isolated and claustrophobic couple or doing things as part of a rowdy 'laddish' or 'laddettish' single-sex group. On the other hand, living with someone, in a heterosexual relationship of commitment, is increasingly being portrayed as an insurance policy for warding off loneliness.

The new 'families of choice' perspective claims that individuals have differing identities and needs that alter as they move through their adult lives. The emphasis by Giddens (1992) on the idea of the postmodern reflexive self and on fragmented selves, and changes in the types of people individuals are prepared to live with and be identified with, justifies serial monogamy and normalises hybridised, hyphenated family meanings and practices. The problem is that moral commitment is anchored in an anachronistic familial framework and concept of romance and yet it operates as a crucial component of the organisation of performance and identity of the self in the formation of a 'familial subject'. Meanwhile, the hybrid family scenario remains deeply troubling for many because it exposes the precarious, provisional and contingent nature of this new code of contingent moral commitment. Interestingly, as we see below, this dilemma is being endlessly played out within the changing popular representations of intimacy in the private lives of predominantly middle-class, heterosexual couples in Hollywood and other mainstream films.

The Recovery of Romantic Love as Identity

Sexual love is the one desire that makes sense of a person's life as the core of one's identity, according to Beck and Beck-Gernsheim (1995), as discussed in Chapter 1. However, a profound tension exists in a society in which erotic desire and passion do not mix with 'family'. The reward for this passion has conventionally been marriage and children, but it is being increasingly acknowledged that traditional family life offers no guarantees of fulfilment of passionate, erotic love or long-term emotional security. The film genre of romantic comedy is an example of a potent battleground for the portrayal of familial performance: love, romance, sex, motherhood and fatherhood (Neale and Krutnik, 1990). Krutnik (1990) identified a group of popular dominant Hollywood films, 'nervous romances', and Neale (1992) then identified 'new romance' comedies, which represent a collective desire to recover old-fashioned values of traditional heterosexual romance and return to the certainties of the old family values.

'Nervous' and 'new romances' belong to an artistic tradition that relies on a very specific and relatively static view of love, sexuality and marriage that fits in neatly with the ideal, heterosexual, middle-class, nuclearised model. Since the 1980s, the genre of romantic comedy has been characterised by a self-conscious acknowledgement of that tradition, an acknowledgement that constitutes a significant defence *against* the postmodern social disruptions within the very institutions on which the genre depends: love, hetero-sexuality and marriage. But Evans and Deleyto (1998) emphasise that cul-tural variations have been incorporated into the genre, allowing it a resilience and flexibility to adapt to historical change. In this way, the central concept of love has undergone important changes in its representa-tions, largely centred in white American culture, and principally produced through Hollywood.

New romantic comedies convey the deep ambiguities surrounding love, sex and marriage in the postmodern era. For Foucault (1978), modern perceptions of sexuality have transformed sex into a secret, into something hidden and repressed but which, if uncovered, will somehow reveal our true identities. Love and sex have come to be seen as key ingredients to indivi-dual identity tied to an idea of the individual's personal narrative (Giddens, 1992: 37–8). As such, cultural representations of romantic love are central to a project of the self (Evans and Deleyto, 1998: 3). Stevi Jackson (1993: 202) observes that '[t]he pervasiveness of love as a representational theme is related to its institutionalisation in marriage and family life'.

Hollywood romantic comedy films grapple with the tension between unruly passion and permanent monogamy by ending the narrative at the moment of marriage, which ensures that romantic passion is fused with monogamy as an eternal state of being (Wexman, 1993: 8). Yet romantic comedy has also acted as a barometer for some key shifts in attitudes towards love, intimate relations and marriage while retaining those endur-ing features that represent preoccupations with sex, love and marriage in the modern world. Kathleen Rowe (1995: 212) states that the genre is enduring because it invests in the utopian possibilities of friendship and joy between couples who are nevertheless hindered by unequal power relations. However, from the 1960s, Hollywood romantic comedy has undergone a number of changes prompted by a series of intense reorientations within intimate relationships from the 'sexual revolution' of the 1960s, to the moral panics of the late 1970s and mid-1980s, followed by a reassertion in the 1990s of the previously discredited values of old-fashioned romance (Krutnik, 1998).

Old-fashioned romance was discredited during the 1960s and 1970s by the values of the 'sexual revolution', in which the conventions of heterosexual monogamy were questioned or discarded. The 'sex comedies' and 'screwball comedies' of the 1960s engaged in relatively frank discussions about sex and questioned some of the repressive elements of marriage (Lent, 1995; Musser, 1995). The ephemeral nature of heterosexual relations represented in mid-1970s films such as *Semi-Tough* (1977) led Brian Henderson (1978) to suggest that romantic comedy was, by the end of the decade, on its way out. But what actually happened was that the genre simply modified its emphasis. As Frank Krutnik (1990) argues, films of that period, such as *Starting Over* (1979) and *Manhattan* (1979), were 'nervous romance' comedies in which white, mainly middle-class, heterosexual men were struggling to regain a sense of self-respect in the face of a post-feminist wave of 'narcissistic' wives who had abandoned them. In this 'post-1960s' era, heterosexual attachments were fraught with danger, but experiencing rather than avoiding them was somehow compulsory and had to be carefully negotiated to avoid the frightening prospect of emotional desolation.

> As they catalogue the perils of loving in the modern world, the nervous romances detail the difficulties men and women face in initiating, establishing and sustaining attachments in an age that has seen the splitting of sex and self from previous guarantees of romantic and emotional fulfilment. (Krutnik, 1998: 18)

Steve Neale (1992) contrasts the 'nervous romances' of the mid-1970s with popular romantic comedies of the mid-1980s. Nervous romances revealed the strong desire *for* romance yet denied its possibility. By contrast, 'new romances' idealised heterosexual unions and confidently pursued them in the narratives. The values of old-fashioned romance that had been dismissed by the nervous narratives of the 1970s were resurrected by the 1980s. To exemplify this, Krutnik compares Woody Allen's *Annie Hall* (1977) with its reconfiguration in *When Harry Met Sally* (1989). The search for self-identity through love and sex is exemplified as an obsessive narcissism in Woody Allen's films of the 1970s. A cluster of distancing devices are used in films such as *Annie Hall* to disrupt and disavow the certainties of heterosexual romance. Puns, ironic counterpoints and self-conscious mocking of courtship, love and intimacy dismantle the traditional features of the romantic comedy. Yet the nervous romance comedy never managed to transcend established gender hierarchies. It conveyed disappointment at the unattainability of the romantic, passionate and equal-partnered companionate couple but offered no solution. Various strategies such as split-screening functioned to disrupt romantic conviction. The certainties of old-fashioned romance, signified in the nostalgic, crooning sounds of Frank Sinatra's 'It Had to be You' withered away within the nervousness of 1970s modern love. By contrast, *When Harry Met Sally* is regarded as a 'new' romance because it transforms 'hesitancy to romantic commitment' (Krutnik, 1998: 25) through the character of Harry, who struggles over his fear of commitment and his feelings for Sally but eventually reveals his love to her, framed by Sinatra's same song as certainty not irony. Romantic music is used to evoke and valorise the authenticity of traditional romance values.

The new romantic comedies from the 1980s could be interpreted as a conservative reaction to a period of crisis in marriage in western societies. But, as Evans and Deleyto (1998) point out, marriage is less centrally part of the happy ending in films such as *Green Card* (1990), *Pretty Woman* (1990) or *My Best Friend's Wedding* (1997). Rather, they refer to Giddens' (1992: 63) idea of 'confluent love', which, as discussed in Chapter 1, has now replaced romantic love. It is a contingent love, not permanent and not necessarily sexually exclusive. It is a relationship founded on intimacy and reciprocal sexual pleasure but rather than being permanent it acknowledges the provisionality of relationships. It is held together 'until further notice'. Friendship rivals or merges with romantic love by collapsing into 'companionate' coupling, and this theme is revisited in the new 1990s version of the romantic comedy.

Drawing on Umberto Eco (1985), Krutnik points out ways in which the new romance comedy contrasts with the metanarrative of old-fashioned romance. It is a product of a 'postmodern culture haunted by the over-presence of the "already said"' (Krutnik, 1998: 28). Love can only be declared, and intimacy achieved, by drawing on discredited past conventions of romance through the use of self-conscious irony as a defence against the disruptions of traditional rituals of love, sexuality and marriage. In this way, films such as *Pretty Woman* (1990) can engage in a Cinderella fantasy. The film acknowledges that the rescuing of a Cinderella prostitute called Vivian (Julia Roberts) by a prince charming asset-stripper, Edward (Richard Gere), is just a fantasy by confirming through its closure that 'This is Hollywood. Always time for dreams, so keep on dreaming.' Significantly, it is the voice of a black male that declares this 'lie of love', so that a white fairy-tale romance is framed by a black narrator. Black and white racial codes are used as a device with which to split heterosexual romance fantasy from reality, desire from knowledge (Radner, 1993). The black orator exposes the fantasy of the story without undermining the authenticity of desire.

It seems, then, that in the era of the postmodern hybrid relationship, the crisis of moral commitment is being repeatedly exposed, panicked about and dissected as the angst of the age. Meanwhile, we find that the white middle-class family is deployed as part of an assimilationist strategy, both for gay and lesbian relationships and for representations of black families in sitcoms such as *The Cosby Show*. Black people can only figure centrally in sitcoms if they represent middle-class success and aspirational qualities and adopt dominant cultural views. The use of black news readers and anchors in local and national news programmes also implies that racism has evaporated. Yet most representations in the news media are negatives ones framed in issues surrounding drugs, crime and riots. The achievements of the Huxtable family imply that the majority of black people are individually to blame for African American poverty, as Jhally and Lewis (1992: 137) point out. Beyond this sitcom, black families, as we have seen, have been typically represented and condemned as matriarchal, chaotic and disordered, and typified as lone-parent welfare scroungers.

For some gay and lesbian relationships, however, the familial metaphor is being used as a potentially liberating set of principles as part of an attempt to gain public acknowledgement of gay and lesbian sexual identities (Weeks et al., 1999). This clearly demonstrates the power of discourses of familial-ism and is a significant project in a global context where citizenship is denied to many positioned outside familial relations. The metaphor of the family becomes a strategic trope yet it retains problems inherited from hetero-sexual and white discourses. Such self-narratives are, nevertheless, part of an important challenging of heterosexed fatherhood and are therefore consi-dered a threat to traditional family values. Conversely, for many heterosexual men and women in search of identities through straight, familial-based relationships, the family remains deeply problematic: a site of profound struggles over gendered power relations that are underpinned by confusing and quite mythical post-patriarchal *and* post-feminist discourses.

These transformations in public and popular representations, which both produce and react to the official coding and categorisation of individuals in relation to 'familyness', may be indicative of a reassessment and reshaping of familial meanings, but not necessarily an erosion of them. Despite the rise of Giddens' (1992) confluent and contingent love, and the disenchantment of discovering that love objects are unstable entities that gradually meta-morphose into something else, the search for fulfilment through love is still so strong that individuals are willing to go through the process again and again. So Beck and Beck-Gernsheim (1995) seem to be right in their claim that love is the obsession of the postmodern era that replaces religion as a kind of faith. It creates 'family trouble'. Family seems to offer the positive values of security and stability, but not long-term passionate love. There is therefore a profound disjunction and tension between erotic and passionate 'love' and 'family' in an age when erotic love is approached as spiritual passion. Under these conditions, infidelity and divorce are likely to remain popular.

Nevertheless, hybrid images and postmodern familial statistics are being perceived as a threat to the white nuclear family. A new kind of white familial fundamentalism is emerging in reaction to a perceived threat to the traditional family, in which attempts are being made to reassert and recover the nuclear version of family. The following chapter looks more closely at this trend. The mythical modern family seems to be more compelling than the muddled reality of postmodern familialism. But in fact, the postmodern family is itself a mythical middle-class construct that embraces lone parents, black families and teenage mothers most uncomfortably. Moreover, it is being invented and reinvented within a number of competing contexts, from the marketing of products to the promotion of a sense of community at work, to sell products and sell labour power. The family is a highly successful marketing device.

The 'families of choice' argument hides class and ethnic factors through its emphasis on *choice*. It remains, therefore, a middle-class debate dependent on this factor of personal choice, which, in turn, is dependent on the material resources with which to make lifestyle decisions that accrue to aspirational lifestyles. Individuals' choices are always marked by and situated within a complex grid of structural constraints. For example, research on teenage pregnancies shows that they take place within the myriad of constraints associated with social disadvantage, including education, employment prospects, poor housing conditions, and so on. Within such a set of circumstances, maternity can be interpreted as an important and emotionally fulfilling option, but it is a form of familial choice that can only be properly understood within a complex framework of material and cultural deprivation. As such it is far away from the notion of 'families of choice'.

These debates about transformations in family life do, however, contribute to an understanding of some important shifts in attitudes towards familial relations and experiments in the *performance of familialism* within everyday lived practices. But we must not lose sight of the fact that this argument is based not on wide evidence but on predominantly white middle-class ideals from western societies in which articulate, affluent individuals can afford to experiment with narratives of self-invention. Although Giddens emphasises that he is referring to emerging ideals and principles that may guide future relations towards sexual equality, this utopian vision hides those current structures and relations of power that indicate future biographies that oppose these postmodern familial utopias. The material reality *beyond* those representational projections and lived *performances* of familialism exemplified in *Ellen*, *The Cosby Show* and the *i-D* exhibition involve unequal power relations that centrally structure intimate and familial relations into much more complex, ambiguous and conflictual experiences and meanings. Raced, ethnicised, gendered, classed and generational dynamics of power continue to form profound material conflicts and constraints residing at the heart of individual and community life narratives. Most individual and institutional abuses of power and human rights violations are, both privately and publicly, excused precisely in the name of familial, community and national cultural identities.

NOTES

1. Quoted by Amanda Stocks and Alison Gordon, 'Debts and doubts of gay millionaires who are expecting surrogate twins' in the *Mail on Sunday*, 5 September 1999, p. 34–5.
2. Quoted by Fiona Barton, 'Gay Couple's Surrogate Twins are Refused Entry to UK' in the *Mail on Sunday*, 2 January 2000, p. 25.
3. Quoted in ibid.
4. The *Sunday Express*, 14 February 1999, p. 34.
5. I am grateful to Kathleen O'Mara for drawing my attention to these themes about *Ellen*. Also see O'Mara (1997).
6. I would like to thank Estella Tincknell for discussions about *The Cosby Show* and American debates about whiteness.
7. ICM interviewed a random sample of 1016 electors thoughout Britain by telephone and published the results in the *Observer*, 25 October 1998.
8. Ibid., p. 1.
9. *The Sunday Times*, 17 October 1999, p. 5.
10. Ibid.

CHAPTER 6

DISCOURSES OF FAMILY CRISIS

Debates about family values in the news media have been characterised by swings between left-wing celebration or tolerance of 'family diversity' and right-wing moral panics about 'family decline' and the disintegration of traditional family values. A gradual acceptance of the idea of the family 'adapting' to changing circumstances was detectable during the 1970s. But a decade later, during the Reagan/Thatcher era, there was a shift again back to the right of the political spectrum when the term 'family decline' was repeatedly used by politicians and echoed by social scientists in their interpretations of changes in family relations. 'The family' was launched as a powerful ideological weapon in a counter-attack on liberationist sexual politics within this post-liberation landscape. 'The family' has continued to be deployed as a powerful myth for organising material reality by consolidating a biologically and racially structured discourse about morality and identity. Popular media, political rhetoric and government policy are three key Arenas that exploit the family as a sign of moral righteousness in mobilising anxieties about acceptance and exclusion within social groupings of national, ethnic and sexual identities. A backlash against political correctness and the syndrome of the 'angry white male' spread through the public sphere in the United States during a wave of resentment that arose against liberal feminist values during the 1980s. It was within this backlash that the functionalist lineage was resurrected and established in the following decade. So the discourse of family crisis has a long history, but it is becoming more 'urgent, fractious and ubiquitous than ever before', as Judith Stacey (1999: 185) remarks. How this discourse continues to be enunciated is the subject of this chapter.

What is significant here is not simply the trends showing that the 'modern' nuclear family is no longer the norm and an increasing public recognition of family diversity as a key feature of today's society, as shown in the previous chapter (Stacey, 1992: 93; Van Every, 1999: 164). It is that *legislative changes* are specifically aimed at halting the 'postmodern family revolution' and that they are shaped by public discourses of family crisis, as Van Every (1999) points out. The serious confusion between family/household, couple/ marriage and marriage/parenthood that Van Every (1999) and others have referred to continues to characterise social scientific research on the family. Although families are often identified by biological ties, by the sharing of residence and basic household tasks, and by ties of intimacy, studies of relationships such as gay and lesbian 'chosen families', single-parent and post-divorce families show that these categories cannot be taken for granted.

A number of prominent institutions and research centres in the United States produced a series of research projects designed to prove that familial arrangements outside the nuclear model were dysfunctional (Stacey, 1999: 191). In particular, the findings of these studies claimed that non-nuclear family life and divorce is detrimental to children. Research on working mothers, single mothers (but, significantly, not single fathers) and on children in child care were all designed to prove that if children were not brought up by their own mothers at home, in the first few years of the child's life, they were likely to be deprived emotionally, become delinquent and educationally illiterate.

These kinds of study continue to be given weight in the news media of western anglophone nations. They are endlessly debated while opposing research is often either ignored or sensationalised. A scientific narrative is used to give authority to the backlash that gained ground in the 1990s.[1] Social scientists who had previously supported social change were now condemning step-families and single-parent families, emphasising that children are being harmed in households and intimate relationships that fail to conform to that of a heterosexual marriage of the biological or adoptive parents (Stacey, 1999: 193). The 'family-values crisis' was blamed on particular social groups and practices in which race and gender were central determinants. A cluster of enemies were identified to fuel the backlash: divorce, single motherhood, teenage mothers, and lesbian and gay 'families'. For example, a large amount of public money was invested in research to prove that divorce inflicts long-term damage on children (see Wallerstein and Blakeslee, 1989). Research on domestic violence, child abuse and familial relationships and practices leading to divorce meanwhile tended to be poorly funded.

This chapter examines the reconfiguring of family-values discourse within a postmodern setting by addressing attempts to retrieve a 1950s model of the white nuclear family through public debate, political rhetoric and policy. It assesses how an ideal white nuclear family form is promoted in certain official, formal and popular cultural contexts, and the ways in which the discourse slides between these contexts as a central feature of its mythologisation. Anxieties surrounding parenthood are being represented within political rhetoric and popular discourses on familialism, starting from the late 1980s and early 1990s. The denouncing of lone mothers is a theme being sustained within the rhetoric of the recent 'Back to Basics' and

'National Moral Purpose' political campaigns in British politics. In this context, familial 'dysfunctionality' is expressed in the form of deviant motherhood, and measured against the standards of a mythical ideal nuclear version of familialism which valorises patriarchal fatherhood. Here I look at the ways in which the promotion of the ideal, white nuclear family by American and then British political rhetoric and public policies hinges on the re-centring of the traditional family by re-centring fathers and outlawing single motherhood. The second discourse I look at is the way in which the idealisation of families is being mobilised and constructed through the moral panics about lesbian and gay 'pretended families' sparked by the debates surrounding the current British Labour government's desire to repeal Section 28 of the Local Government Act of 1988.

AMERICAN POLITICAL RHETORIC ON NEO-FAMILY VALUES

A striking feature of present day western anglophone nations is the way in which familial ideology is mobilised within government attempts to control people's lives through state welfare policies that echo the strategies of the early twentieth century and even stretch back to those of the nineteenth century. Public policies continue to shore up the ideal of the male breadwinner and to pathologise mothers without a male partner or who wish or need to enter paid employment, and also other types of living arrangements and sexual relations that do not conform to the nuclear ideal.

During the mid-1960s counter-culture, when a questioning of family values took place, public figures in the USA like Daniel Patrick Moynihan (1965) rose to battle against what was labelled an 'amoral' younger generation. Moynihan became a central crusading figure, proclaiming the crisis in family values and imminent break-up of the American family. Promiscuity, dysfunctional African American families, single motherhood and fatherless families were all identified as 'the enemy' that was undermining modern family values. A right-wing 'moral majority' was formed in reaction to the sexual and familial experiments of privileged middle-class white youth on campuses across America. Even white middle-class families were thought to be contaminated by a wave of defamilialisation, once thought to be confined to black and working-class families. Moynihan actually provoked a backlash among students of the counter-culture. He became a symbol of sexual and racial bigotry, condemned for blaming the victims (Stacey, 1999: 188).

By the early 1990s, nearly half of America's population of children were living outside nuclear family arrangements, as Stacey (1999) points out. Double the number of children were living in single-parent families than in families defined by the male breadwinner and female homemaker. The emergence of a new cluster of 'postmodern' family forms was viewed with deep suspicion by the state. Postmodern family statistics of divorce, remarriage, step-families, single parenthood, joint custody, abortion, domestic partnership, cohabitation, two-career families, and so on, generated public debates about the family characterised by a state of normative and definitional instability. Stacey points out that a troubling collaboration is now taking place between electoral politicians and revisionist family-values social scientists. These scholars are promoting a return to nuclear family values and providing 'substantial ideology, rhetoric and legitimacy to post-Cold War politicians in both major political parties' (Stacey, 1999: 187). Many academics are working alongside politicians engaged in the search for the origins and solutions for the 'fall of the modern family system'. Politicians and institutions who promote the idea of a crisis of family values claim it to be related to a crisis of gender identities that can only be resolved by a return to traditional gender roles. This sense of a moral emergency played out through political rhetoric and government policy is figured in the media as a postmodern malaise. Politicians are even engaging in morality battles with popular television drama as a way of expressing outrage at wayward mothers.

In order to attract disaffected middle-class voters, right-wing pro-family crusading politicians in the US have been shifting their position on traditional family values. Neo-family values institutions and campaigners such as the Institute for Family Values, the Council on Families in America, the American Family Panel, Communication Network, the Progressive Policy Institute, and Republicans and leaders of the right-wing Christian Coalition are promoting a new (post-)familism that grudgingly admits to the demise of the 1950s-style male breadwinner family and the presence of working mothers as central to family life but that evades analysis of power, conflicts, gender and ethnic hierarchies as Stacey (1999: 198) points out. The 1992 party platform of the Republican Party, televised at the national convention, employed a militant pro-family rhetoric that proved to be unpopular by the 1994 election.

Within their pro-family stance, prominent Republicans tried to shake off their image of intolerance. Dan Quayle, William Bennett and leaders of the right-wing Christian Coalition modified their approach in order to appear more tolerant of divorce, abortion and gay rights. Acknowledging that there was no longer the 'political support to make it illegal' when referring to abortions, Quayle urged voters to concentrate on lowering the demand for abortions, and to change people's attitudes. Similarly, Bennett advised participants at the Christian conference to dampen down their homophobia by stating that homosexuality had done less damage to children than divorce.[2] As we have seen in Chapter 1, Republican Quayle and Democrat Clinton delivered remarkably similar speeches about family values during the 1994 US election. Stacey refers to Richard Sennett's (1994) observation that the popular rhetoric of 'family values' 'is a barely disguised language of sexual prohibitions'. The subtext is that sexual explicitness and promiscuity cause the breakdown of family values, which, in turn, causes the breakdown of the moral fibre of the nation. Republicans and other pro-family campaigners are defenders of sexual prohibition.

During a bizarre episode of the 1992 presidential campaign, Vice President Dan Quayle publicly reprimanded the heroine of an American sitcom, *Murphy Brown*, for celebrating unmarried motherhood. The sitcom scripted a response through the character of Murphy, who reacted by blaming the Vice President for being 'out of touch' with the problems of 'real' families. That particular episode of the sitcom was widely publicised, and ended up being watched by millions of American viewers. In fact, Quayle took full advantage of the hype by inviting a small group of single mothers, and a television camera, to view the episode with him, thereby turning the event into an electoral drama. *Murphy Brown*'s sentiments were supported by the majority of political commentators who felt that Quayle had a serious problem in distinguishing between real and fictional families. The incident became a media event which betrayed the Republican Party's anachronistic approach to the nation's ordinary families and so it worked in Clinton's favour (Stacey, 1999: 199).

Yet Dan Quayle actually benefited from the episode in the longer term because his campaign advisers realised that contemporary family-values rhetoric is a vote catcher that relies fundamentally on powerful symbols that are rooted both in the fictionalising of family life and in the public shaming of lifestyles that threaten those values. Quayle's campaign against single mothers eventually recovered. As Stacey (1999: 199) says, Quayle's campaign scriptwriters 'recognised that Murphy Brown could function symbolically as a wayward stepdaughter of Ozzie and Harriet Nelson, the mythical couple who lodge, much larger than life, in collective nostalgia for the world of 1950s families'.

THE POLITICS OF ANXIETY: BRITISH MORAL PANICS ABOUT LONE MOTHERS AND 'PRETEND FAMILIES'

The perceived 'crisis in family values', fuelled by empirical evidence of a decline in the nuclear family, was blamed on particular social groups and practices in which race, class, gender and sexuality were central determinants. As Anne Phoenix (1991) has documented, black single mothers are portrayed through a whole cluster of negative associations in the UK, as if black women were predetermined to be single parents. And we have seen, in Chapter 1, how African American women in the United States have been typecast as 'welfare queens'. They continue to be represented as demonic single mothers who exist outside normal patriarchal family boundaries as dependants on the welfare state (Lubiano, 1993). In 1980s and 1990s Britain, the Conservative government promoted and celebrated the myth of a fixed and unchanging nuclear familial type as essentially white, heterosexual Anglo-Saxon Protestant. Official discourses, in the form of government policies, actively promote the 1950s model of the white nuclear family, thereby creating a seamless continuum with a distinctive idealised version being figured in advertising and other media images yet challenged in everyday lived practices. Both rhetoric and policy have stigmatised lone mothers, working mothers, immigrants, Afro-Caribbean families and gay and lesbian 'families' and blamed them for undermining the *proper* family.

However, political leaders' use of family-values discourse can often backfire dramatically, as both the British Conservative government and US President Bill Clinton discovered in the late 1990s. In fact, this kind of spectacular failure is happening with such frequency that it has come to characterise public political and news media life. A direct correlation can be detected between politicians' use of family-values discourse and the 'naming and shaming' of politicians exposed in the media for their sexual indiscretions.

As mentioned in Chapter 1, the marketisation of research in Britain and the USA has influenced the kinds of topics selected for study, leading to a lack of attention being paid to rising levels of poverty among children and to children's rights. In Britain, the most prominent policy debate is centred on fears about declining parental responsibility and the 'inadequate' socialisation of children due to high levels of family breakdown, hence the 'Back to Basics' campaign of the former Tory government and the Labour government's Green Paper *Supporting Families* (Stationery Office, 1998).

The Moral Panics about Lone Mothers

Motherhood continues to be a site on which many of the family-values debates and the call for the return to a traditional family have been fought. Significations of motherhood have always been contingent on the patriarchal structure and, more recently, the nuclear form. 'Motherhood' is being problematised today in ways that seem to echo nineteenth- and early twentieth-century government targeting of 'bad' (lower-class) motherhood as the cause of child neglect. As a consequence, contemporary political debates and policy solutions continue to be directed at educating mothers in 'parenting skills', concealing the wider socio-economic causes of child poverty. As the 1989 Children Act in Britain shows, the state's role in engendering greater parental responsibility is mainly confined to guidance and advocating partnership between parents and professionals such as teachers, day-care workers, social workers and other 'child experts'. This policy concern refers to children only indirectly and addresses parental responsibility for children's behaviour in a variety of domains like the education system, the law and divorce. The most recent shift echoes the preoccupations of the fatherhood films discussed in Chapter 4. It concerns attempts to involve fathers directly in parenting so as to recover a particular version of fatherhood, that is, the recovery of the male breadwinner, as part of the reassertion of the patriarchal nuclear family form. Yet this cannot be retrieved because there has been an irrevocable redefinition of men's labour and male identities – a theme centrally addressed and enacted within mainstream cinema, as we have seen. Central to the debate about recovering fatherhood has been the discrediting of the kind of motherhood that excludes the father.

Atkinson et al. (1998) have undertaken an important investigation into the ways in which policy agendas, political rhetoric and news interweave to produce a definition of lone parents as undeserving scroungers. They point out that the New Right ideologies of the family that dominated public discourse during the 1980s Reagan/Thatcher era relied on targeting single mothers as political scapegoats by blaming them as the cause of a collapse of the moral infrastructure of society. In 1993 the British Prime Minister, John Major, launched a 'Back to Basics' campaign in order to recover the golden era of economic self-reliance, prescriptive morality and traditional family values. The theme was played out across a number of social policy areas during the years leading up to the General Election of 1997. It was evoked in educational debates and Conservative Party policy to demand a return to the 'three R's' of reading, writing and arithmetic. It was used to problematise non-traditional family relationships through a reassertion of a 1950s vision of white nuclear family values and culture and led to the condemnation of lone mothers as undeserving scroungers of the welfare purse. The whole agenda backfired during the run-up to the General Election when a series of Cabinet members' adulterous affairs were exposed, one after another, by the news media.

But before its collapse, the 'Back to Basics' agenda was used to create a sense of public indignation about 'unmarried mothers'. In their incisive study of the treatment of single mothers by politicians and the press during that period, Atkinson et al. (1998) showed how lone mothers were demonised, particularly by the tabloid press, as 'scroungers'. They were held responsible for a 'welfare benefit crisis' and even seen as the cause of the breakdown of the family. They were stigmatised for increasing the welfare debt, for criminalising their children and for creating a shortage in public council housing. When James Bulger was murdered by two 10-year-old boys in 1993 the news media suggested that the murder was committed because they came from broken homes, and their mothers were publicly condemned. In these ways, then, single mothers were targeted as the root cause of juvenile crime and the breakdown of the nuclear family. The resulting moral outrage was fully exploited by the Home Secretary of the period, Michael Howard, who amplified alarm by claiming that the escalation in lone parents was endangering the very foundations of traditional family values.[3]

These strategic attacks on single mothers were aimed at justifying the Conservative government's decision to freeze one-parent benefit in 1993 and to eradicate the lone-parent premium in their budget of November 1996. A moral panic took hold by the early 1990s, exemplified by news headlines such as 'SINGLE PARENTS CRIPPLE LIVES'.[4] In 1993, Peter Lilley MP accused mothers who had never married as 'benefit-driven' and 'undeserving' compared to mothers who had been through a traditional family relationship and were widowed, divorced and separated 'against their will'. He asserted that the fastest growing group of single parents were those who had never married: 'Since the 'sixties their numbers have risen seven-fold because throughout that period it has been 'politically incorrect' to uphold the traditional family as an ideal ... earlier this year I decided that it was time to break that taboo'.[5] As Atkinson et al. (1998) point out, this kind of rhetoric directly contradicted government statistical data upon which it supposedly depended. Although births outside wedlock rose from 11.8 per cent in 1980 to 30.2 per cent in 1991, the proportion registered by both parents rose from 50 per cent to 74 per cent in 1991 and more than half were registered by parents who lived at the same address and were probably cohabiting couples. Lone mothers were accused of encouraging a culture of welfare dependency for their children and becoming a new underclass of scroungers even though the statistical evidence directly contradicted this rhetoric. Mothers who chose not to be dependent on men were vilified morally so as to justify being punished financially by welfare benefit reduction.

Single teenage mothers were accused of getting pregnant as a way of ensuring that they be placed at the front of the council housing waiting list. They were therefore being blamed for a council housing shortage when the real cause of the shortage was the government sale of council houses through the 'right to buy' scheme of the 1980 Housing Act. As a result, new constraints were placed on single mothers' access to housing, and couples with children in traditional family relationships were favoured over lone parents. Yet only 0.3 per cent of people housed in council homes were made up of single mothers under the age of 20. There was no evidence to support the view that lone parents were being favoured over two-parent families (Atkinson et al., 1998: 3).

The news media followed the government in pursuing a moral crusade about unmarried mothers by publishing stories of sexual promiscuity among teenage girls. Michael Howard joined the outrage by claiming that unmarried mothers should give their children up for adoption. After visiting St Mellons, a housing estate in Cardiff, in June 1993 where he discovered a large number of lone parents, the Secretary of State for Wales, John Redwood, made the following speech two days later at the Conservative Political Summer School, which made national news headlines:

One of the biggest social problems of our day is the surge in single parent families. Everyone would wish to help the young family that has suddenly lost the father through death, or if the mother has been abused or badly treated by the father and the relationship has broken down. What is more worrying is the trend in some places for young women to have babies with no apparent intention of even trying a marriage or stable relationship with the father of the child. ... On a recent visit to a housing estate where I was told that more than half the families were single parent families, I asked what action if any was being taken to involve the men folk of the community rather more in helping bring up the children they had fathered. The reply was interesting. I was told 'there aren't many fathers around here'. In that community people had begun to accept that babies just happened and there was no presumption in favour of two adults creating a loving family background for their children. It is that which we have to change. ... The natural state should be the 2-adult family caring for their children.[6]

The father is appropriated in this speech as the single critical figure who can legitimise the mother and child unit as a 'family'. His absence leads directly to the condemnation of the mother, regardless of the circumstances. The traditional nuclear family, in which the father is firmly defined as the only criterion that validates the family and provides stability, is used to pathologise the young single-mother family. Curiously, the fact that 'there aren't many fathers around here' is taken by Redwood to mean that girls/women must be promiscuous and morally repugnant, since this sentence is prefigured by the earlier remark that 'what is more worrying is the trend in some places for young women to have babies with no apparent intention of even trying a marriage or stable relationship with the father of the child'. The fact that fathers are absent is interpreted as the fault of the young mothers as if they have somehow been banishing young men. The father's role in absenting himself, first in the act of conception and then in fathering, seems to be disavowed in this discourse in the rush to blame paternal absence on the mother.

Redwood's speech acted as a springboard for further media indignation and outrage about the collapse of the nuclear family and erosion of moral values. Suggestions were made in current affairs programmes that lone mothers and their children should be denied access to welfare benefits. Mothers who chose not to be dependent on men were condemned morally in order to justify financial punishment by welfare benefit reduction. Interestingly, the local press in Wales realised that single mothers were being witch-hunted and began to do careful research on the experiences and predicament of the single mothers on the St Mellons estate, which were reported in a more sympathetic light. For example, the *Western Mail* (5 July 1993) discovered what the local community knew all along: that the root of the problem was related to levels of poverty and lack of decent community facilities (Atkinson et al., 1998). Certain national newspapers began to follow suit and report more accurate and more sympathetic stories about single mothers.

These kinds of attacks were used to justify the vilification of lone mothers within welfare policy. The Child Support Act of 1991 was introduced in Britain to reduce the Treasury's expenditure by forcing 'absent parents' to be financially responsible for their children under the age of 18. The Act established the Child Support Agency with the objective of locating 'recalcitrant fathers', mainly post-divorce fathers, so as to 'shift the burden of debt' away from the government and on to parents. Currently, a third of fathers fail to pay any child maintenance and another third pay only in part. The Agency has been given the power to place financial penalties on claimants who did not provide information about the child's father. In this way, withholding welfare benefit and threatening poverty are used as weapons to punish those mothers who choose not to abide by the traditionalist values of dependency on men. After being stigmatised as deviant, single mothers could be effectively disenfranchised (Atkinson et al., 1998).

While lone mothers were being discredited, a wave of Conservative MPs' sexual infidelities were being exposed by the news media. It was even discovered that the Junior Environment Minister had fathered an illegitimate child. In the light of these revelations, Redwood was forced to qualify his earlier statement by claiming that he had not 'suggested we watch every bedroom door and have views on how every relationship should be conducted' (*Guardian*, 27 December 1993). During the months leading up to the May 1997 General Election, it was recognised that this rhetoric was actually losing, not gaining, votes. The press was reporting the views of single mothers and other members of the public who argued that new policies were needed to suit new family arrangements. The *Guardian* (24 April 1997) pointed out that the whole 'family-values' debate was losing women voters. When the lone-parent discourse of pathologisation had backfired it became clear that the New Right ideology of the family was in need of a marketing face-lift. The Conservative government switched attention to educational policy by proposing that a moral code be taught in schools. But the traditionalists in the Party demanded that children be taught the moral superiority of the nuclear family, which led to further controversy centred, once again, on the treatment of non-nuclear family forms as inferior and on the condemnation of homosexual relationships through 'Section 28' of the Local Government Act, discussed below.

The 'New National Moral Purpose': *Supporting Families*

Meanwhile, public debate in the press was moving towards a recognition of family diversity fuelled by the realisation that millions of children were being condemned as 'dysfunctional' families for living in single-parent and cohabiting couple families. A more caring approach to teenage mothers was detectable. As the election loomed, both major parties developed schemes to help single mothers gain employment, called 'Parent Plus' by the Conservative Party and 'Welfare-to-Work' by the Labour Party. Yet the objective of both parties was a set of welfare policies designed to shift the responsibility for children away from the state and to gain more rigid control over the lives of lone parents. Single mothers continued to be linked with benefit fraud and crime (Atkinson et al., 1998: 7). The Labour Party's pre-election document on parenting set out its plan to introduce parental responsibility orders to force parents of offending children to attend counselling and guidance sessions (Straw and Anderson, 1996).

After the General Election of 1997, when the new squeaky-clean British Labour government won power from the Conservatives, the political triumph was underlined by news media images of the new Prime Minister's own perfect, traditional nuclearised family, which invoked the wholesome morals of New Labour (see Figure 1.1. in Chapter 1). These images worked as a visual spectacle, acting as a sharp counterfoil to the sleaze and sexual scandals that led to the Tory government's downfall. Blair's prominent 'family man' image conveyed a crucial revival of both universal moral values and youthfulness in government, and implicitly reinforced a patriarchal familial structure. It was in this manner that Blair was able to construct himself, in terms of his personal and political identity, as 'a modern man'. His youthfulness and dynamism relied on the idea of a young family man (that is, young for a PM) with young children, which was associated with the image of an open-minded and sensitive 'new man'. But his image of newness did not extend to embrace the postmodern 'new family' of diverse family forms whether rhetorically or in terms of material welfare support. The following year, New Labour published a Green Paper called *Supporting Families*, which promised a radical blueprint on family policy to protect traditional nuclear families, signifying the preservation of the configuration of bread-winner father and full- or part-time housewife mother with dependent children.

By 1999, when Tony Blair launched his 'new moral crusade' on family values, teenage and pre-teenage pregnancies were targeted as the subject of a moral panic to boost the pro-family message of the campaign. The Labour government followed in the footsteps of the previous Tory government by interpreting official statistics on key trends in actual household arrangements as a distressing indication of societal decline. Ultimately condemning alternative living arrangements such as single-parent families as 'dysfunctional', Jack Straw, Home Secretary and chair of the Ministerial Group on the family, claimed that 'stable families' are probably the single most effective crime prevention strategy available to the government. Stable families signified the traditional nuclear ideal. Home Office research supports the view that 'problem families' bring up problem children. Children therefore need the stability of two (heterosexual) participating parents. It is also emphasised that married couples are more likely to stick together than are cohabitees. Rather than positively supporting the diverse range of relationships in society to ensure *their* stability, the Labour government privileges a narrow ideal nuclear familial form and discredits alternative living arrangements with proposals to make it harder to marry and get divorced by introducing marriage support services, prenuptial advice and childrearing advice. If welfare support is concentrated on traditional nuclear family arrangements, it is little wonder that they have a better chance of stability.

Jack Straw and the leader of the Conservative opposition party, William Hague, were interviewed on BBC Radio 4's *Women's Hour* on the day of the deadline for submissions to the Green Paper consultancy document, *Supporting Families* (15 March 1999). The similarities in their opinions were more striking than the differences. Hague said he wanted divorce to be much more difficult for married couples to obtain because of evidence that married relationships are longer lasting than cohabiting ones. Curbing people's rights to move out of bad marital relations is here defended by the claim that the state's role is to support children, and children *ought* to be supported only within stable circumstances, which can only be guaranteed within the legally endorsed version of the family. Moreover, because the problems that lead to divorce are not addressed in this context (poverty, poor housing and health care, domestic violence, child abuse), this view implies that couples who find it difficult to create an emotionally and economically stable living environment should be forced to stay together and bring up children in what could clearly become an intolerable, unstable relationship and environment.

Jack Straw arranged for the British Labour government to provide health visitors to give advice and guidance to parents in order to enhance the 'emotional well-being' of families. He emphasised that these health visitors are to be seen not as 'agents of social control' by the government, but as 'independent' of the state. This action appears to be a strong echo of state interference in people's lives during the first half of the twentieth century within attempts to induce women to have more babies. Having produced a consultative document entitled *Supporting Families*, Straw's claim that the government is neutral on marriage and not judgemental about how people should manage their relationships sounded somewhat hollow and contradictory. The protection and support of children is claimed as the key motivation for the construction of family policy in nations such as Britain and the United States. However, while bringing up children involves public as well as private responsibilities, current familial ideology is designed to privatise the care of children. The underlying structural problems of poverty, bad housing and education, crime and unemployment are not tackled as causes of poor child care or familial breakdown. On the contrary, family breakdown is claimed as the cause of these forms of social deprivation. By focusing on the family as the root cause of social problems and the principal route to social reform, the government attempts to hide evidence of structural material problems in society and hijack the emotive discourse. This is the broad context in which policy is designed and that shapes the research agenda in western anglophone nations.

Repeating the post-war forms of discrimination in favour of married mothers, we find that today's divorced mothers have little support from the Children Act 1989, the legal profession or the mediation services. None of them give priority or even much consideration to the needs of the mother, but they do support the father. The main policy concern is to attach men to their children, as Smart (1999: 112) points out, so that men rather than the state will pay for children's welfare. These policies have been developed as correctives to what have been perceived as past errors in family law policy. The priority given to children and fathers after divorce does nothing to help mothers in the transition to full citizenship since it reasserts patriarchal structures of power.

After the discovery of 12-year-old mothers and 14-year-old fathers, the government announced on 4 September 1999 that it intends to provide information packs for parents to encourage them to contribute a personal and moral dimension to the improved sex education provided for children aged 10 and above. Also, a government guide to fatherhood is intended to encourage the new father to take a central role in bringing up his family by addressing his anxieties and helping him to relate to his children, and advising on nurturing and how to treat his partner in her new role as mother. Prompted by the fear that fathers are evading their responsibilities, the guide is intended to make fatherhood 'acceptable' during a period when fathers are likely to be surrounded by female relatives. Once again, the subtext is to pathologise lone motherhood and recuperate fatherhood in order to take the burden off the state.

Moral Panics about Lesbian and Gay 'Pretended Family Relationships'

The legitimacy of non-heterosexual relationships has become a topic of profound political controversy in western anglophone nations. An example of this is the term 'pretended family relationships', identified in Section 28 of the British Local Government Act 1988 (see Weeks, 1991), suggesting that heterosexual familial relationships are the only authentic ones and that non-heterosexual relationships are false. In legal terms, the word 'pretend' means *claimed* as in 'a pretender (claimant) to a throne'. Unfortunately however, the news media's manipulation of this legal term has fuelled the incorrect idea, now in common usage, that 'pretend' in fact means *make believe* or *imaginary*. This had led to much confusion and inaccuracy. Section 28 (also referred to as 'Clause 28') was introduced to prevent local councils from 'promoting' homosexuality in schools. In 1999 the Labour government wished to fulfil a general election pledge to repeal the Section 28 ban in England and Wales in order to remove 'a symbol of intolerance and a source of confusion' and to remove the barrier against teachers in tackling homophobic bullying in schools. The announcement of the government's decision to repeal Section 28 prompted a tidal wave of moral outrage and public protest by church leaders and pro-family campaigners who made up the Moral Right anti-repeal lobby. This group evoked a family-values discourse, based on the moral panic of 'family decline', in their claim that the repeal of Section 28 would undermine the traditional nuclear family. What is of interest, here, is the way in which the political rhetoric, news media moral panic and the policy have interwoven to produce a war of morality about sexual and familial values during the government's attempts to repeal Section 28. The wording in the Act of 1988 is as follows:

> 28.–(1) The following section shall be inserted after section 2 of the Local Government Act 1986 (prohibition of political publicity) – 'Prohibition on promoting homosexuality by teaching or by publishing material.'
> 2A.–(1) A local authority shall not –
> (a) intentionally promote homosexuality or publish material with the intention of promoting homosexuality;
> (b) promote the teaching in any maintained school of the acceptability of homosexuality as a pretended family relationship.

Section 28 was introduced in response to the former Tory government's fears of a breakdown in family values during a period when local government councils, including the Greater London Council (GLC), were accused of promoting a homosexual political agenda. The Tory government and right-wing press claimed at the time that Labour-controlled local councils were sponsoring lesbian and gay groups and actively promoting homosexual and anti-family values financed through taxpayers' money. There was a fear, but a lack of substantial evidence, that 'homosexual propaganda' was flooding into schools. One particular children's storybook, *Jenny Lives with Eric and Martin* written in 1981 by Danish author Susanne Bosche and published in the UK in 1983, was singled out as an example of the kind of literature that was unleashing homosexual propaganda on British schoolchildren. The book was a photo-narrative that showed a little girl who lived with her gay father and his homosexual partner. One picture, which caused alarm among anti-gay groups, showed the girl having breakfast in bed with the two men. The book has been retrieved by the pro-family lobby as a symbol of depravity in the argument for retaining Section 28.

Lessons in Marriage and 'Stable Relationships'

In 1999, pro-family campaigners and Church of England leaders insisted that the new Labour government should privilege marriage and the traditional two-parent family in its new curriculum guidelines for lessons in citizenship and Personal, Social and Health Education (PSHE). The Campaign for Real Education said it hoped that the traditional two-parent family would not be taught about as 'just another lifestyle choice alongside homosexuality and one-parent families and will be given the importance it deserves'.[7] Two in five marriages end in divorce, which means that at least 25 per cent of all children are likely to experience family divorce by the age of 16. One would therefore expect moral leaders to be sensitive to the fact that children need to be reassured that the diversity of family relationships is normal and that if children do not experience a nuclear family upbringing themselves it does not mean they are somehow 'odd' or 'abnormal'. Instead, pro-family campaigners used the decline in the nuclear family form as an argument for teaching that it is the only version which *is* 'normal'.

Amid mounting panic over the decline of marriage and the rise in one-parent families, the *Daily Mail* (26 January 2000) published an invited piece by Tory leader William Hague in a double-page spread in which he defended Section 28. The two pages were linked by a caption that spread across both: 'A Matter for Your Conscience' and, significantly, was placed right next to a report about the gay couple, Drewitt and Barlow, who joint-fathered the surrogate baby twins (discussed in Chapter 5). It was accompanied by a large, provocatively positioned photograph of the two gay men, side by side, one with his arm around the other and both holding a baby in each. The twins were permitted to stay in Britain after all. The positioning of this report and photograph next to Hague's views gave justification for his continued support of Section 28 with the headline: '"MR BLAIR IS SHOWING NOTHING BUT CONTEMPT FOR PARENTS", BY WILLIAM HAGUE'. In the article, Hague defended the introduction of Clause 28 a decade before, stating that a series of Labour councils had been using public money

> to support a campaign that homosexuality was not simply a sexual tendency freely practised by a minority of individuals but something more, *a new form of family life*. As such it should be seen equal to marriage as a suitable way of bringing up children and similarly widespread. This campaign was particularly targeted at schools.

He went on to say:

> It is intolerable to teach children lessons about family relationships which people may deeply disapprove of for moral or religious reasons. Section 28 respects these majority rights without unduly infringing those of a minority. (p. 6, my emphasis)

The insistence that minorities should respect the beliefs of majorities was dubiously supported by the argument that taxpayers' money was used to promote homosexuality as a form of family life. Taxpayers are interpreted as a silent 'moral majority' who disapprove of homosexuality. The argument also rested on the fear of innocent children being misled by homosexuality within the assumption that it is somehow more predatory and dangerous in misguiding young people than much more numerous forms of heterosexual crimes such as date rape, indecent assault, sexual harassment, forced prostitution, and so on.

On the same double page, the *Daily Mail* published a column called 'CLAUSE 28 WATCH', below the photograph of the gay parents of surrogate twins. In classic witch-hunt style, the aim of Clause 28 Watch was to target daily a local council's use of 'taxpayers' money' on 'homosexuality as a pretend family'. On this particular day it reported in indignant tones that the Labour-run East London borough of Tower Hamlets advertised for eleven youth workers to join PHASE, a Lesbian, Gay and Bi-sexual Youth Project. The report went into detail about the workers' contact with children and duties to work with and provide services for children. The piece was worded in such as way that readers could have easily drawn the conclusion that the gay, lesbian or bi-sexual staff were acting in sexually predatory ways towards children, evoking fears of paedophilia. After weeks of reporting on the gay couple's fight to keep the surrogate baby twins in Britain with them, the *Daily Mail*'s final report on the couple's success is framed in a 'public backlash' discourse against Section 28 that exposes the gay couple as a pretended, that is self-claimed, family relationship. This framing device is a common one used in the tabloid press as a way of fuelling the moral panic.

Tabloid and right-wing newspapers produced a flurry of homophobic articles that denounced homosexuals for imposing their agenda on New Labour and on wider society. The *Sun* newspaper (9 November 1998) declared that a 'gay Mafia' was running Britain. This headline referred to the existence of three gay Cabinet ministers in government the day after the Agriculture Minister, Nick Brown, decided to come out and publicise his gay identity, with the Prime Minister's support. The *Mail on Sunday* in turn published the headline: 'THE GAY GAULEITERS SURROUNDING BLAIR' (13 February 2000). These examples demonstrate some of the ways in which the tabloid media reportage colluded with the Moral Right in demonising lesbian and gay identities as sexually predatory agents, self-proclaimed families and Mafia-style criminals. The pro-family campaigners and tabloids used the Section 28 debate and traditional family-values discourse to publicise and legitimise homophobic behaviour by suggesting that homosexuality was being declared as a new form of family life that would cause the destruction of the traditional family.

Moral Leaders and the Moral Majority

In its attempt to repeal Section 28 in England and Wales, the government was confronted by a wall of homophobia not only from many quarters of

Britain's press but also from Britain's elite institutions of 'moral leaders', the House of Lords, which has an in-built majority of Conservative members, church leaders, and other pro-family campaigners. The criterion of 'majority' was regularly evoked to defend the ruling. The Christian Institute, an evangelical think tank who have been leading the opposition to repeal Section 28, claimed that the law is necessary because 'the great majority of parents think homosexual practice is wrong'.

Realising that the attempted repeal of Section 28 was likely to be defeated in the House of Lords, the Education and Employment Secretary, David Blunkett, attempted a compromise. He produced an amendment to the Learning and Skills Bill and new sex education guidance in a new framework for personal, social and health education to appease the House of Lords. He announced, in February 2000, that teachers would be required to promote 'marriage' and 'stable relationships' yet would be required to instruct children of 11 to 14 not to pass judgement on individual sexuality. As David Charter pointed out in *The Times* this is an 'apparent contradiction'.[8] Blunkett's main challenge was how to reconcile pressures to privilege marriage and, at the same time, avoid accusations of homophobia.

The Education and Employment Secretary found himself attacked on all sides within the ensuing political row. In response to the amendment, David Hart of the National Association of Head Teachers stated that the emphasis on marriage sent a negative message to one-parent families and prevented schools being sensitive to the family backgrounds of children.[9] But Blunkett dismissed fears that an emphasis on traditional family values would lead to the stigmatisation of children whose parents were not married. He said:

> For many children, rather than being a stigma it will be an indication of what for many of us is an ideal that doesn't always work out. ... We are not ordering or dictating to anyone, we are simply saying for many children that there are no role models.[10]

One of the outcomes of the public political row was the recognition that homophobia is a prejudice that has been legitimised by Section 28. Tragic cases of homophobic bullying in schools have been reported in the news media, such as the suicide of a Burton-upon-Trent schoolboy who was bullied by taunts of 'gay boy' and 'poof' because he liked cookery and drama.[11] Teachers have been left uncertain as to how to deal with such incidents in the light of Section 28. In a House of Lords debate responding to a claim by then Chief Inspector of Schools, Chris Woodhead, that he had not come across any evidence of Section 28 having an effect on homophobic bullying in schools, Lord Tope pointed out that there is, in fact, ample evidence. Lord Whitty agreed, citing that 44 per cent of teachers felt that they had difficulty in 'meeting the needs of gay and lesbian pupils', and 28 per cent felt that Section 28 'may leave them open to legal proceedings'. Baroness Thornton also referred to a report of the Institute of Education of 1997.[12]

Debbie Epstein's research on teachers' views of Section 28 was quoted in *The Times*.[13] In the article she is quoted as saying that there is great confusion among teachers about Section 28: 'Teachers don't fully know what it says and they believe it means they cannot say anything at all positive about lesbian or gay or bisexual people'.[14]

By February 2000, paranoia about discussing sex education in schools was widespread, prompted by the moral panics reported in the press. Head teachers were admitting, but only off the record, that 'they consider sex education to be terribly important, but if they are seen to encourage an overly liberal or broad approach to the subject, they could create havoc'.[15] As Simon Hattenstone comments: 'Hence the fierce and diverse opposition from the likes of Cardinal Thomas Winning, who called homosexuality a "perversion" and likened the gay lobby's campaign to bombardment by Nazi war planes'.[16]

Remarkably, during the very same period, the government introduced a new curriculum subject on citizenship, which will be compulsory for 11- to 16-year-olds from 2002. It is intended to encourage pupils to develop skills of inquiry and critical thinking, discussion, debate and negotiation. Presumably, however, this is so long as it is not about changing family values or alternative families. This new subject is supposed to include the study of legal and human rights and responsibilities; diversity of national, regional, religious and ethnic identities in the UK; and the need for mutual respect and understanding. The right-wing press condemned the curriculum on citizenship for other reasons, of state interference in schools, with headlines such as 'HEADS ARE ANGRY AT BLUNKETT'S "NANNYING" BLUEPRINT'.[17]

While the new subject of citizenship is intended to enhance schoolchildren's understandings of tolerance and respect for others, it seems likely that, given the moral panic around homosexuality circulating during the very moment that this new curriculum subject is announced, this subject will be taught with quite different emphases. The concept of citizenship is itself highly problematic. The key problem is how citizenship is to be defined in the context of the national curriculum. And what are its limits? Within the guidelines for teachers in *The National Curriculum Handbook for Secondary Teachers in England*, it states under the heading 'The Importance of Citizenship':

> Citizenship gives pupils the knowledge, skills and understanding to play an effective role in society at local, national and international levels. It helps them to become informed, thoughtful and responsible citizens who are aware of their duties and rights. It promotes their spiritual, moral, social and cultural development, making them more self-confident and responsible both in and beyond the classroom. It encourages pupils to play a helpful part in the life of their schools, neighbourhoods, communities and the wider world. It also teaches them about our economy and democratic institutions and values; *encourages respect for different national, religious and ethnic identities*; and develops pupils' ability to reflect on issues, and take part in discussions.

> *Citizenship is complemented by the framework for personal, social and health education* at key stages 3 and 4. (Department of Education and Employment and Qualifications and Curriculum Authority, 1999: 183, my emphases)

Citizenship is a form of identity through which individuals are granted rights and obligations within political communities. Although the intention is to advance a diversity of values and ideas in a democratic framework, all forms of identity and policy regulation enact some kind of exclusion. Citizenship's rights tend to be defined by governments in the narrow political context of the nation-state and are therefore focused on fostering feelings of commitment to national identity that may promote xenophobia if taught in a particular way. Moreover, with the political directive being misinterpreted to discredit gay and lesbian families as pretend, that is make believe or false families, it seems likely that citizenship will be defined in a limited way to promote an intolerance of certain identities, values and ideas. This is all the more worrying, given that citizenship is to be taught in such a way as to complement the Personal, Social and Health Education in which sex education, and the promotion of a particular version of family values, is taught. And this is why it falls short in its list of identities for whom children should be encouraged to have respect, by excluding sexual identity. Yet, as Bauman (1991: 256) puts it, '[s]urvival in the world of contingency and diversity is possible only if each difference recognises another difference as the necessary condition of the preservation of its own'.

The Morality Debate in the House of Lords

Despite its attempt at a compromise, the government's plan to repeal Section 28 was defeated in the House of Lords in February 2000. The debate in the Upper House was explosive and took some bizarre turns. The government's proposed legal guidelines were intended to show that the repeal would expose pupils to inappropriate material in the classroom. But the Tories were concerned that schools may use explicit sexual material in the teaching of sex education. The Conservatives objected that a reference to 'stable relationships' would still allow teachers to claim that homosexual relationships were as valid as marriage. Baroness Young, the Tory former leader of the Lords who led the campaign against the repeal of Section 28, denied that her supporters were motivated by a hatred of homosexuals, insisting that their campaign was aimed only at protecting children and family life. She declared that: 'There is not a moral equivalence between heterosexual and homosexual relationships. We need to set in front of children an ideal by which they should live'.[18]

Lord Moran, a crossbencher, said the term 'stable relationships' could include any type of union outside marriage, including necrophiliacs, transvestites and sadomasochists, and questioned whether they should be interpreted as 'key building blocks of society'. Earl Russell interjected: 'Are you suggesting that necrophiliacs have relationships?' Lord Moran continued, stating that the government amendment would encourage a minority of homosexual teachers to endanger children in ways reminiscent of the scandal surrounding a North Wales children's home in which the wardens were accused of paedophilia. The only openly gay peer, Lord Alli, accused those who voted to retain Section 28 of having the same 'morality of hate' as the bomber who blew up a gay pub in Central London's Soho a year earlier.[19] He stated: 'This is indeed a debate about morality. For me it is about the morality of hate. I believe that hate exists because we teach our children to hate.'[20]

After the government's defeat in the House of Lords the front-page headline in the *Daily Mail* the next day (8 February 2000) was 'PRAISE BE TO THE LORDS: PEERS VOTE BY A MAJORITY OF 45 TO THROW OUT LABOUR'S BID TO LIFT THE BAN ON PROMOTING HOMOSEXUALITY IN SCHOOLS'. And in large bold letters in the front page 'comment' box it said: 'Despite Labour's bid to emasculate them, the Lords have shown they are truly representative of the people. It would be outrageous if the "people's government" rejected their wisdom.' 'Emasculate' and 'people' are evocative terms, linking the controversy over legitimate sex/ gender identities with the issue of power and citizenship to conjure notions of a war of masculinity won by the patriarchs who chivalrously defended the nation, the *real* people.

Blunkett was pressurised to make changes to an amendment to the Learning and Skills Bill to replace Section 28. He issued new guidelines for 11- to 14-year-old pupils in state schools, to 'learn about the nature of marriage and its importance for family life and raising children; learn about the significance of marriage and stable relationships as key building blocks of community and society; learn the reasons for delaying sexual activity and the benefits to be gained from such delay' as well as to be 'protected from inappropriate teaching and materials; learn to understand human sexuality; learn about obtaining appropriate advice on sexual health'.[21]

Although the amendment to the Bill was a compromise arrived at through consultation with Bishops of the Church of England to ease the repeal of Section 28, pro-family campaigners remained opposed to the repeal. The *Express* reported that church leaders remained divided over the new guidelines. Some Anglican churchmen voiced opposition to the amendment, complaining that children's rights to protection against 'inappropriate material' were being eroded. Jewish leaders said they were not even consulted, and Muslim leaders claimed the proposals were a 'mockery' because they legitimised gay couples and gay 'marriage'. The Family and Youth Concern director, Valerie Riches, stated that the guidelines were too loosely worded: 'There is nothing that prevents the promotion of homosexuality.' Colin Hart of the Evangelical Christian Institute said that the guidelines would not stop local authorities from promoting homosexuality and that 'there is no doubt that some of them would want to'.

By contrast, the gay and lesbian group Stonewall supported the consultation document, stressing that it acknowledges that homophobic bullying exists in schools, and that 'stable relationships' does not exclude homosexual partnerships. However, teachers' unions did not support the guidelines, claiming that it was not the role of schools to advocate a 'model' family unit. Nigel de Gruchy, leader of the National Association of School Masters and Union of Women Teachers, described the move as

> insulting, patronising, superfluous and bureaucratic. ... Teachers are being made to pay the price for a government scared to face down its critics in the wake of the decision to repeal Section 28. We now witness the absurd spectacle of Government ministers, with all kinds of non-conventional lifestyles and broken marriages, lecturing the nation on traditional family values.[22]

Inventing Enemies of the Traditional Family

Throughout this public war over sexual morality and family values, various sections of society were being labelled as the enemy by the Moral Right. For example, on its front page of 17 March 2000, the *Daily Mail* announced 'TEACHERS SABOTAGE LABOUR'S NEW SEX LESSONS'. Teachers, the state, homosexual members of Cabinet and MPs, the working class, teenagers and so on, were being blamed, one after the other, for the decline in family values. The right-wing press accused the state of believing that most parents are incompetent at bringing up their own children, and that teachers can somehow perform miracles. Teachers were attacked by the press for their own moral impurity and regarded as unfit to teach moral education to the nation's children. In the *Sunday Telegraph* Theodore Dalrymple claimed that 'many of the teachers themselves have descended into the moral morass from which they are now expected, by means of mere homily, to extricate their pupils'. She goes on to say that:

> Teachers have slid so far down the social class – or the underclass way of life has ascended so far up it – that their manner of conducting their private life is often indistinguishable from that of their pupils' parents. They themselves have illegitimate children and violent relationships with obviously unsuitable 'partners' (a word they unashamedly use, the word 'husband' or 'wife' being considered implicitly 'judgmental').[23]

In response to the fear that 'marriage' is about to become extinct, contributors to the family crisis discourse held up the 'Indian immigrant population' as exemplary in preserving traditional family values and condemned the white working class. This highlights the alliance between Christian and Muslim fundamentalism and Tories in sharing traditional family values:

Seventy per cent of the children born in the hospital in which I work are illegitimate (which is, after all, only twice the national average). If it were not for the presence in the area of an Indian immigrant population, there would be practically no legitimate births at all. Marriage isn't struggling in the slums of England: it was dead and buried a long time ago, and will hardly be resurrected by pedagogic exhortation.[24]

The pitching of the goodness of 'Indian immigrants' against the badness of the slums of England also reveals the fact that the family-values discourse operates centrally within a white familial context in which the main fear is that the white family is under siege from inside, from its own members. It is, crucially, the white family that is being threatened by the enemy from within: the actions of white people.

The right-wing press claimed that teenage pregnancies have risen as a consequence of sex education: 'Teenage pregnancy, be it remembered, was much less frequent before the advent of sex education.'[25] These kinds of myths are popular reactions within the discourses of family crisis and revisionist family values and are difficult to shift. As mentioned in Chapter 1, teenage pregnancies are no higher today than they were in the 1970s. England and Wales boasted one of the fastest drops in teenage birth rates during the 1970s up to 1976 (from 34 per 1000 in 1973 to 23 per 1000 in 1976). Since then, when the rates were expected to have dropped much further, they increased again albeit quite moderately, from the 1980s (peaking at 27 per 1000 in 1990 and 1991). Meanwhile, in the Netherlands, the sharpest decrease in birth rates of teenagers was between 1973 and 1976, like England and Wales. But a dramatic reduction then took place in the Netherlands, now among the lowest teenage pregnancy rates in Europe, showing a decrease from 14 per 1000 in 1973 to 4 per 1000 in 1995 which remains the current rate (Social Exclusion Unit, 1999). The Dutch achieved this reduction by reducing levels of poverty among children, by making sex education more explicit and by improving access to services within a multi-agency approach consisting of the Catholic and Dutch reform churches, the government and education authorities. At the end of Theodore Dalrymple's spectacularly misleading article in the *Sunday Telegraph*, the advice given to the government was to stop 'indulging in patently insincere moralising' and, instead, to privilege the traditional family by giving large tax advantages to married couples and withdraw them from those who do not conform to marriage.

CONCLUSION

After a series of embarrassing defeats, bitter arguments and continued opposition in the House of Lords, ministers are now, at the time of writing

(November 2000), apparently considering shelving the repeal of Section 28 in England and Wales[27]. The repeal of the Local Government Bill was defeated once again in the House of Lords on 24 July 2000 but with an even heavier defeat, despite the introduction of more Labour peers. Nicholas Watt of the *Guardian* stated that:

> The decision will fuel speculation that Tony Blair is caving in to pressure from the right-wing tabloids to be more family oriented. In a memo leaked last week, the prime minister said that the government appeared to be weak on the family because of its stance on 'gay issues'.[26]

The powerful cross-party alliance of peers and church leaders has proved to be a formidable political force within the processes of regulating the formation of 'sexed' and 'familial' subjects. The Section 28 saga demonstrates that the family remains a topic of turbulent political debate. The Local Government Act clause has carved out a public space that harbours and legitimises deep cultural prejudices evoked within a moral fundamentalist nuclear family-values discourse. It has acted as an effective ideological device for the policing and regulation of patriarchal familial heterosexuality and for discrediting members of society such as the teaching profession.

As this chapter has shown, the neo-family movement together with the right-wing elements of the news media have not only excused the disenfranchisement of lesbian and gay citizenship and subordinated the experiences of family life of children from post-divorce, cohabiting, lesbian and gay, and single-parent families. They have also singled out certain groups as particular enemies of traditional family values: namely single mothers and lesbian and gay couples. As Kathryn Woodward (1997: 257) states, 'Mothers are constructed as the nation's and the family's moral guardians', but when they are single parents they generate hostility as dependants on the welfare state, particularly during an era when the role of the welfare state is being cut back to make way for the market and privatisation. Moreover, single mothers pose a threat to male authority by unhinging the traditional patriarchal family in the same way that homosexuality challenges heterosexual normativity.

NOTES

1. For example, by people like David Popenoe (1988, 1992, 1993, 1994) and Norval Glenn (1994) in the United States (see Stacey, 1999).
2. R.L. Berke, 'Two top Republicans soften their tone', *New York Times*, 17 September 1994, p. A8.
3. 'Single parents: the facts of life', *The Economist*, 16–22 October 1993. As Atkinson et al. point out, only 17 per cent of British families with children under 18 were then composed of single-parent families.

4. *Daily Telegraph*, 2 August 1991.
5. Conservative Party Conference, 1993, quoted in Atkinson et al. (1998: 2).
6. John Redwood MP, speech to the Conservative Political Summer School, Trevithick Building, The Parade, Cardiff, 2 July 1993.
7. Quoted in Alison Gordon, 'Climbdown means marriage lessons', *Mail on Sunday*, 5 September 1999, p. 9.
8. David Charter, 'Sex education to be neutral, teachers told', *The Times*, 8 February 2000, p. 2.
9. John Clare, 'Blunkett's mini-curriculum too much for unions', *Daily Telegraph*, 10 September 1999.
10. Quoted in John Carvel, 'Heads are angry at Blunkett's "nannying" blueprint', *Guardian*, 10 September 1999, p. 10.
11. James Meek, 'Jenny and Eric and Martin are still living happily', *Guardian*, 29 January 2000, p. 11.
12. Quoted in Paul Foot, 'It's the sex inspector', *Guardian*, 8 February 2000, p. 21.
13. Debbie Epstein (independently and with Richard Johnson) has conducted extensive research on and analysis of Section 28 and sex education. See, for example, Epstein (2000a, 2000b), Epstein and Johnson (1998).
14. Debbie Epstein quoted in David Charter, 'Sex education to be neutral, teachers told', *The Times*, 8 February 2000, p. 2.
15. Discussed in Simon Hattenstone, 'Why no one wants to talk about it', *Guardian Education*, 8 February 2000, p. 2.
16. Ibid.
17. See note 9 above.
18. Quoted by Lucy Ward in 'Peers uphold schools gay ban clause', *Guardian*, 8 February 2000, p. 13.
19. Lucy Ward, 'Ministers suffer heavy defeat on Section 28', *Guardian*, 8 February 2000, p. 13.
20. Quoted in Ward, 'Peers uphold schools gay ban clause', see note 18 above.
21. Patrick Wintour, Stephen Bates and John Carvel, 'Section 28 deal faces new attacks', *Guardian*, 17 March 2000, p. 1.
22. Dorothy Leprowska, 'Happy family lessons "insult single parents"', *Express*, 17 March 2000, p. 7.
23. Theodore Dalrymple, 'Teachers cannot preach, nor perform miracles', *Sunday Telegraph*, 19 March 2000, p. 37.
24. Ibid.
25. Ibid.
26. Nicholas Watt, 'Section 28 could survive', *Guardian*, 24 July 2000.
27. Section 28 has been repeated in Scotland after a similarly accrimonious battle.

CHAPTER 7

CONCLUSIONS

One of the main themes in this book is a recognition that meanings and values of family are formed and contested through a multiplicity of discursive sites. Official, formal and popular discourses are systems of representation that produce regulatory ideals and control and survey meanings and practices of family. Political rhetoric, academic discourses, family policy, popular media discourses and private representations of the family, such as the family photograph album, are all vital interlocking cultural sites across which distinctive versions of family are articulated and framed. But they are not the only sites, and although the messages emitting from them come together to constitute a discursive field as a system of representation, they do not necessarily operate as a seamless united voice. What these discourses indicate is that the family is one of the most urgently contested signs within global struggles for control over changing definitions and structures of civil society, as Giddens (1999) argues.

We have seen how the public arguments about what constitutes a 'stable relationship' and what gets included in and excluded from that category have given rise to a spate of homophobia in the news media through the treatment of lesbian and gay relationships as sexual dissidents (Weeks, 1998). As such, sexual orientation has proved to be a core issue within these debates about definitions of family. The troubled arena of individualisation versus familism has been evoked in a number of different ways through feminist demands for democracy within what Giddens calls 'pure relationships'. Again, lesbian and gay relationships have come to the fore as a crucial site of transformation. They have been deployed as a model for 'families of choice' by those sociologists, such as Giddens and Weeks, engaged in theorising the postmodern condition. The potential for forming alternative definitions and practices of family are clearly founded more on choice than on tradition or inherited moralities. But some of these debates tend to skirt round the problems of inequality and thereby inadvertently invent a 'new family' myth, a virtual perfect family that exists in the public imagination but is not experienced by anybody.

This concluding chapter begins by approaching the family as a site of struggle over cultural values, ideals and morality, and between tradition and modernity. First it examines global tendencies towards a return to a familial fundamentalism and then it addresses the opposing significations of the new family narratives that, as Chapter 5 shows, have been articulated through representations of what I call 'hybridised' families. Finally, the chapter assesses the value of a broadly cultural approach to the family by asking what it offers that other accounts do not.

THE FAMILY AS A SITE OF CULTURAL STRUGGLE

As a process through which global struggles about tradition and modernity are being articulated, postmodernism involves an undermining of authority by de-centring the orthodoxies of western culture. Its critique of universal values and fixed identities provides the political wherewithal for resisting racism, unitary nationalisms and other essentialist ideologies. As such it has been a critical force within the project of de-centring familism and exposing it as an essentialist ideology. The family plays a central role in the expression of the core values of civil society and as such has become a key site of struggle over cultural values surrounding social hierarchies of class, race, nationhood, sexual morality, child socialisation, which can be articulated as characteristics of the tensions between tradition and modernity. So the obsession with family values constitutes a critical feature of the postmodern condition. Giddens (1999) emphasises that, as the site for the democratisation of intimate relationships, the family becomes a major platform on which debates about moralities and ethics get staged. The rise in familial diversity generates a crisis of authority so that patriarchal relations of power are increasingly exposed and discredited. I have examined some of the main discursive contexts in which these struggles and debates about traditional versus postmodern family values have been articulated, both historically as well as contemporarily. The contemporary public debates about what is a 'proper family' can be contextualised by examining some of the historical precedents and preconditions to these ideas, in terms of the ideological investment in a contemporary reinvention of white nuclear family origins.

The family was vital to the historical formulation of nationhood and colonial expansion at the level of ideas and structures in nineteenth-century Britain and continues to act as a powerful metaphor and cultural institution for fixing ideas about identity today. It has come to stand for moral order in the public sphere, which is one of the reasons why it is fought over with both such relish and such bitterness in the context of political rhetoric, the news media and public welfare policies. The kinds of hybridised cultures and identities being represented in the popular media are imaginarily purified and united by being linked to, rather than challenging, white nuclear familial discourses. These discourses indicate the continuities and differences surrounding race, ethnic identity and familial belonging through a culture of inclusion and exclusion. Lived as a dimension of cultural identity, whiteness is rarely recognised as a *racial* category invested with power or privilege in studies of representations of the family. Tensions and anxieties surrounding familial identity are being experienced at this historical juncture because a reordering and reassessment of national and international economic, political and cultural links and ties is taking place. Nationhood and the traditional links between western anglophone nations, such as Britain and the USA, are being re-evaluated on a number of levels as a consequence of national and transnational shifts such as Britain's ambivalent moves towards Europeanisation, and decentralised government within the United Kingdom. Such factors are leading to a reassessment of traditional continuities and links and the opening up of cultural spaces for new modes of interaction and independence. As Roland Robertson (1995) states, globalisation concerns the construction and global spread of ideas of 'home', 'community' and 'locality' and so it centrally involves the contested meanings of familialism.

It seems, then, that two distinctive trends are emerging as part of the process of globalisation within the postmodern condition that, as Giddens (1992) argues, are having a direct impact on changing meanings of family. The first is cosmopolitanism, plurality and celebration of difference resulting from the increased movement of peoples through colonialism, war and economic migration, leading to the proliferation of diaspora cultures and communities. The growth of multiculturalism and the liberalisation of sexual mores through the promotion of equality are transforming meanings and values of familyness on a global scale. The second is a kind of fundamentalism that is resulting from a fear of change, a sense of invasion, exploitation and inferiorisation by the global forces of cultural, economic and social transformation.

The white anglophone nuclear family may remain a trope for the communication of material aspirations: the potential of success, individual satisfaction and long-term fulfilment, played out in the advertising media and echoed in the private visual displays of family in family photographs and albums. But at another level, this rigid version of the family is being questioned and challenged within global discourses in which either the white nuclear family fails to have significance or deviations from this version and the rise of the 'new family' are viewed with deep hostility, as exemplified in the debates about Section 28 in the House of Lords and the news media. On the one hand, new diaspora cultures, immigration, hybrid cultures and new urban cosmopolitanisms (see Tomlinson, 1999) are generating major challenges to family conventions. On the other hand, there is a cultural polemic taking place between western and third world cultures and being articulated along racial, ethnic and religious lines in which the family is both the site of contestation and the excuse for violating women's rights in both regions.

According to Giddens, globalisation has contributed to the reconstitution of agency and democracy and, because this has particularly impacted on the lives of women, it has affected the structures and meanings of family. But globalisation does not guarantee the proliferation of social justice, especially as there is no global agreement about what human universal rights and values should be. The acknowledgement of difference within international human rights debates has not necessarily led to genuine pluralities. International law has not yet been stabilised, and there is no evidence of a process of democratisation taking place on a global scale. As the previous chapter shows, a revisionist model of the nuclear family is being recuperated through a rising moral fundamentalism in western anglophone nations, spearheaded by the Moral Right, ethical socialists and certain religious groups to regulate meanings and practices of family and halt the processes of increasing individualisation. A growing sense of agency among formerly subordinated and inferiorised groups, including women, gay men and people who are treated as ethnic 'minorities', threatens modern family values. Modern family values have been the very site in which those social and cultural inequalities have been reproduced. Their demise would erode those key mechanisms of regulation. The privileging of nuclear family values is therefore being sharply defended, policed and fought over.

The Moral Right condemnation of postmodern familialism and its call for a return to basic moral values is founded on a profound paradox. On the one hand, neo-liberalism has promoted a laissez-faire, free-market economy in which old forms of state regulation were dismantled during the Reagan/Thatcher years to make way for unhampered profit making. On the other hand, censorship, tight controls and state regulation have been enforced in the name of the family and sexual morality, fanned by a series of moral panics about the potential for corruption through forms such as television violence, pornography and the promotion of gay sex (Bocock, 1997; Hall, 1997). As Giddens (1999) infers, within the desire for a return to old values something new is produced: a fear and persecution of plurality. Fundamentalism is, then, a reaction against the demands for diversity and difference.

NEW FAMILY NARRATIVES

A spectacularisation of postmodern family values and practices is taking place within the western anglophone media context. Is there evidence, within popular media and 'expert' discourses, of an authentication of the postmodern family, and the overturning of the modern family-values orthodoxy?

The postmodernist challenges to social theory have stressed the fluid, negotiable and contingent nature of all social identities. This means that sexual identities are no longer treated simply as pre-given. As we have seen, lesbian and gay assertion of identities is now gradually being recognised, among much resistance, as just one aspect of a wider construction of identities (Weeks et al., 1999: 84). The transformation of intimacy that Giddens outlines is the product of the breakdown of traditional narratives and legitimising discourses under the impact of long-term cultural, social and economic forces, making it possible for people to adopt diverse styles of life and forms of partnership that cut across the heterosexual/homosexual dichotomy (Weeks et al., 1999: 85). As 'family' comes increasingly to signify subjective meanings of intimate connection rather than formal, objective blood or marriage ties, so the emphasis is increasingly on 'doing family' (Bernardes, 1987; Finch and Mason, 1993; Morgan, 1996).

The 'family' is being recovered, revamped and reasserted by incorporating a range of practices, including gay and lesbian relationships, work relationships and friendships, within a new, hybrid form whose meanings are being explored in the popular media. The family is being recuperated as a pure relationship within a democracy of the emotions. But we need to interrogate these cultural shifts continuously by always asking: 'on *whose* terms, using *whose* version of "family" and emotional equality, and for whose benefit are they being produced?' We find that the marketing of difference is just as useful to global capital as the marketing of the ideal, white nuclearised family. But that 'difference' is still necessarily judged by and against a set (sub)text of western-centred white familism which is profoundly structured by inequalities of race, class, gender, sexuality and generation.

Nardi (1992) notes that friends can provide a sense of commitment and shared responsibility that kin relationships traditionally offer in a 'friends as family' model. Weeks et al., (1999: 86) admit that the emergence of new ways of expressing basic needs and desires may be the expressions of a minority, but they apparently 'resonate with broader changes in intimate life'. The narrative of self-invention is important for lesbian and gay relationships because the story of creating one's own life is a powerful signifier of a new sense of belonging as a way of asserting a homosexual way of life (Plummer, 1995). The traditional word 'family' and 'community', 'with all its historical baggage and ambiguity' (Weeks, 1999: 88), offers a context for claiming personal values and for putting homosexuality on the public agenda. 'Identity' and 'community' and 'choice' are words that have been central to the formation of the 'queer construct family'. In this sense, lesbian and gay relationships have come to operate as a sign of transformation and hope – for all familial relationships. It seems, then, that families of choice have become an icon for postmodern familialism.

Gender difference and the normality of heterosexual familism are being affirmed in the everyday routines and narratives of social life by structuring and guiding, and placing limits on, the meanings and forms of intimate relationships beyond heterosexual familial ones to encompass gay and lesbian relationships (Dunne, 1999: 71, 73). Like the performativity of gender, being part of a family is something that must be culturally inscribed and accomplished as an ongoing performance. Familialism is something that has to be reinvented and continuously achieved in everyday interactions with others – we *do* rather than simply *have* family. The sense of 'doing' family, of performance and performativity, has operated as a critical thread running through the book, with, as Spigel (1992, 1997) shows, the post-war popular cultural treatment of the home as a theatrical space and family members as actors in a play about 'family', which is followed through in terms of self-representation within family photography.

Although in the past, during the 1950s, this theatricality was a crucial device for fixing the family as a hierarchicalised nuclear model, today it is treated as a feature of the family's ability to change and respond to shifting demands for new forms of social relationships. If we recognise that family life is reinvented on a daily basis within lived cultures and representations, through narrative and performance, then it is possible to acknowledge that changes in the plot, the characters and even the stage can be made without necessarily being inherently amoral and dysfunctional. 'Doing' rather than just 'having' family implies knowledge of wider social conceptions of what constitutes the attitudes and activities/practices regarded as appropriate ingredients for 'happy families'. Individual action and subjectivity are constrained because they are subject to evaluation on the basis of how far they 'measure up' to the familial criteria which are specific to the particular context within which the performance takes place. This implies an ongoing self-monitoring and self-censorship within the management of our sexed and gendered identities as familial identities, whether heterosexual, gay or lesbian, single-parent, post-divorce family, and so on.

The category of 'normal sexuality' is being subverted by lesbian and gay families of choice and by hybridised representations by the act of untying sexuality from gender. Following Butler (1990), we can say that the family is the site of performativity through which gender and sexuality are reproduced by the convention of repeated performances. Subversive possibilities come to the fore within the families of choice, making 'gender trouble', and spearheading the shift towards the democratic 'pure relationship'. Lesbian and gay families of choice undermine old binary restrictions, and have the potential to disrupt and weaken those dominant family discourses based on the heterosexual/reproductive code.

However, the transgressive performance can be defused by public discourses that consent to lesbian and gay couples calling themselves 'families' – as long as they conform to the moral criterion of a 'stable relationship'. The 'de-traditionalisation' of the family and the redefinition of marriage to include lesbian and gay marriages is a crucial move towards saving certain treasured meanings of family. In this respect, the family still acts as a regulatory ideal, reproducing the legitimacy for the exercise of heterosexual norms. Opposition to same-sex marriage is often defended by the claim that sexual relationships between gay men are inherently promiscuous and regarded as a sexual perversion that undermines and betrays marriage as an institution.

The real threat to pro-family campaigners, then, is instability: that is, sexual relationships regarded as transient, illicit, transgressive. Bisexuality and predatory gay sex are therefore seen as the deepest threat to family values as they cannot be contained. They undermine the social order by undermining those core familial values based on stable relationships. This threat is no longer 'external' but comes from inside, through the desire for individuality and experimentation. And it is depicted as a *white* problem. This white fear is revealed in some of the public responses to the explicit gay sex drama series *Queer as Folk*, screened on Britain's Channel 4 television in 2000. The series featured three gay white men living in Manchester's famous gay 'village' and, within a fast-paced narrative, showed them engaged in explicit sex in club public toilets as well as bedroom scenes. Rather than labelled a late night 'specialist' gay programme as would be expected, it was broadcast during the prime evening time slot and attracted high audience ratings. Arguments took place over whether the series was popularising and even celebrating the negative stereotype of gay men as pleasurably predatory in their sexual habits and undermining the sensitive, caring and stable forms of gay relationships that exist, as depicted in the news story of the gay couple who adopted the surrogate twins. The 'stable relationship', as long-term commitment, is an important sign that has the potential to authenticate relationships that are troubling. Marriage and the family discursively regulate the sexual transgression.

Sexual Dissidents

On 23 April 2000, the *Sunday Times*' front-page headline, which declared 'BLAIR TO LET GAY COUPLES ADOPT', was followed by a report that announced:

Tony Blair is preparing to give gay couples the right to adopt children, putting them on a par with married heterosexual couples. ... The prime minister recognises that the move towards parity will be controversial but believes many homosexuals in stable relationships are being unfairly denied the chance to adopt. ... The disclosure dismayed family campaigners, who described the move as another 'nail in the coffin' for marriage. Valerie Riches, director of Family and Youth Concern, said: 'This government is beholden to the gay lobby. It is very serious for the institution of marriage, which is the safest and best way to bring up children.'

The demand for same-sex marriage, and for lesbian and gay couples to be able to adopt children, have, then, become vital sites of struggle. The continuing disenfranchising of those who cannot legally marry presents itself as a serious problem. Immigration law is an example where biologically essentialist and traditional nuclear family norms are reinforced in the interpretation of immigration as a major source of family reunion. It excludes those who do not conform to the traditional nuclear family model. For example, current immigration law in Britain and the USA prevents same-sex cohabiting couples from the same entitlements as married, heterosexual couples. Immigration law and practice has failed to catch up with the social, political and cultural changes leading to postmodern family forms, such as the rise in same-sex and heterosexual cohabiting households (Weeks, 1998: 41). Weeks (1998: 35) refers to those who do not conform to the heterosexual norms of marriage as 'sexual dissidents'.

This sexual citizen is a 'hybrid' who breaches the norms of heterosexual relationships (see Bell, 1995; Binnie, 1997; Weeks, 1998). But successful lobbying by Stonewall on the issue of immigration has led to the reinstatement of a clearer, more defined concession within immigration law, allowing same-sex couples to be treated in the same way as married couples. This concession now applies to unmarried couples, and people applying for it must show they cannot legally marry under UK law. Some countries such as Denmark, Sweden and the Netherlands do recognise cohabitation and same-sex partnerships for immigration purposes, but, like the UK, France treats migrants on a discretionary basis. Same-sex couples whose partnerships have not been recognised for immigration purposes have had their claims rejected by the European Court of the European Convention of Human Rights[1] as it does not view same-sex couples as a 'family'. Scandinavian countries and the Netherlands are allowing the extension of marriage to lesbian and gay couples in 2001, having acknowledged that its denial is a violation of human rights.

THE NEW FANTASY OF POSTMODERN FAMILIALISM

Postmodernism critiques universal values and fixed identities, providing an opportunity for resisting racism, unitary nationalisms and other essentialist ideologies. However, in doing so, it evokes a neo-universalism and new humanism to which other cultures are encouraged to aspire. While exposing the model of the nuclear family as a myth, the postmodern family replaces it as a mythical construct, as a fantasy and idealisation. As yet, within heterosexual relationships, the hegemonic status of the nuclear family with male breadwinner head has not been deposed. As we have seen, even sociology is still having trouble shifting away from its 1950s paradigm of the modern family, despite the interventions of feminism in the 1970s. That is to say, the nuclear family exists in the public imagination, as a set of powerful representations projected from a number of discursive sites such as the media, popular culture, consumerism, political rhetoric and welfare policy, and so on. On the one hand, this virtual family is, like a computer animation, more pure, more perfect and more real than the real thing. It invents the 'real'. It performs on our behalf as the ideal nuclear family. On the other hand, while we hold up and celebrate hybrid families and 'families of choice' as a way of challenging such orthodoxies, we still need to remind ourselves that many people who live in alternative arrangements, such as lone-parent families, cohabiting and same-sex couples, and post-divorce families, are not only disenfranchised by the political rhetoric and welfare policies of the Moral Right, but are also suffering severe economic deprivation. Postmodern familialism remains contaminated by aspects of the pre-existing nuclearised familialism. It continues to operate on the assumption that we are 'all middle class now'.

The narrative of self-invention may be emerging as a crucial element in the democratising of pure relationships, especially for same-sex couples, but we need to be cautious in holding up such relationships as new models because the old hierarchies are not disintegrating. Gillian Dunne's (1999) research on the Lesbian Household Project investigated the extent to which lesbian partners were able to put into practice egalitarian ideals within their domestic arrangements. Since gender is something accomplished and ascribed, it implies an audience, as Dunne (1999: 72) says, in the sense that 'the gender of the person we are doing our gender with/for and who does it to us matters'. However, she found that gender scripts are so strong that they even operate and guide relationships in same-sex cohabiting households (Dunne, 1999: 73). One wonders what hope there is for heterosexual couples in finding equality in relationships, especially when child care, deferred career, gender discrimination in employment and welfare are operating against diversity and in favour of the traditional nuclear family form. For heterosexual and same-sex couples with children, the care of children is a crucial constraining factor. Performing tasks and caring roles in the sphere of intimate relationships is at the heart of the reproduction of gender inequality. It is at this level that democracy is fought out, on a daily basis.

Moral Individualism

We have found a crisis of commitment articulated in areas of the popular, such as romantic comedy, as a response to the provisional nature of commitment that evolves out of hybridised family and personal relationships, as discussed in Chapter 5. This privately and publicly expressed crisis of commitment has profound implications for government policies on parenting given that such policies are based precisely on the assumption of monogamous and long-term commitment. This is the strong subtext of the *Supporting Families* consultation document produced by Britain's Labour government in 1998 (Stationery Office, 1998). The treatment of parents who 'walk out' on their families as potential tax burdens demonstrates that the crisis is located within the breakdown of the reliance on women as carers and men as providers. Within debates about the growing diversification in family forms accompanying increasing individualisation, Cheale (1999, originally 1991) argues that contemporary family relations take the form of a moral individualism. A year later, Giddens (1992) importantly emphasised the gender specificities of such shifts. Pointing to the rise of a new form of individualised contractual governance within anglophone liberal democracies, Anna Yeatman (1996) states that this new contractualism consists of a form of individualised regulation that approaches the parties as individuals in their relation to governance and constitutes them as consenting equals (O'Connor et al., 1999). Individual contracts are replacing collective agreements in employment relations. Publicly funded services are being contracted out to external suppliers, including competitive tender and individualised forms of 'case management' for care.[2]

Certain versions of this new contractualism were part of the neo-liberal social policies of Reagan and Thatcher, but Yeatman points out that other versions may signify a shift in forms of governance towards a more substantive individualism. This creates serious problems for women, who have not been given full liberal personhood. Liberal thought is flawed because its liberalism and universalism deny the interdependencies and interconnections of society, which impinge on women, who, as carers, cross the ideological divisions of social life into public and private spheres. As O'Connor et al. (1999: 64) put it:

> There is an enduring contradiction between the liberal individualism of economy and society, in which men and women are separate and equal persons with individual rights, and the collective bonds of private life joining men and women in marriage, kin relations and the upbringing of children. Operating at the conjunction of state and civil society, *social policy* mediates this contradiction. (my emphasis)

Social policy steps in, then, to patch up the wounds wrought by the loss of the long-term companionate marriage. In doing so, lone mothers and post-divorce mothers are named and shamed at various junctures and contexts, as the cause of the breakdown of the fabric of society through the disintegration of family values, while teenage and post-divorce fathers are wooed and retrieved as masculine carers both by welfare policies and by popular culture.

Friendships may have come to be authenticated through the metaphor of family and vice versa, but notions of 'pure relationships' undermine the complexities of family practices, which include caring and love for children. The idea of pure relationships as a central goal in late modernity actually masks the burden of caring for children as well as the desire to do so. As Morgan (1999) says, the pursuit of individually-based adult relationships may provide further sources of instability for family-based practices. Brannen (1999: 145) states that, '[a]s marriage and co-residential parenthood becomes less common, children are increasingly significant to the symbolic order of family life'. Given that children are central symbols and practices of family, parenthood as a form of caring and affection, remains a central issue within the desire to forge 'post-patriarchal' family relationships. Parenthood will therefore constitute an ongoing site of bitter struggle within post-divorce families.

Troubled Parenthood

This ongoing site of struggle of post-divorce parenthood is precisely the reason why new discourses are being articulated around masculinity through explorations of fatherhood in the popular media, as discussed in Chapter 4. While motherhood has traditionally been the object of the public gaze across a range of discourses within the popular media, fatherhood has been largely absent, until now. The fact that the 'fatherly' side of the male is now on display in a wide range of films is generated by profound anxieties around divorce. The family has become a battlegound in which men and women are fighting over individual identity, love and control of children and the formation of family life as something stable, secure and permanent. Not only do rising divorce rates expose the problems, anxieties and desires surrounding fatherhood, but postmodern diversity exposes the redundancy of 'the rule of the father' and dethrones patriarchy as a legitimate source of bonding. As discussed in Chapter 4, contemporary public concerns surrounding fatherly desires are embodied in the spectacles of the white male in Anglo-western cultures in Hollywood and mainstream films in Britain, Australia and the USA. Questions are being raised in popular culture about ways in which men perform fatherhood through the circulation of 'troubled' images of white male sexuality, parenting and male performativity. Fatherhood has therefore become a site, along with same-sex 'families of choice', for the exploration of a new set of meanings through which to deal with issues about power, hierarchy, democracy, fairness and morality.

A high price is being paid for idealising the nuclear family form and using it to defend and promote fixed moral virtues. Tensions between individualism and familialism are dominant preoccupations within anglophone media discourses centred on public morality. The ongoing sex scandals concerning men in public office and preoccupations with fatherhood are proof that the idealised space of nuclear familism is imaginary and that, through the daily *performance* of familism within lived cultures, nobody can live up to the high expectations set by it. Popular media representations of the family confirm the deep struggle between the innocence and sanctity of the ideal family versus the guilty, perverse individualism of family members. Hollywood alerts us to the problems that besiege the white nuclear family and identifies the enemy as one that lies within. Representations of the hybrid arrangements of actual families are showing the ambiguous status of fatherhood while motherhood remains condemned as biological caring or threatening power.[3] Paternally generated familial crises have come to signify the dysfunctionality of familialism. They signify ongoing discursive struggles to come to terms with the massive discrepancy between complex lived experiences of human relationships and those popular discourses that invent and promote an imaginary nuclear familialism. Without guarantees of life-long monogamy and life-long male employment, middle-class fatherhood has to be reinvented as a sensitive role founded on masculine affection.

Contemporary public rhetoric contains a persistent undercurrent concerning the legitimacy of an ideal white male breadwinner *against* postmodern, post-patriarchal familial values. The growing preoccupation with reaffirming white fatherhood as a form of masculine care which is no longer crisis-ridden is dependent on a pathologisation of mothers who fail and refuse to position themselves within a dependency relationship with men and do not conform to the nuclear ideal. This is expressed in terms of declining maternal responsibility, bad mothers and the 'inadequate' socialisation of children due to the high level of family breakdown. Thus, moral panics surrounding pre-teenage motherhood are directly connected to the ways in which fatherhood is represented in public discourses and the popular media. In Britain, official discourses and government rhetoric are centred on fears about the increasing independence and individualisation of women and the economic and cultural discrediting of the concept of male breadwinner. Although the crisis of fatherhood has been located in the news media, the 'ideal' nuclear and the 'dysfunctional' discourses actually work together to reassert the authority of white fatherhood as a reaction against this crisis.

Anxieties surrounding perceptions of these dislocations are leading to a search for traditions, for the reassertion of authority and the search for absolute truths in familial values. They are being expressed through the investment in traditional nuclear familial discourses, which, like genetic discourses, act to defend hierarchical, heterosexual relations as 'natural'. During a crucial period of global economic activity in which the welfare state is being eroded and replaced by a market state, popular media representations such as Hollywood films are preoccupied with representing men *performing* fatherhood as an active 'project of the self' (Giddens, 1992). Unable to 'find themselves' in the post-Reagan/Thatcher era of high unemployment and unstable national and international financial markets, we find that male heroes are being located back in the home to recover paternity as a central rather than a marginal identity alongside their professional career. White paternity is being used as a device to reproduce and universalise the authority not of hard, aggressive white men but of sensitive, nurturing white men. Masculinity is being recuperated in a domesticated, feminised and paternal version but refuses to relinquish its power (Davies and Smith, 1997).

THE VALUE OF CULTURAL APPROACHES TO THE FAMILY

This book has set out to examine the relationship between moral regulation and representations by approaching the family as a key site of social regulation, and for conferring sexual, ethnic and national identities. I have taken the privileging of whiteness and the regulation of heterosexuality as two principal factors that have become central to the promotion of patriarchal family-values discourses in western anglophone nations. This kind of inquiry into the processes through which whiteness and a patriarchally structured heterosexuality are inscribed in representations of the modern family requires a study of the discursive fields that work to naturalise and perpetuate ideologies and myths of familism. The institutions of law, education, medical and welfare services have constituted discursive sites of moral and social conduct through which the state, in relation to the church, has sought to regulate human subjects' actions and identities. It is a patriarchal, raced and class-based morality that relies on the reinvention and perpetuation of a middle-class, white ideal model of the family.

Importantly, the moral campaigns being conducted by past and present politicians and religious leaders to promote family-values codes and to curtail the perceived decline in moral standards are not only centred on legal and policy issues but also being fought out prominently at the level of *representations*. Television, school books and the national curriculum, films and other public cultural media and information channels have constituted core sites of contestation through censorship and regulation in the arguments over issues such as Section 28, teenage and pre-teenage pregnancies, divorce, abortion and demands for lesbian and gay marriages. Representations have become a critical battleground in the conflicts over family and family values, leading to the spectacularisation of the family as the platform on which society's profound debates about sexual and personal morality are performed. The family is being treated as a theatrical stage upon which society's deepest disputes and ruptures about sexual and personal morality are struggled over. As such, family values are being argued over at the level of representations, leading to a spectacularisation of 'the family' as a monolithic unit, to be defended or dismantled.

So in approaching the family as a set of powerful, yet often contradictory, meanings produced and circulated through a range of key discourses, it has been examined through a broadly cultural lens to show how cultural representations are deeply implicated in the policies and practices of family life. As such, this broadly cultural approach has deployed and combined film studies, media and cultural studies, queer theory and sociological debates to examine the interconnections between official, academic and popular discourses that contribute to the circulation of dominant representations of familyness. Until now, 'the family' has been hijacked by the social sciences, and yet within sociology, for example, the study of 'the family' has been condemned to a low status until it was incorporated into mainstream social theory through the work of Giddens (1992), Beck (1992) and Beck and Beck-Gernsheim (1995).

Although much work has been undertaken in cultural studies and related areas, such as film studies and queer studies, that impinge on representations of the family, the key debates have been entered into under other headings, such as the body, sexuality, television and audiences, postmodernism and globalisation. Clearly, the ground-breaking empirical research and analyses of sociologists such as those referred to throughout the book, including Gillian Dunne, David Morgan, Bren Neale, Elizabeth Silva, Carol Smart, Judith Stacey, Jo Van Every and Jeffrey Weeks, have challenged traditional sociological views of the family by documenting and theorising about current transformations in family life around the idea of the 'new family' and postmodern families. I have drawn considerably on their important findings and ideas, as well as the work of key social theorists such as Anthony Giddens and Ulrich Beck, who have developed major channels of inquiry and debate about the postmodern condition of familialism.

Elsewhere in the social sciences, such as more conventional approaches in sociology and psychology, there has, however, been an overemphasis on political and economic processes concerning material conditions and patterns of behaviour. As contributors to the 'new family' and postmodern debates agree, this overemphasis has prevented certain important questions from being addressed directly. Such disciplines have lacked a commitment to a form of cultural politics in which the 'cultural' is understood as a crucial mode of intervention across cultural movements that involve racial politics, feminism, queer studies and lesbian and gay politics, and neo-colonial studies. These latter approaches treat the discursive formations composed of signs, images, representations, meanings and ideologies that make up the 'cultural' as important areas of analysis interconnected with, rather than subordinate to, economic and social structural factors. Thus, as Annette Kuhn (1982: 4) states in her important classic work on feminism and cinema,

> everything that might come under the heading of the ideological – a society's representations of itself within and for itself and the ways in which people both live out and produce these representations – may be seen as a vital, pervasive and active element in the constitution of social structures and formations.

As I have argued in Chapter 1, the social sciences have, until recently, proved to be remarkably unreflexive by taking representations at face value and thereby often colluding with the myth of the ideal modern family in political rhetoric and popular moral discourses on the family. In fact, looking back across two centuries, we find that this collusion has been central to the continued construction and circulation of the ideal modern family. Nevertheless, the 'cultural' now has a more prominent place in the social sciences. Although the 'cultural' contains its own effects and dynamic within wider social conditions, it is no longer seen as simply a reflection of economic or political structures but 'regarded as being as constitutive of the social world as economic or political processes', as Paul du Gay (1997: 2) states.

Du Gay points to two key strands within the contemporary turn to culture: the *substantive* and the *epistemological*. The former is about matters of empirical substances, which refers to the impact of changing cultural practices and institutions, and the latter is concerned with the production and circulation of knowledge. Within the study of representations of family and family-values discourses, these two strands have been central to an understanding of how familial meanings are organised across a number of discursive fields. He goes on to say that the production of social meanings is a fundamental precondition for the operation of all social practice, so 'an account of the cultural conditions of social practices must form part of the sociological explanation of how they work. Cultural description and analysis is therefore increasingly crucial to the production of sociological knowledge' (du Gay, 1997: 2).

The value of this broadly cultural standpoint, then, is that it is able to offer an articulation and analysis of the family across a multiplicity of discursive sites: political rhetoric, public policy, academic discourses and the popular media. Public debates involving complex issues about the moral rules and values that regulate representations of the family and sexual practices and identities can be effectively interrogated by drawing on cultural methods such as Foucauldian theory. A cultural approach combined with social theory allows us to analyse the representations used to describe, regulate and celebrate the family both as a monolithic category and as a fluid and changing set of meanings and identities. It constitutes a necessary part of understanding the interconnections between the way people are represented by official and popular discourses and the way people represent themselves in relation to those public modes of signification.

Through this approach, we can acknowledge that there is an important dynamic relationship between how people are portrayed, how they portray themselves and how they actually live their social relations and give meaning to them. We can begin to trace the ways in which welfare policy and political rhetoric are intertwined within the continuous reinvention of the modern family in the face of social change. The objective of a cultural approach is to question the basis of the traditional world view of the modern family and to reveal and explore the contradictions, ambiguities, oppositions and differences that seem to make up a postmodern set of alternatives that are being experienced, lived, struggled against, pathologised and also celebrated. In this way, the impossibility of considering familism in terms of fixed social or textual attributes is foregrounded by emphasising that meanings about the family do not reside solely in behaviour, social structures or representations but mediate across these organising principles as part of the contested nature of cultural production.

NOTES

1. Under article 8 of the European Court of Justice, the right to 'family and private life'.
2. For example, the UK Citizen's Charter and the 1994 Australian Employment White Paper.
3. See Kathryn Woodward (1997) for an insightful discussion about the investment in biological discourses within meanings and myths surrounding motherhood.

BIBLIOGRAPHY

Aschbrenner, J. (1978) 'Continuities and variations in Black family structures', in D.B. Shimkin, E.M. Shimkin and D.A. Frate (eds) *The Extended Family in Black Societies*, The Hague: Mouton.

Atkinson, K., Oerton, S. and Burns, D. (1998) 'Happy families? Single mothers, the press and the politicians', *Capital and Class*, 64: 1–11.

Babb, P. (1994) 'Teenage conceptions and fertility in England and Wales 1971–1991', *Population Trends*, 74: 12–17.

Barrett, M. and Macintosh, M., (1982) *The Anti-social Family*, London: Verso.

Barthes, R. (1972) *Mythologies*, London: Jonathan Cape.

Bauman, Z. (1991) *Modernity and Ambivalence*, Cambridge: Polity.

Beck, U. (1992) *Risk Society: Towards a New Modernity*, London: Sage.

Beck, U. and Beck-Gernsheim, E. (1995) *The Normal Chaos of Love*, Cambridge: Polity.

Bell, D. (1995) 'Pleasure and danger: the paradoxical spaces of sexual citizenship', *Political Geography*, 14: 139–52.

Bell, D. and Valentine, V. (eds) (1995) *Mapping Desires*, London: Routledge.

Berger, J. (1980) *About Looking*, London: Writers and Readers Publishing Cooperative Ltd.

Bernardes, J. (1987) '"Doing things with words": sociology and "family policy" debates', *The Sociological Review*, 36 (2): 267–72.

Bernardes, J. (1997) *Family Studies*, London: Routledge.

Billingsley, A. (1968) *Black Families in White America*, Englewood Cliffs, NJ: Prentice Hall.

Billingsley, A. (1992) *Climbing Jacob's Ladder: The Enduring Legacy of African American Families*, New York: Simon and Schuster.

Binnie, J. (1997) 'Invisible Europeans: sexual citizenship in the New Europe', *Environment and Planning*, 29: 237–48.

Blount, M. and Cunningham, G.P. (eds) (1996) *Representing Black Men*, London: Routledge.

Bocock, R. (1997) 'Choice and regulation: sexual moralities', in K. Thompson (ed.) *Media and Cultural Regulation*, London: Sage/Open University Press.

Boddy, W. (1998) 'The amateur, the housewife, and the salesroom floor: promoting postwar US television', *International Journal of Cultural Studies*, 1 (1): 129–42.

Bourdieu, P. (1990) *Photography: A Middle-Brow Art*, Stanford, CA: Stanford University Press.

Bowlby, J. (1953) *Child Care and the Growth of Love*, London: Penguin.

Brannen, J. (1999) 'Reconsidering children and childhood: sociological and policy perspectives', in E.B. Silva and C. Smart (eds) *The New Family?*, London: Sage.

Brunt, R. (1982) '"An immense verbosity": permissive sexual advice in the 1970s', in R. Brunt and C. Rowan (eds) *Feminism, Culture and Politics*, London: Lawrence and Wishart.

Burgess, E. (1973) *On Community, Family and Deliquency*, Chicago: Chicago University Press.

Burgess, E. and Locke, H. (1945) *The Family*, New York: American Book Company.

Butler, J. (1990) *Gender Trouble: Feminism and the Subversion of Identity*, London: Routledge.

Butler, J. (1994) 'Gender as performance: an interview with Judith Butler', *Radical Philosophy*, 67 (Summer): 32–7.

Callan, T., Nolan, B. and Whelan, C.T. (1993) 'Resources, deprivation and the measurement of poverty', *Journal of Social Policy*, 22 (2): 141–72.

Campbell, B. (1993) 'A teenage girl's passport to womanhood', *The Independent*, 12 May.

Chamberlain, M. (1995) 'Family narratives and migration dynamics', *New West Indies Guide/Nieue West Indische Gids*, 69 (3/4): 253–75.

Chamberlain, M. (1999) 'Brothers and sisters, uncles and aunts: a lateral perspective in Caribbean families', in E.B. Silva and C. Smart (eds) *The New Family?*, London: Sage.

Chambers, D. (1997) 'A stake in the country', in R. Silverstone (ed.) *Visions of Suburbia*, London and New York: Routledge.

Chambers, D. (2000) 'Representations of familialism in the British popular media', *European Journal of Cultural Studies*, 3 (2): 195–214.

Chambers, D. (2001) 'Picturing domestic space: a cultural study of the family photograph album', in J. Ryan and J. Schwartz (eds) *Picturing Place: Geography and Photography*.

Cheale, D. (1999) 'The one and the many: modernity and postmodernity' in G. Allan (ed.) *The Sociology of the Family: A Reader*, Oxford: Basil Blackwell (originally Chapter 5 of *Family and the State of Theory*, Hemel Hempstead: Harvester Wheatsheaf, 1991).

Chodorow, N. (1978) *The Reproduction of Mothering*, Berkeley: University of California Press.

Chopra, R. (1999) 'Retrieving the Father: Gender Studies, "Father Love" and the discourse of Mothering', University of Delhi, paper presented at the Women's Studies Network Conference, Warwick University, July.

Collier, R. (1999) 'Men, heterosexuality and the changing family: (re)constructing fatherhood in law and social policy', in G. Jagger and C. Wright (eds) *Changing Family Values*, London: Routledge.

Collins, P.H. (1990) 'Learning from the outsider within: the sociological significance of Black feminist thought', *Social Problems*, 33: S14–S32.

Coltrane, S. (1998) *Gender and Families*, Thousand Oaks, CA: Pine Forge Press.

Comfort, A. (ed.) (1972) *The Joys of Sex*, New York: Simon and Schuster.

Connell, R.W. (1995) *Masculinities*, Cambridge: Polity.

Cooper, D. (1998) *Power in Struggle: Feminism, Sexuality and the State*, Milton Keynes: Open University Press.

Creed, B. (1993) *The Monstrous-Feminine: Film, Feminism, Psychoanalysis*, London: Routledge.

Darwin, C. (1871) *The Descent of Man, and Selection in Relation to Sex*, 2 vols, London: John Murray.

Davidoff, L. and Hall, C. (1988) *Family Fortunes: Men and Women of the English Middle Class, 1780–1850*, London: Hutchinson.

Davidoff, L., Doolittle, M., Fink, J. and Holden, K. (1999) *The Family Story: Blood, Contract and Intimacy, 1830–1960*, Harlow: Addison Wesley Longman.

Davies, J. and Smith, C.R. (1997) *Gender, Ethnicity and Sexuality in Contemporary American Film*, Edinburgh: Keele University Press.

Davin, A. (1978) 'Imperialism and motherhood', *History Workshop Journal*, 5 (Spring): 9–56.

Delphy, C. (1984) *Close to Home: A Materialist Analysis of Women's Oppression*, London: Hutchinson.

Dench, G. (1996) *The Place of Men in Changing Family Attitudes*, London: Institute of Community Studies.

Denzin, N. (1987) 'Postmodern children', *Society*, 24: 32–6.

Department of Education and Employment and Qualifications and Curriculum Authority (1999) *The National Curriculum Handbook for Secondary Teachers in England*, London: Qualifications and Curriculum Authority/HMSO.

Dewdney, A. (1991) 'More than black and white: the extended and shared family album', in J. Spence and P. Holland (eds) *Family Snaps: The Meanings of Domestic Photography*, London: Virago.

Doane, M.A. (1987) *The Desire to Desire: The Woman's Film of the 1940s*, Bloomington and Indianapolis: Indiana University Press.

du Gay, P. (1997) 'Introduction', in P. du Gay, S. Hall, L. Janes, H. Mackay and K. Negus (1997) *Doing Cultural Studies: The Story of the Sony Walkman*, London: Sage/Open University Press.

Dunne, G. (1999) 'A passion for sameness?', in E.B. Silva and C. Smart (eds) *The New Family?* London: Sage.

Dyer, R. (1997) *White*, London: Routledge.

Eaton, M. (1977) 'Television situation comedy', in T. Bennett, S. Boyd-Bowman, C. Mercer and J. Woolacott (eds) *Popular Television and Film*, London: British Film Institute.

Eco, U. (1985) 'Postmodernism, irony, the enjoyable', in P. Brooker (ed.) *Modernism/Postmodernism*, London: Longman.

Edgell, S. (1980) *Middle-Class Couples: A Study of Segregation, Domination and Inequality in Marriage*, London: George Allen and Unwin.

Ellis, H. (1946) *Psychology of Sex*, London: William Heinemann (first published 1933).

Epstein, D. (2000a) 'Sexualities and education: Catch 28', *Sexualities, Special Issue: Sexualities and Education*, 3 (4): 387–94.

Epstein, D. (2000b), Promoting homophobia', *ChildRIGHT*, 164 (March): 14–15.

Epstein, D. and Johnson, R. (1998) *Schooling Sexualities*, Buckingham: Open University Press.

Evans, P.W. and Deleyto, C. (1998) 'Introduction: Surviving Love', in P.W. Evans and C. Deleyto (ed.) *Terms of Endearment: Hollywood Romantic Comedy of the 1980s and 1990s*, Edinburgh: Edinburgh University Press.

Fairclough, N. (2000) *New Labour, New Language*, London: Routledge.

Finch, J. and Mason, J. (1993) *Negotiating Family Responsibilities*, London: Routledge.

Finch, J. and Summerfield, P. (1991) 'Social construction and the emergence of companionate marriage, 1949–59', in D. Clark (ed.) *Marriage, Domestic Life and Social Change*, London: Routledge.

Foote, N. (1955) 'Family living as play', *Marriage and Family Living*, 17 (4): 297–9.

Forty, A. (1986) *Objects of Desire: Design and Society, 1750–1980*, London: Thames and Hudson.

Foucault, M. (1978) *The History of Sexuality*, Vol 1 Harmondsworth: Allen Lane/ Penguin.

Foucault, M. (1980) *Power/Knowledge*, Brighton: Harvester.

Fox Harding, L. (1996) *Family, State and Social Policy*, London: Macmillan.

Frankenberg, R. (1993) *White Women, Race Matters: The Social Construction of Whiteness*, Minneapolis: University of Minnesota Press.

Frankenberg, R. (ed.) (1997) *Displacing Whiteness: Essays in Social and Cultural Criticism*, Durham, NC: Duke University Press.

Franklin, B. (1997) *Newszak and the News Media*, London: Arnold.

Frazier E.F. (1932) *The Negro Family in Chicago*, Chicago: University of Chicago Press.

Frazier, E.F. (1939) *The Negro Family in the United States*, Chicago: University of Chicago Press.

Frazier, E.F. (1949) 'The Negro Family in America', in R.N. Anshen (ed.) *The Family: its Function and Destiny*, New York: Harper and Row.

Friedan, B. (1963) *The Feminine Mystique*, Harmondsworth: Penguin.

Friedan, B. (1981) *The Second Stage*, Summit: New York.

Gabriel, J. (1998) *Whitewash: Racialized Politics and the Media*, London: Routledge.

Gagnon, J. and Simon, W. (1973) *Sexual Conduct: The Social Sources of Human Sexuality*, Chicago: Aldine.

Gavron, H. (1966) *The Captive Wife: Conflicts of Housebound Mothers*, London: Routledge and Kegan Paul.

Gee, E. (1986) 'The life course of Canadian women', *Social Indicators Research*, 18: 263–83.

Giddens, A. (1992) *The Transformation of Intimacy: Sexuality, Love and Eroticism in Modern Societies*, Cambridge: Polity.

Giddens, A. (1999) *Runaway World: How Globalisation is Reshaping our Lives*, London: Profile Books.

Gillespie, M. (1993) 'Soap viewing, gossip and rumour among Punjabi youth in Southall', in P. Drummond, R. Paterson and J. Willis (eds) *National Identity and Europe: The Television Revolution*, London: BFI.

Gillespie, M. (1995) *Television, Ethnicity and Cultural Change*, London: Routledge.

Gillis, J. (1996) *A World of Their Own Making: Myth, Ritual and the Quest for Family Values*, London: Basic Books.

Giroux, H.A. (1993) 'Living dangerously: identity politics and the new cultural racism: towards a critical pedagogy of representation', *Cultural Studies*, 7 (1): 1–27.

Giroux, H.A. (1997) 'White Squall: resistance and the pedagogy of whiteness', *Cultural Studies*, 11 (3): 376–81.

Gittins, D. (1982) *Fair Sex: Family Size and Structure: 1900–39*, London: Hutchinson.

Gittins, D. (1993) *The Family in Question: Changing Households and Familiar Ideologies* (Second Edition), London: Macmillan.

Glenn, N.D. (1994) 'There-evaluation of family change by American social scientists', paper presented to the Committee for the International Year of the Family of the Catholic Archdiocese of Melbourne.

Grey, C. (1991) 'Theories of relativity', in J. Spence and P. Holland (eds) *Family Snaps: The Meanings of Domestic Photography*, London: Virago.

Griffiths, N. (2000) 'America's First Family', *The Times Magazine*, 15 April.

Gutman, H.G. (1973) 'Persistent myths about the Afro-American family', in M. Gordon (ed.) *The American Family in Social-Historical Perspective*, New York: St Martin's.

Gutman, H.G. (1976) *The Black Family in Slavery and Freedom: 1750–1925*, New York: Vintage.

Hall, C. (1992) *White, Male and Middle Class: Explorations in Feminism and History*, Cambridge: Polity.

Hall, S. (1991) 'Reconstruction work: images of post-war black settlement', in J. Spence and P. Holland (eds) *Family Snaps: The Meanings of Domestic Photography*, London: Virago.

Hall, S. (1997) 'The work of representation', in S. Hall (ed.) *Representation: Cultural Representations and Signifying Practices*, London Sage/Open University Press.

Harwood, S. (1997) *Family Fictions: Representations of the Family in 1980s Hollywood Cinema*, London: Macmillan.

Henderson, B. (1978) 'Romantic comedy today: semi-tough or impossible?', *Film Quarterly*, 31 (4): 11–23.

Hobsbawm, E. and Ranger, T. (eds) (1983) *The Invention of Tradition*, Cambridge: Cambridge University Press.

Hobson, D. (1982) *Crossroads: The Drama of a Soap Opera*, London: Methuen.

Holland, P. (1991) 'Introduction: history, memory and the family album', in J. Spence and P. Holland (eds) *Family Snaps: The Meanings of Domestic Photography*, London: Virago.

i-D (1998) 'Family future positive', London: Terry Jones and Tony Elliott.

Ignatiev, N. (1995) *How the Irish Became White*, New York: Routledge.

Irigaray, L. (1981) 'And the one doesn't stir without the other', *Signs*, 7 (1): 60–7.

Jackson, M. (1987) '"Facts of life" or the eroticization of women's oppression? Sexology and the social construction of heterosexuality', in P. Caplan (ed.) *The Cultural Construction of Sexuality*, London: Tavistock.

Jackson, S. (1993) 'Even sociologists fall in love: an exploration in the sociology of emotions', *Sociology*, 27 (2): 201–20.

Jackson, S. and Moores, S. (1995) 'Introduction', in S. Jackson and S. Moores (eds) *The Politics of Domestic Consumption: Critical Readings*, London: Prentice Hall/Harvester Wheatsheaf.

Jebb, M.A. and Haebich, A. (1992) 'Across the Great Divide: gender relations on Australian frontiers', in K. Saunders and R. Evans (eds) *Gender Relations in Australia*, Sydney: Harcourt Brace Jovanovich.

Jeffords, S. (1993) 'The big switch: Hollywood masculinity in the nineties', in J. Collins, H. Radner and A. Preacher Collins (eds) *Film Theory Goes to the Movies*, New York and London: Routledge.

Jhally, S. and Lewis, J. (1992) *Enlightenment Racism: The Cosby Show, Audiences, and the Myth of the American Dream*, Boulder, CO: Westview Press.

Kennedy, L. (1996) 'Alien nation: white male paranoia and imperial culture in the United States', *Journal of American Studies*, 30: 87–100.

Kinsey, A.C., Pomeroy, W.B. and Martin, C.E. (1948) *Sexual Behavior in the Human Male*, Philadelphia: W.B. Saunders.

Kinsey, A.C., Pomeroy, W.B., Martin, C.E. and Gebhard, P.H. (1953) *Sexual Behavior in the Human Female*, Philadelphia: W.B. Saunders.

Kristeva, J. (1983) *Powers of Horror*, New York: Columbia University Press.

Krutnik, F. (1990) 'The faint aroma of performing seals: the "nervous" romance and the comedy of the sexes', *The Velvet Light Trap*, 26 (Fall): 57–72.

Krutnik, F. (1998) 'Love lies: romantic fabrication in contemporary romantic comedy', in P.W. Evans and C. Deleyto (eds) *Terms of Endearment: Hollywood Comedy of the 1980s and 1990s*, Edinburgh: Edinburgh University Press.

Kuhn, A. (1982) *Women's Pictures: Feminism and Cinema*, London: Routledge and Kegan Paul.

Lees, S. (1999) 'Will boys be left on the shelf?', in G. Jagger and C. Wright (eds) *Changing Family Values*, London: Routledge.

Lent, T.O. (1995) 'Romantic love and friendship: the redefinition of gender relations in screwball comedy', in K.B. Karnick and H. Jenkins (eds) *Classical Hollywood Comedy*, New York and London: Routledge.

Lewis, J. (1991) 'The power of popular television: the case of *Cosby*', in *The Ideological Octopus: An Exploration of Television and its Audience*, London: Routledge.

Lewis, O. (1959) *Five Families: Mexican Case Studies in the Culture of Poverty*, New York: Basic Books.

Lewis, O. (1966) *La Vida: A Puerto Rican Family in the Culture of Poverty – San Juan, New York*, New York: Random House.

Lubiano, W. (1993) 'Black ladies, welfare queens and state minstrels: ideological war by narrative means', in T. Morrison (ed.) *Race-ing Justice, En-gendering Power*, London, Chatto and Windus.

Luhmann, N. (1986) *Love as Passion*, Cambridge: Polity.

Lupton, D. and Barclay, L. (1997) *Constructing Fatherhood: Discourses and Experiences*, London: Sage.

Lury, C. (1998) *Prosthetic Culture: Photography, Memory and Identity*, London and New York: Routledge.

McClintock, A. (1995) *Imperial Leather: Race, Gender and Sexuality in the Colonial Context*, London: Routledge.

McCray, C.A. (1980) 'The Black woman and family roles', in L. Rodgers-Rose (ed.) *The Black Woman*, Beverly Hills, CA: Sage.

Malinowski, B. (1913) *The Family Among the Australian Aborigines*, London: London University Press.

Malinowski, B. (1932) *The Sexual Life of Savages in North-Western Melanesia*, 3rd edn, London: Routledge and Kegan Paul.

Mansfield, P. (1999) interviewed on *Woman's Hour*, BBC Radio 4, 20 October.

Masters, W. and Johnson, V. (1970) *Human Sexual Inadequacy*, Boston: Little Brown.

May, E.T. (1988) *Homeward Bound: American Families in the Cold War Era*, New York: Basic Books.

Mirande, A. (1985) *The Chicano Experience: An Alternative Perspective*, South Bend, IN: University of Notre Dame Press.

Modleski, T. (1984) *Loving With a Vengeance: Mass Produced Fantasies for Women*, London: Methuen.

Modleski, T. (1991) *Feminism Without Women: Culture and Criticism in a 'Post-feminist' Age*, New York and London: Routledge.

Moore, H. (1988) *Feminist Anthropology*, Cambridge: Polity.

Morgan, D.H.J. (1975) *Social Theory and the Family*, London: Routledge and Kegan Paul.

Morgan, D.H.J. (1996) *Family Connections: An Introduction to Family Studies*, Cambridge: Polity.

Morgan, D.H.J. (1999) 'Risk and family practices: accounting for change and fluidity in family life', in E.B. Silva and C. Smart (eds) *The New Family?*, London: Sage.

Morley, D. (1986) *Family Television: Cultural Power and Domestic Leisure*, London: Comedia.

185

Moynihan, D.P. (1965) *The Negro Family: A Case for National Action*, Washington, DC: Government Printing Office.

Mulvey, L. (1989) 'Notes on Sirk and melodrama', in *Visual and Other Pleasures*, Bloomington and Indianapolis: Indiana University Press (originally published in *Movie*, Winter, 1977–8).

Musser, C. (1995) 'Divorce, DeMille and the comedy of remarriage' in K.B. Karnick and H. Jenkins (eds) *Classical Hollywood Comedy*, New York and London: Routledge.

Nardi, P. (1992) 'Sex, friendship and gender roles among gay men', in P. Nardi (ed.) *Men's Friendships*, London: Sage.

Neale, S. (1992) 'The big romance or something wild? Romantic comedy today', *Screen*, 33 (3): 284–99.

Neale, S. and Krutnik, F. (1990) *Popular Film and Television Comedy*, London: Routledge.

Nobles, W.W. (1974) 'Africanity: its role in Black families', *The Black Scholars*, 5 (9): 10–17.

Oakley, A. (1974) *The Sociology of Housework*, Oxford: Basil Blackwell.

Oakley, A. (1976) 'Wisewoman and medicine man: changes in the management of childbirth', in J. Mitchell and A. Oakley (eds) *The Rights and Wrongs of Women*, Harmondsworth: Penguin.

O'Connor, J.S., Shola Orloff, A. and Shaver, S. (1999) *States, Markets, Families: Gender, Liberalism and Social Policy in Australia, Canada, Great Britain and the United States*, Cambridge: Cambridge University Press.

O'Mara, K.O. (1997) 'Historicising outsiders on campus: the re/production of lesbian and gay insiders', *Journal of Gender Studies*, 7 (1): 17–31.

Padilla, F. (1987) *Puerto Rican Chicago*, South Bend, IN: University of Notre Dame Press.

Pahl, R. (1995) *After Success*, Cambridge: Polity.

Pahl, R. (1999) Interviewed on *Woman's Hour*, BBC Radio 4, 20 October.

Parsons, T. (1951) *The Social System*, Gencoe, IL: Free Press.

Parsons, T. (1971) 'The normal American family', in B. Adams and T. Weirath (eds) *Readings on the Sociology of the Family*, Chicago: Markham.

Parsons, T. and Bales, R. (1956) *Family Socialisation and Interaction Process* New York: Free Press.

Paul, K. (1997) *Whitewashing Britain: Race and Citizenship in the Postwar Era*, Ithaca: NY: Cornell University Press.

Pfeil, F. (1995) *White Guys: Studies in Post-Modern Domination and Difference*, London: Verso.

Phillips, M. (2000) *The Sex Change Society: Feminised Britain and the Neutered Male*, London: Social Market Foundation.

Phoenix, A. (1991) *Young Mothers?*, Cambridge: Polity.

Plummer, K. (1995) *Telling Sexual Stories: Power, Change, and Social Worlds*, London: Routledge.

Popenoe, D. (1988) *Disturbing the Nest: Family Change and Decline in Modern Societies*, New York: Aldine de Gruyter.

Popenoe, D. (1992) 'The controversial truth: the two-parent family is better', *New York Times*, 26 December, p. 13.

Popenoe, D. (1993) 'American family decline, 1960–1990: a review and appraisal', *American Journal of Marriage and the Family*, 55 (3): 527–44.

Popenoe, D. (1994) 'What's behind the family values debate?', American Sociological Association Meetings, Los Angeles, 7 August.

Radner, H. (1993) '"Pretty is as pretty does": free enterprise and the marriage plot', in J. Collins, H. Radner and A. Preacher Collins (eds) *Film Theory Goes to the Movies*, New York and London: Routledge.

Rieger, K. (1985) *The Disenchantment of the Home*, Melbourne: Oxford University Press.

Rieger, K. (1987) 'All but the kitchen sink: on the significance of domestic science and the silence of social theory', *Theory and Society*, 16: 497–526.

Robertson, R. (1995) 'Glocalization: time-space and homogeneity-heterogeneity', in M. Feathersone, S. Lash and R. Robertson (eds) *Global Modernities*, London: Sage.

Roediger, D. (1994) *Towards the Abolition of Whiteness*, London: Verso.

Roman, L.G., Christian-Smith, L.K. with Ellsworth, E. (1988) (eds) *Becoming Feminine: The Politics of Popular Culture*, Philadelphia, PA: Falmer Press.

Roschelle, A.R. (1997) *No More Kin: Exploring Race, Class and Gender in Family Networks*, Thousand Oaks, CA: Sage.

Rowe, K. (1995) *The Unruly Woman: Gender and the Genres of Laughter*, Austin: University of Texas Press.

Ryan, J. (1997) *Picturing Empire: Photography and the Visualization of the British Empire*, London: Reaktion Books.

Ryan, J. and Schwartz, J. (2001) (eds) *Picturing Place: Photography and the Geographical Imagination*, London: I.B. Tauris and Co.

Sanders, N. (1980) 'Family Snaps: images, ideology and the family', Occasional Papers in Media Studies, No. 8, Faculty of Humanities and Social Sciences, New South Wales Institute of Technology.

Sanders, N. (1989) 'Angles on the image', in G. Kress (ed.) *Communication and Culture*, Sydney: New South Wales University Press, pp. 131–154.

Santaolla, I.C. (1998) 'The fever and the itch: matching plots in Spike Lee's *Jungle Fever*', in P.W. Evans and C. Deleyto (eds) *Terms of Endearment: Hollywood Romantic Comedy of the 1980s and 1990s*, Edinburgh: Edinburgh University Press.

Scanlon, T. (1986) 'Pure and clean and true to Christ: black women and white missionaries in the North', *Hecate* 7 (1–2): 82–105.

Sedgwick, E.K. (1985) *Between Men: English Literature and Male Homosocial Desire*, New York: Columbia University Press.

Selman, P. (1996) 'Teenage motherhood then and now: a comparison of the pattern and outcomes of teenage pregnancy in England and Wales in the 1960s and 1980s', in H. Jones and J. Millar (eds) *The Politics of the Family*, Aldershot: Social Policy Association; Avebury: Ashgate Publishing.

Sennett, R. (1994) 'The new censorship', *Contemporary Sociology*, 23 (4): 487–91.

Silva, E.B. (1999) 'Transforming housewifery: dispositions, practices and technologies', in E.B. Silva and C. Smart (eds) *The New Family?*, London: Sage.

Silva, E.B. and Smart, C. (1999) 'The "new" practices and politics of family life', in E.B. Silva and C. Smart (eds) *The New Family?* London: Sage.

Slater, D. (1991) 'Consuming Kodak', in J. Spence and P. Holland (eds) *Family Snaps: The Meanings of Domestic Photography*, London: Virago.

Slater, D. (1995) 'Domestic photography and digital culture', in M. Lister (ed.) *The Photographic Image in Digital Culture*, New York and London: Routledge.

Smart, C. (1997) 'Wishful thinking and harmful tinkering? Sociological reflections on family policy', *Journal of Social Policy*, 26 (3): 1–21.

Smart, C. (1999) 'The "new parenthood": fathers and mothers after divorce', in E.B. Silva and C. Smart (eds) *The New Family?*, London: Sage.

Smart, C. and Neale, B. (1999) *Family Fragments?*, Cambridge: Polity.

Smith, D. (1988) 'Femininity as discourse', in L.G. Roman, L.K. Christian-Smith with E. Ellsworth, *Becoming Feminine: The Politics of Popular Culture*, Philadelphia, PA: Falmer Press.

Social Exclusion Unit (1999) *Teenage Pregnancy*, London: Stationery Office.

Sontag, S. (1977) *On Photography*, Harmondsworth: Penguin.

Spence, J. (1991) 'Soap, family album work … and hope', in J. Spence and P. Holland (eds) *Family Snaps: The Meaning of Domestic Photography*, London: Virago.

Spigel, L. (1992) *Make Room for TV: Television and the Family in an Age of Uncertainty*, Chicago: University of Chicago Press.

Spigel, L. (1997) 'From theatre to space ship: metaphors of suburban domesticity', in R. Silverstone (ed.) *Visions of Suburbia*, London and New York: Routledge.

Spillman, L. (1997) *Nation and Commemoration: Creating Identities in the United States and Australia*, Cambridge: Cambridge University Press.

Spring Rice, M. (1939) *Working-Class Wives: Their Health and Conditions*, London: Penguin.

Stacey, J. (1992) 'Backward toward the postmodern family: reflections on gender, kinship and class in the Silicon Valley', in B. Thorne and M. Yalom (eds) *Rethinking the Family: Some Feminist Questions, Second Edition*, Boston: Northeastern University Press.

Stacey, J. (1999) 'Virtual social science and the politics of family values in the United States', in G. Jagger and C. Wright (eds) *Changing Family Values*, London: Routledge.

Staples, R. and Mirande, A. (1980) 'Racial and cultural variations among American families: a decennial review of the literature of minority families', *Journal of Marriage and the Family*, 42 (4): 157–73.

Stationery Office (1998) *Supporting Families, A Consultation Document*, Norwich: Her Majesty's Stationery Office.

Stopes, M. (1918) *Married Love*, London: Fabian Society.

Straw, J. and Anderson, J. (1996) *Parenting*. London: Stationery Office. Labour Party Publication, November.

Sullivan, A. (1995) *Virtually Normal: An Argument About Homosexuality*, London: Picador.

Taylor, F.W. (1974) *Scientific Management*, New York: Harper (originally published in 1911 as *The Principles of Scientific Management*).

Tincknell, E. and Chambers, D. (1998) 'Sites of desire, sights of sexuality: new communities of identity?', paper presented at the Fourth Annual Conference of the Lesbian and Gay Study Group, Department of Film and and Television, Humanities Research Centre, Warwick University, 'Film: Queer/Homosexual/ Lesbian/Gay/Queer', April.

Tomlinson, J. (1999) *Globalization and Culture*, Cambridge: Polity.

Traube, E.G. (1992) *Dreaming Identities: Class, Gender and Generation in 1980s Film*, Boulder, CO and Oxford: Westview Press.

Van de Velde, T.H. and Smyth, M. (eds) (1980) *Ideal Marriage: Its Physiology and Technique*, Westport, CT: Greenwood Press.

Van Every, J. (1999) 'From modern nuclear family households to postmodern diversity? The sociological construction of families', in G. Jagger and C. Wright (eds) *Changing Family Values*, London: Routledge.

Viviani, C. (1980) 'Who is without sin? The maternal melodrama in American film 1930–3', *Wide Angle*, 4 (2): 7.

Wallace, M. (1992) '*Boyz N the Hood* and *Jungle Fever*', in G. Dent (ed.) *Black Popular Culture*, Seattle: Bay Press 1.

Wallerstein, J.S. and Blakeslee, S. (1989) *Second Chances: Men, Women and Children a Decade After Divorce*, New York: Ticknor and Fields.

Warner, M. (1985) *Monuments and Maidens: The Allegory of the Female Form*, London: Picador.

Watney, S. (1991) 'Ordinary boys', in J. Spence and P. Holland (eds) *Family Snaps: The Meanings of Domestic Photography*, London: Virago.

Weeks, J. (1985) *Sexuality and Its Discontents*, London: Routledge and Kegan Paul.

Weeks, J. (1989) *Sex, Politics and Society: The Regulation of Sexuality Since 1800*, 2nd edn, London: Longman.

Weeks, J. (1991) 'Pretended family relationships', in J. Weeks (ed.) *Against Nature: Essays on History, Sexuality and Identity*, London: Rivers Oram Press.

Weeks, J. (1995) *Inventing Moralities: Sexual Values in an Age of Uncertainty*, Cambridge: Polity Press.

Weeks, J. (1996) 'The idea of a sexual community', *Soundings*, 2, Spring, 71–84.

Weeks, J. (1998) 'The sexual citizen', *Theory, Culture and Society*, 15 (3–4): 35–52.

Weeks, J., Donovan, C. and Heaphy, B. (1999) 'Everyday experiments: narratives of non-heterosexual relationships', in E.B. Silva and C. Smart (eds) *The New Family?*, London: Sage.

Westermarck, E. (1921) *The History of Human Marriage* (5th Edition, rewritten), London: Macmillan & Co. (first published 1891).

Weston, K. (1991) *Families We Choose: Lesbian, Gays and Kinship*, New York: Columbia University Press.

Wexman, V.W. (1993) *Creating the Couple: Love, Marriage, and Hollywood Performance*, Princeton: Princeton University Press.

Wiegman, R. (1991) 'Black bodies/American commodities: gender, race and the bourgeois ideal in contemporary film', in L.D. Friedman (ed.) *Unspeakable Images: Ethnicity and the American Cinema*, Urbana and Chicago: University of Illinois Press.

Williams, N.M. and Jolly, L. (1992) 'From time immemorial? Gender relations in Aboriginal societies before "white contact"', in K. Saunders and N.M. Williams (eds) *Gender Relations in Australia: Domination and Negotiation*, Sydney: Harcourt Brace Jovanovich.

Williams, R. (1974) *Television, Technology and Cultural Form*, London: Fontana.

Willmott, P. and Young, M. (1967) *Family and Class in a London Suburb*, London: New English Library.

Wilson, W.J. (1991) 'Studying inner-city social dislocations: the challenge of public agenda research', 1990 Presidential Address', *American Sociological Review*, 56: 1–14.

Winship, J. (1984) 'Nation before family: *Woman, The National Home Weekly* 1945–1953', in Formations Editorial Collective, *Formations of Nation and People*, London: Routledge and Kegan Paul.

Winship, J. (1987) *Inside Women's Magazines*, London: Pandora.

Woodward, K. (1997) 'Motherhood, identities, meanings and myths', in K. Woodward (ed.) *Identity and Difference*, London: Sage/Open University Press.

Wright, C. and Jagger, G. (1999) 'End of century, end of family? Shifting discourses of family "crisis"', in G. Jagger and C. Wright (eds) *Changing Family Values*, London: Routledge.

Yeatman, A. (1996) 'Interpreting contemporary contractualism', *Australian Journal of Social Issues*, 31 (1): 39–54.

INDEX